JIMMY SHARMAN'S BOXERS

Australia's legendary travelling boxing troupe

First published 2023

Big Sky Publishing Pty Ltd
PO Box 303, Newport, NSW 2106, Australia
Phone: 1300 364 611
Fax: (61 2) 9918 2396
Email: info@bigskypublishing.com.au
Web: www.bigskypublishing.com.au

Cover design and typesetting: Think Productions

A catalogue record for this book is available from the National Library of Australia

Title: Jimmy Sharman's Boxers
ISBN: 9781922896865

Cover image: Jimmy Sharman's Boxing Troupe, Ballarat [Photographer; Jack Walton, Jimmy Sharman's Boxing Troupe, Ballarat, 1934, Museum Victoria].

Back Cover image: Prest (left) versus Lewis and the referee Jimmy Sharman [Photographer H Coates, Prest (left) versus Lewis and the referee Jimmy Sharman, 1910, National Library of Australia PIC/8395/903 Arnold Thomas boxing collection].

JIMMY SHARMAN'S BOXERS

Australia's legendary travelling boxing troupe

Stephen McGrath

Dedication

For Esther, Lawrence and Michelle and all my widespread kith and kin.

Also, I dedicate this book to the real people portrayed here and in doing so I hope for two things: first, that I have returned some truth to your life story where there may have been some deviation; and second, that your story can now be shared and celebrated more widely.

Cultural Safety Warnings

First Nations people are depicted in this work. They are fictionalised. No real-life First Nations people are named. This work has been reviewed and edited to fulfil the Australia Council for the Arts' *Protocols for Using First Nations Cultural and Intellectual Property in the Arts* (ICIP).

There is racist and prejudice language used in this work reflecting the social norms of the time portrayed. These may not be considered appropriate today. These views are not the views of the author. Although the information may not reflect current understanding, it is provided in an historical context.

There are also depictions of violence and war in this work.

(Please refer to the appendices for further details on these matters.)

Brush the cymbals gently,
Muffled be the drum
Voices whisper softly,
Tread lightly as you come.
By canvas tent bereft of sound
No more the 'spruiker' cries;
Life has lost the final round
And Death has claimed the prize.

Tribute to James ('Jimmy') Sharman Snr
Camden News, 1966

Contents

CHAPTER ONE

Beginnings

Trundle, NSW

There is no firmer or friendlier handshake than the handshake of a pugilist.

He introduces himself: 'Jim Cowan, heavyweight. But you can call me Jimmy.'

He seems to accept me straightaway, regardless of my deficiency …

My turned-in foot.

The claw of my left hand.

My walk.

I walk like a broken marionette.

I have a palsy. 'God's revenge for my ancestors' sins', my Aunt Adelaide is always reminding me and telling others.

He is here to help carry my luggage because Trundle's main

street is as wide as it is long and muddy.

He has stories …

The time at the Shepparton Show when some lads threw a monitor lizard into one of the luncheon tents. Inside, a dozen or more men, New Zealanders from the Wellington Brass Band, ran in all directions.

Not used to the habits of such creatures, several men climbed onto the trestle tables, where upon the reptile, also scared, did as scared reptiles do and climbed to the highest point, resting on the head of the euphonium player.

Another story about the baker's apprentice knocked out very hard at Beechworth. How when he came to, sat up, turned to Mr Sharman, and said with a queer look on his face, 'I would really love a piece of orange.'

'You are joining a great adventure, Archie.'

We are outside the hotel now. Jimmy points up to a man standing at a window, staring.

'That's Mr Sharman up there.'

The man steps back into the darkness.

'So, the last bookkeeper Mr Sharman had was either stupid with numbers or stupid enough to steal from Mr Sharman, I don't know what, but watch yourself, Archie; you don't want to get on the wrong side of Mr Sharman and his money,' Jimmy whispered.

'Mr Sharman, Archie Blackmore the bookkeeper is here for interview.'

The man appears at the window again.

'The interview is at one o'clock, that's the arrangement we made. It's a quarter to. Wait; he will see you then.'

The man steps back into the darkness.

It is still raining. Jimmy Cowan leaves me and my luggage, whispering again.

'Stay right where you are, lad, this is how Mr Sharman does things.'

'But I have the job promised to me by a letter from Mr Sharman already.'

'Stay right there, don't move.'

Jimmy is now inside the warm and dry hotel.

I stand there.

I see a couple of wet stray dogs, but that is all.

I stand alone. At least the rain has stopped.

At 2 o'clock a window opens and Mr Sharman appears. It has been him along.

'Archie Blackmore?' Mr Sharman shouts from the window. 'From Camden?'

'Yes, you wrote to my father confirming a bookkeeper position with the boxing troupe and told me to come here to Trundle,' I say.

'I did, but the position's not quite confirmed as yours just yet,' he says.

'What do you mean?'

'See, the last chap did me wrong; he cooked the books and he stole from me. Tell me why you won't go and do that. Yes? Tell me.'

'I don't know, Mr Sharman, I just wouldn't.'

'You wouldn't until you were tempted by something I reckon. Do you drink? Do you gamble? Horses? Dogs? Cards?'

'No, Mr Sharman, no, I don't do any of that.'

'Well, not yet you don't.'

'Mr Cashmere, the accountant, your last employer, told me

that he deeply regretted losing you. Why do you want to join a boxing troupe?'

'My father said I could learn a great deal from you. That you were a canny businessman,' I say.

* * *

My father knew Sharman.

Poor and Catholic, he said.

His family had a small dairy farm in the wettest part of Narellan, which the good Lord would choose to fill with water at least three or four times a year.

One of thirteen children.

Got about clothed in only old sugar bags, no shoes.

A good, honest man, hard but fair, my father said.

Careful with his money, a shrewd businessman.

A man I could learn a great deal from if he chose to take me under his wing.

* * *

'A canny businessman, your father said?'

'Yes,' I say.

'Good answer. Your father is James Blackmore, the farmer on Cawdor Road?'

'Yes.'

'Yes. A good family. Two brothers, yes?'

'Yes.'

'Frank and Albert, yes?'

'Yes.'

'Yes, I know them; useful boxers, they are in my book. Useful.'

'Yes, they fought at your Campbelltown show.'

'What's two pounds ten shilling and twelve pence a week over forty weeks total? Quick!'

'One hundred and twenty pounds, two shillings and two pence.'

'Correct. How do you spell agriculturalist?'

'A-g-r-i-c-u-l-t-u-r-a-l-i-s-t.'

'Good. I hear that you have a remarkable memory of detail. Is this true?

* * *

Yes. It is true. I do remember everything.

My foot makes me slow, but it does not make me a dimwit, although it is often useful to be underestimated.

Being a pace slower than others gives me the chance to look around, observe, to take things in, to remember the details, to savour, and to catalogue. I have more time to marvel at all of the world's subtleties.

I am unique … I can remember everything … I can never forget.

Every spoken word I have ever heard can be replayed if I choose it, as if my mind is a gramophone and there are wax recordings of everything ever said, everything I ever hear.

It is the same for whatever I see. Places, events, objects. Ask me to recall anything in the written form and I see each numbered page of everything I have ever read, the words, the sentences, and its grammar, I can even recall the typeface.

It is as if everything has been photographed and then stored away in great everlasting vaults.

A gift? Yes … and also a curse.

I can often see, like a dream, like moving pictures, the scene that words or a conversation describes. It is as if I am there, a witness through the mind's eye.

Most people whose memory is not as accurate as mine can simply reconstruct or even just abandon any of their painful past. They can reconfigure any events or memories so all of it becomes more pleasant.

With a large, exact and stubborn memory such as mine, the details refuse to be reconfigured and can leave me to dwell in dark times, dark places.

* * *

'Right, then, demonstrate your famous memory to me,' Mr Sharman asks.

'Right, Mr Sharman. I have read the 1914 New South Wales Agricultural Show calendar; ask me something regarding that.'

'Who is the President of the Trundle Agricultural Show Society?'

'Mr Daniel John Burford Casey.'

'Yes, correct, I only need the surname but good show anyway. Who is the President of the Goulburn Agricultural Show Society?'

'Mr Chipford.'

'Yes, correct. Good, then. You need to reply to Mr Chipford on my behalf. Have you ever lied, Archie?'

'No … I mean, yes. Yes, I have. I try hard not to.'

'Good, you would be lying if you said you never lied,' he says with a tiny smile cracking on his hard face.

'Mr Piggott will come down to fetch your luggage and you

come to the parlour to sign the contract and understand your roles and your responsibilities.'

'Thank you, Mr Sharman.'

'Yes. One other thing: Mr Blackmore, if I find even a single zac unaccounted for, whether that's through your own error or skulduggery, I'll have your guts for garters, boy.'

The window slams shut.

A man with a big mouth of teeth and wide eyes is suddenly here in front of me.

'Hello. Mr Piggott, tent boss. Archie, nice to meet you. Let's get you inside, yes?'

He takes off at a quick pace, banging my luggage up the stairs to the parlour. I struggle behind upstairs and into the parlour.

There is a long table with a number of papers at one end and at the other end is Mr Sharman. He is smaller and thinner than I imagined. He looks very serious. He points to the contract: 'Read and sign.'

CONTRACT made between JIMMY SHARMAN of Narellan Athletic Promoter and Showman (hereinafter called the employer) of the one part and ARCHIBALD BLACKMORE of Camden (hereinafter called the athlete and general assistant) of the other part on the third of August 1914.

There were the standard conditions about employment dates and renewals of contracts for further periods. There is one clause that concerns me.

3. For each week that the troupe are operating in any Town, Carnival, or Show whilst on tour the employer shall pay to athlete and general assistant the sum of £4.

4. The employer shall retain the sum of £2 each week out of the sum to be paid to the athlete and general assistant as and

by way of a bond and/or guarantee against any breach of this contract by the athlete and general assistant during his term of employment under and by virtue of this contract and in the event of any breach of this contract by the athlete and general assistant all moneys held and/or retained by the employer shall be deemed to have been forfeited by the athlete and general assistant and in addition thereto the athlete and general assistant shall pay to the employer the sum of £50 as and by way of liquidated damages.

5. The athlete and general assistant shall keep himself strictly law-abiding and shall refrain from all intoxicating liquors and injurious drugs and shall keep himself in a thoroughly fit condition to carry out his duties at any time or place as directed by the employer or his representatives. In the event of the said athlete and general assistant becoming incapable of performing his duties in a fit and proper manner through insobriety, sickness, injury or any other cause whatsoever the athlete and general assistant shall be deemed to have committed a breach of this contract and the employer shall be at liberty to exercise the rights and powers conferred on him by clause 4.hereof and the employer shall also have the right to terminate this contract forthwith and the athlete and general assistant shall then be responsible for his own transport without any further claim upon the employer whatsoever.

There are other clauses regarding

The proper care of costumes, gear or property.

The requirement to use only the transport directed by the employer, obeying all directions given.

The devotion of the athletes and general assistants' entire services to the employer, being ready and prepared to work or train no later than eight thirty in the morning until the closing down.

'When is the bond returned?' I ask.

'You didn't come down in the last shower did you, Archie Blackmore?'

'No, but I just want to clarify this point; if a legal agreement is unclear it must be explained.' I say that before really thinking about it.

'So, you don't think it's fair then, Mr Blackmore? Every other man just signs the contract and gets on with it.'

'It is just that you don't get full pay until the end of the season.'

'So, you are thinking about taking off already? Is it all this talk of war? Am I not paying you a pretty penny? If you don't want to sign on the next train is at four.'

'I will sign, Mr Sharman, I will, it's just an interesting clause.'

'The thing is, Mr Blackmore, if I have any of my boxers taking off, or my wrestler, even though he's just a big soft pudding, I can't show a class of boxing fights and I know nothing about wrestling. I lose challengers, I lose money and word spreads that Jimmy Sharman's Boxing Troupe is going to the pot.'

I sign.

Mr Sharman is beside me now and offers a firm and friendly handshake.

'You have an eye for detail. You're a thinker too. I like that. Useful. Good. Excellent.'

Mr Piggott shows me to my room. Dinner is at six.

* * *

I am introduced to each of them …

Jackie Green, flyweight,

Stanley Hill, the Aboriginal boxer,

Alf Preston,

Frank Burns, middleweight, the blacksmith from Temora,

Tommy Murphy,

Billy Spiers, the wrestler.

At the dinner table the troupe tell me about touring, things to watch out for.

The tricks some men played in pubs, where a bloke leaves a one pound note on the floor just in front of the bar, no-one near it; then he says it's his when you bend down to pick it up. You beg to differ and five of his mates have an excuse to set loose on you.

Or another instance where some little fella gives you lip and invites you outside to fight it out, and down the alley are twenty others ready to beat the life out of you.

Frank told me to watch out for illywhackers at the Maitland show.

Watch out for Frater too, Tommy said, and they all smile.

Mr Sharman had a hard-hitter style of hat and a face that matched. He reminds us that our contractual obligations did not include fights in or outside public houses.

It is only when all of them are together in one small room and I have spent some time with them that I notice their collective features.

Their hard heads.

Faces, foreheads, scuffed, shadowed or scrubbed.

Ears bent inside out, compressed into small hard lumps.

Eyes steely and hooded close.

Eyebrows pushed to wrong parts or half rubbed off.

Mouths, thick rubbery curtains over missing teeth.

Noses, pushed flat behind cheekbones or made crooked.

And their smiles, their big outside voices, their laughs, their playfulness and their friendship.

After dinner Mr Piggott calls me into Mr Sharman's room where he outlines his expectations.

I am responsible for all tasks of a generally minor administrative nature. I will arrange lodgings, print and distribute flyers, organise drays and make enquiries about trains. I will assist as directed on show days. I am responsible for the banking. Each evening I will assist Mr Sharman, reconciling petty cash and the day's takings. I will also be responsible for recording all new details into the cashbook. These and the other notebooks are all kept in an old heavy bag that has seen several repairs. This is the bag he wears with a thick strap over one shoulder and is never far from.

I can see one notebook has pages of neatly lined columns for expected profits and outgoings for each site, and the variations from one year to the next. It is an impressive ledger, both in its detail, its design and in its neatness.

There is a second notebook, a blue one, full of names and details listed alphabetically … I steal a glimpse … with my photographic memory I see some more detail …

James Clark, featherweight, bootmaker, 12 Victoria Ararat, Victoria, southpaw with good combinations.

Harry Devon, heavyweight, miner, c\o Railway hotel, Aratula, Queensland, heavy punch, courage.

Bill Franklin, welterweight, farmer, Arawata Road, Arawata, Victoria, good mover, thinker, fights with guile.

He spends any free time he has making notes.

There is the letter from Mr E Chipford, the show president from Goulburn, who writes that the streets are full this time of year with young fit lads. Mr Chipford respectively requests Mr Sharman's troupe pay a visit soon as possible as a spectacle of fistic fun is in the offing.

I am to draft a reply for Mr Sharman's signature suggesting a possible future visit, apologising as this year's tour is now underway.

Before I leave he gives me the year's remaining itinerary. His neat copperplate hand lists the dates and venues from this instant until November.

* * *

Billy Spiers, the wrestler, sees the list and calls the others in. They fill the room.

'Any changes?'

As they study it carefully they add their remarks.

Trundle.

Temora, Ardlethan, Leeton, Wagga Wagga, Narrandera

… Shearing season … lots of shearers … all well used to fighting …

Albury

… The local constable …

Shepparton

Royal Melbourne Show

Port Fairy

… Fishermen …

Mount Gambier, Castlemaine

… Big farm boys raised on mutton …

Warrnambool

… Good Irish stock coming in from Koroit …

Ballarat … no good … flogging a dead horse there …

Bairnsdale,
... The timber workers ...
Dandenong, Lilydale, Camperdown and Daylesford.
Melbourne Cup. Then the summer break.

* * *

At the showgrounds the next morning canvas banners have been raised behind a platform. Bright yellow and red lettering ... Prizes to be won by all comers ... A sporting treat for men and women ...

There are pictures of Tommy and Jackie. Mr Sharman has added, for effect, Jack Johnson and Les Darcy, their big fists poised, tight waists wrapped in champion belts.

More words ...

Australian Champions of all weights to challenge and meet all comers ... Contests arranged for local and district champs ... The best by test ... Sharman's Boxing Troupe producer of Champion Boxers and Champion Wrestlers.

One of the largest banners has Jimmy Sharman spelt out in large letters and within the border of each letter of his name is a figure in a boxing or wrestling repose. I also notice in small letters a warning ... *Imitators, note all banners or paintings of the Jimmy Sharman Boxing Troupe are original designs of the proprietor. Signed Pat Piggott (Manager)*

The local men are making themselves known to Mr Sharman. He is smiling now, sitting on an orange ladder propped up against shipping crates. He is throwing out jokes, greeting everyone like old friends, slapping people on the back.

'What's your name, son? Had a few fights?'

Overnight it is as if he has undergone a strange kind of metamorphosis; he is suddenly someone else, reborn. He seems a foot taller, his voice louder. He has taken a new form, adapted, transformed, become new. As if emerging from a chrysalis, letting wet wings dry, he now sits on the ladder just waiting for the right wind.

* * *

Mr Sharman's hints on how to do well in life:

Never be a knocker.

Always wear the same sized hat.

Always extend a happy hand to an honest trier.

* * *

Before the first session we wait in the tent and talk about old fights.

The tent is a tough place … you have to want to be there.

Sometimes a father would push a sickly or tentative boy forward to fight. Asking Mr Sharman to match him, so a belting might toughen him up, or to make a man out of him, to give him a taste of manhood. Mr Sharman would take the father aside and whisper excuses as to why a fight could not be arranged …

a full card,

no-one in the same weight,

a fictitious Australia Boxing Association age limit policy.

Frank tells me that sometimes Mr Sharman will need to talk up a man to give him confidence or create the impression of a closer fight. He will say, 'He's built like a bullock … he's as brave as Britannia.'

Billy told me about a time when a tiny wee little man drunk as a skunk challenged the whole troupe to fight him. He was too small to match up; so drunk and clumsy he wouldn't make it past the first punch. He would not take no for an answer, kept pestering and pestering; despite his arguments Mr Sharman could not discourage him.

Mr Sharman found a compromise: Jackie, the smallest of the boxers we had would box him on his knees. The fight started and despite his reduced mobility Jackie bopped the little fella a few times. Told by Mr Sharman to let in a few, the angry little man landed several rabbit punches in the next round but in the last Jackie reminded Tiny Tim of the true nature of things with a well-placed uppercut.

Mr Sharman, to the cheers of the local crowd, awarded the fight to the little one and both were showered with at least ten pound of coin.

* * *

I notice we are beside the publican's booth. Mr Piggott tells me that it is a stipulation Mr Sharman makes very clear with each of the show committees when booking.

'Having a skinful of grog always helps them get up.'

* * *

'Mr Sharman keeps his ear to the ground,' says Mr Piggott. Hoping to arrange bouts between any of the townspeople … always on the lookout for local grievances …

Old feuds, unfinished fights, differences of opinion, petty squabbles, jealousies, rivalries …

Disputes based on slow racehorses, stolen horses, missing hay, lost sweethearts …

Bets, dares …

Fights that can be based on rumours, slurs, backhanders, allegations …

Comments about another's character; yellow, cheap, lying, light fingered, thin-skinned, having no zip …

Societal differences … Mr Sharman's expert matchings are always bridging the gap …

Labourer versus Salvationist,
Publican versus Rechabite,
Lodge Man versus Bushman,
Full Forward versus Fullback,
Tally Man versus Carter,
Shop Steward versus Overseer.

Nationhood … The Fijian Cannibal versus the Kanaka.

Place … City versus Country. New South Welshman versus Victorian.

History … Dublin versus London.

Creed … Catholic versus Protestant …

A matching of two locals did two things; it brought in the crowds and spared some of his own troupe.

'Provides a civic service too,' said Mr Piggott. 'A venue for people to resolve their differences, a fistic court of law, things resolved fair and square, we leave the town a better place.'

* * *

Mr Piggott calls me across. I am to stick by him and learn some of the tricks of the trade.

In front of the tent is a row of old piano case boards lying flat across scaffolds erected to chest height. This is the line-up board. Twenty feet long now, bigger at the capital shows, more fighters, more challengers. The orange ladder up on the line-up board, that Mr Sharman stands on, is known as the bridge. The area in front of the line-up board is known as the pitch or ground.

The crowd is building, feeble with excitement.

'Mugs,' Mr Piggott calls them, 'or sheep … first one in to pay – that one we call the ram … if things are slow Mr Sharman might get you to do that … go in first to get the sheep moving. There are gees and takes as well, but I will explain these later. You'll see a bit of that today, so keep it quiet. We don't want any of them twigging the goose.'

Mr Sharman is walking around in front of the line-up boards busy doing nothing.

'He's waiting for the right moment; he's checking, looking for the signs,' says Mr Piggott.

'What's he looking for?'

'See there, see how he turns to study the Ferris wheel?'

'That is how he tells whether the numbers are right, he checks the Ferris wheel, I reckon; he sees how many are on it and he'll times by ten,' Mr Piggott marvels.

And now Mr Sharman is on the ladder. He nods to Mr Piggott. The ground in front of the stand does not seem as full as earlier.

Mr Piggott nods back, now on the stage. He heaves up a big yellow bass drum across his chest, slinging straps over his shoulders. He has the queerest of looks on his face, wide eyes and mad grin. He swings back both arms striking the drum.

Boom … Boom … Boom

Now yelling …

'Hi! Hi! Hi!'

Boom … Boom … Boom.

The drum beats through me, the yelling makes me tingle.

'Hi! Hi! Hi!'

Boom … Boom … Boom.

A bell now rings.

'Hi-ah! Hi-ah! Hi-ah!'

Ding, ding, ding.

Boom … Boom … Boom.

'Hi-ah! Hi-ah! Hi-ah!'

Ding, ding, ding.

Boom … Boom … Boom.

Mr Sharman starts his shouting, a deep growling voice. It is louder than a man of his size would be expected to broadcast.

'Ladies and gentlemen, come see the world's best, the worst and the in-between. Come and see Jackie Green fight, a man with so many title belts he uses a new one every day to hold up his trousers, one for each day of the week.'

'Show us what you got.

'Trundle's a rough n tough kind of town, there must be a few more Les Darcys standing out there among you! Come up, come up, show us what you got.

'A round or two for a pound or two!'

'Who'll take a glove?'

* * *

From all corners, townspeople appear, walking with urgency. Showground grass becomes the jostling tops of straw boater hats.

One by one the fighters are introduced and stand, arms folded across the line-up board. Each one is dressed in 'combinations' as they call them. A pair of black tights under their shorts. A vest, also black, with the white words 'Jimmy Sharman's Troupe' sewn on the front. Each of them wears the heavy flat sole boots. Each boot has a heavy lace and has a high cut inches above the ankle to support the rigours of sparring.

Billy is to be the last up. I ask him where Frank is. 'Frank's in the stew,' he replies. I do not understand.

'A stew is the big fight, end of the night, something special to keep the punters back. Frank's a gee. Pretends to be a punter, a challenger, gets the crowd interested,' Billy whispers. 'Mr Sharman matches him with one of the boys and they have a stew, a scrap a real ding-dong, show the public real fighting.'

Mr Sharman announces Billy Spiers, Australia's most unbeaten wrestler, inventor of the fearsome Hammerlock, and Billy smiles and leaps onto the line-up board. I hear the crowd gasp at his size.

* * *

I find Frank dressed in a suit, tie with a high starched American collar and a straw hat, walking between the sides of tents. Frank tips his boater at me. 'This week I am William St Clair, a wealthy landowner from Kickastickalong down this way for the stock sales.'

I smile. 'Billy told me.'

'Next week a boilermaker from Bandywallop or Boondocktown;

the week after I think Mr Sharman has me pencilled down as a sailor, or a Greek cook. Anyways, best get on; see you out front.'

* * *

Surrounding the line-up board are hundreds of punters. Potential fighters and spectators. Both are important; one cannot work without the other. Mr Sharman works with both. Those keen to fight walk promptly to the front.

Others pushed towards the front by friends now stand in the middle ground.

Those who still need convincing stand at the back studying their shoes.

Mr Sharman will throw the matching glove at potential passers-by, or get down off the ladder and go into the crowd to personally present the matching glove to a potential fighter. Seldom do they refuse. Mr Sharman knows what a useful fighter looks like.

* * *

One by one, challengers step forward and wait to meet Mr Sharman at the ladder.

Mr Piggott keeps banging the drum.

Boom … Boom … Boom.

'Hi-ah! Hi-ah! Hi-ah!'

Ding, ding, ding.

Boom … Boom … Boom.

'A round a two for a pound or two and away!'

* * *

The challengers arrange themselves along one side of the line-up board. Mr Sharman likes to make up names for the challengers; after a quick chat, he makes names up on the spot – often cruel, often flattering or witty.

Names based on occupation:

'The Brutal Bricklayer'

He adapts the challengers' names or surnames:

'Stone Fist Smith'

'Rumbling O' Riley'

'Peter the Perfect'

Names also are made up about appearance:

'Red Terror'

A man with hairy arms … 'The Woolly Mammoth' …

There is one particularly large fellow called John.

Mr Sharman calls him 'Normus' … as in 'John-Normus'.

He gives them names from towns the challengers hail from …

'The Wellington Walloper'

'The Goblin from Condobolin'

Frank is introduced as a pastoralist, William St Clair, up from Scone to attend the sales. Frank is his pompous best; he states that he was Kings School champion and that he is supremely confident he can wipe the floor clean with any one of Sharman's men.

* * *

Into the tent.

Fighters, challengers and their seconders in first. The punters line up outside, their voices and shadows stroking the sides of the tent.

The challengers are herded to one side of the ring; the troupe returns to the back of the tent.

They have their shirts off, waiting. Some remain in shoes, one has boxer's boots, and others are barefoot.

* * *

The ones who go barefoot know the game … the need to grip … they are the ones worth watching out for.

* * *

The bright red V of sunburn on the chest denotes the farmers: 'sons of the soil', Mr Sharman calls them.

Those with the big fists are the miners,

those with the sticking-out ribs are the men who are down on their luck.

Seconders, best friends, mates, mingle. They rub the shoulders of their challengers, they whisper, instruct, embolden. Like dog handlers at coursing. They talk tactics, techniques that were practised, imagined, weeks before or in the last hurried half-hour.

* * *

It isn't hard to spot the cream puffers ... Mr Sharman tells us …

The bark and sawdust always show up the ballet dancer …

* * *

Some appear confident, others menacing, or mad, even deranged.

Some fidget and won't stay still.

Some are quiet or frightened.

The drunks, possibly two or three of the group, vary in noise, according to the amount of liquor consumed. Some have Dutch courage; just enough grog swilling around in their heads to be dangerous – an extra sense of self belief that they will overcome whatever is thrown at them.

Others are further on. More drunk, numb to pain, stupid, sick, slower or a confused kind of angry. Lost. Rudderless.

Some are dared by mates. As a rule, according to Mr Piggott, the drunker the fighter, threefold the drunker his seconder could well be.

Some are there to defend the town's pride.

Others have probably bragged to friends for the last year about their prowess.

Some are there to gauge their own 'usefulness'.

Some may have proven their abilities in pub brawls or on the football field and now wish to step up to bigger things to enhance their own pugilistic reputations.

* * *

Mr Sharman walks among the challengers, chatting; on the line-up board he has made his mind up about matching. I follow him. He tears off paper from a small notepad and gives them to challengers:

Fight one

Stone Fist Smith

Lightweight

vs

Alf Preston

Fight two

The Brutal Bricklayer
Welterweight
vs
Stanley Hill

Fight six

The Woolly Mammoth
Welterweight
vs
Stanley Hill.

Fight nine

Red Terror
Lightweight
vs
Alf Preston

Fight ten

William St Clair
Middleweight
vs
Tommy Murphy

There are no local versus local fights today … Trundle is a happy, harmonious town … for now.

Billy has a willing suite of prospective wrestling challengers. Twelve. The bouts are shorter, he only needs to pin them for ten seconds. More seem to sign on for the wrestling; perhaps, unlike the boxing, they are more likely to emerge unscathed, or perhaps it is because all men since boyhood have always wrestled and often recall beating younger brothers or smaller or weaker friends.

* * *

The tent flap is opened. The punters flood in. They are almost throwing the tickets at us to get a space at the front. Soon the crowd's breath, their shouting, clapping, jeers, laughter inflates the tent. It is close, sweaty and hot.

Fight one: Stone Fist Smith vs Alf Preston

The challenger stuck fast to the spot; Alf wanders around chipping away until Mr Sharman calls it off.

Fight two: The Brutal Bricklayer vs Stanley Hill

The Bricklayer has paid the price after someone in the crowd called Stanley a dumb black coon.

Fight three: The Goblin from Condobolin vs Jackie Green

I see Jackie preparing before entering the ring, punching into Mr Piggott's outstretched hands. Gentle, affable Jackie is transformed … animal quickness … brutal as a shotgun or a butcher's knife. Despite its brutality, I begin to see the intense athletic beauty of this sport.

Fight four: John Normus vs Jimmy Cowan

Giant slow punches, Jimmy's are faster. Heavyweights more or less have to win by knockout. John's just a big, nice but dim chap put up by his mates. Jimmy throws a few in the right places to put him on his backside. Jimmy wins narrowly on points.

Fight five: Peter the Perfect vs Alf Preston

Alf goes in close, ignoring instructions, punches here and there, fast but light. Peter the Perfect proves he is anything but.

Fight six: The Woolly Mammoth vs Stanley Hill.

Woolly Mammoths are extinct.

Fight seven: The Wellington Walloper vs Jimmy Cowan

Jimmy deconstructs him slowly, punches in the gut, face, enough to hurt but not drop him … the man throws in the towel soon enough. Mr Sharman can pick out a bully. They have a swagger.

He very much enjoys matching them with better opponents.

Fight eight: Rumbling O'Riley vs Jackie Green

The in-fighting is fierce: quick hurting jabs, rushes and retreats back and forth, leather hitting flesh, staggering away from a quick left right left, no quarter is given. Ducking … sideslipping. A brittle crack of bone somewhere on either O'Riley or maybe Jackie. O'Riley tires and drops his guard. Jackie gets in and under, wins on points. Mr Sharman notes O'Riley's details in his little book of names.

Fight nine: Red Terror vs Alf Preston

The man runs in, even before the bell. There is a furry of mad swings, Alf ducks under, counterpunches and the Red Terror is on the deck having a brief kip.

Mr Piggott: 'Probably the most at peace that mad bastard has been for quite a while.'

* * *

Billy Spiers has his list of wrestling techniques, between the boxing bouts, which he catalogues on the residents of Trundle:

Referee grip for the butcher's apprentice,
short arm scissors on the blacksmith,
the full nelson efficiently provided to the carpenter,
half nelson on the farrier,
he holds a plumber in a wristlock,
the flying head scissors, for the town bully,
he leaves a storekeeper trapped in the step over toe hold.
Then the infamous hammerlock …

Afterwards I overhear the hapless hammerlock victim exclaim to friends,

'Oh, the power ... the terrible power … '

* * *

I have noticed how expert Mr Sharman's matching has been; it is uncanny how he does this.

A few questions (boxed before? Trained with anyone?),

A check of the challenger's condition (breathing hard, nervous, overweight),

Size and shape (tall, long reach, torso).

These are like signposts for the later fights. He schedules the easier less technical fights first, the more difficult, more exciting last.

A fistic chessboard; pawns, then rooks, then bishops, then knights, kings and queens. It is clear he favours Jackie; everyone knows this, and they all agree Jackie is the best boy going around.

In his mind he is measuring all these men. How much fight

each of them has within them. How they may go up against others. A human yardstick …

Sharman's human scale.

Mr Sharman plans all his moves. After matching fighters and critiquing their skill Mr Sharman has also determined how a fight should run. I have overheard some of his instructions to his fighters before bouts …

To Alf vs Peter Perfect, 'He's new to all this, stay on yer bike and conserve your strength.'

To Jackie vs the Goblin, 'He's short and stocky, watch for the close in uppercut, up to you after that.'

To Alf before fighting the Red Terror, 'Those eyes don't look right, he's going to be fast in, block then drop him quick as you can.'

To Jimmy Cowan before he fronts the Walloper, 'Watch for a sneaky shot, he needs to be taught a lesson, he's the town bully, take it up to him and make him pay.'

* * *

Fight ten: Frank pretending to be Mr William St Clair vs Tommy Murphy

'Mr St Clair claims he's learned to box at Kings School and Sydney University. Well, he's challenged one of the country's best … Tommy's no mug … anyways we like to give a young man a chance to make a name for himself so it's a round or two for a pound or two. How's that? Ok? Good luck, son! Three three-minute rounds … may the best man win … come out fighting …'

For show, Tommy has a few wild swings from a safe distance.

Frank (or Mr William St Clair) throws thundering punches landing on arms and shoulders.

Then Tommy steps in with a fierce combination: right lead, left low, left low, right hook catching Frank on the ear.

Frank is in next with a combination of his own: in close, ducking under left uppercut, left jab, backing out, then a right roundhouse into ribs, left uppercut.

Sitting up close to the front I see that punches might land on faces but are lighter.

Tommy in again with a flurry.

Frank has a bloody nose. He seems surprised.

Tommy backs off and Frank moves in; now Tommy is showing a bit of claret from the nose as well.

Mr Sharman holds up both hands. It's a tie!

Then a shower of coins from the crowd:

deeners,

zacs,

all bouncing in.

Applause.

Cheers.

Children throw in their pocket money.

Treys.

Pennies.

* * *

Dusk now. Under the taste-in-the-mouth flavour of kerosene lamps the tent is rolled up. Frank and Tommy laugh about the blood noses: 'Remember next time when I make an O with my mouth it's time to go in with a round left and I will know to turn so you hit my cheek, ok?'

'Yeah, sorry, mate, got it.' Sheepish grins and smiles, no hard feelings.

* * *

I journal in the Trundle takings Mr Sharman has counted:

£84 2/6

Outgoings

Site hire £5

Lodgings £4

The takings are counted and the coins put into three brown paper bags inside one another with a tag that records the denomination and the total value of contents. Notes all bound in tight rolls with a tag again with denomination and total.

* * *

Mr Sharman's advice again:

Your best friend is your bank book ...

CHAPTER TWO

The old lie

Bells are ringing, at schools, churches, the fire brigade tower …

War! War has been declared!

Dispatch riders rip through the town's wide street at breakneck speed.

Hats and coats are waved.

Those even with the smallest of Union Jacks are raised above the crowd. 'Rule Britannia' and 'Soldiers of the King' are sung until we are all hoarse.

Newspapers sell out … Headlines shout …

Britain at war!

Invasion of Belgium.

France entered.

War fever! Flag torn down off SS Germania *while in port.*

Waves of enthusiasm.

All parts of the empire uniting for a common cause.

Rush of volunteers.

The shire council has met immediately, formally pledging loyalty to its King and Empire.

That night the pub is full. Great excitement. It is hard not to be caught up in the fervour at a time like this ... It's like the horses are turning into the final straight; Christmas morning and fireworks all together at the very same time.

Public meetings are held where motions of loyalty to the throne are passed by acclamation.

'So, some archduke and his missus get shot by a madman and every bloke has to stop what they are doing and go off to war. Beware of the old lie,' Mr Piggott said.

* * *

A dream I had last night ...

Green farms and sunlight, birds installed, singing in the trees.

Then lines of men. I stand by the road as they march past. Hundreds and hundreds of them.

Turning I see the horizon.
All is fire, screeching, rumbling.
Then mud, fog, smoke, a green mist.
Holes and bones and tangles of wire.

* * *

Trundle railway station.

We wait for the train. Hundreds of men are trying to buy tickets to Sydney to enlist. We are going the other way. Some old men, including the mayor, make rambling speeches. Shouting so much their cheeks glow red as they huff and puff. I need to go to the toilet and I push through the urgent, purposeful crowd.

The toilets stink of piss. I hear three men behind me as I stand at the urinal. They are arranging themselves.

'There he is, the cripple, he's not going off to fight. He's going to stay here with his mum. Let's see if you've got a bent, crooked dick as well.'

A push in the back and I lose my balance. My arm, my back and my leg are wet now as I lie in the urinal looking up at them.

Someone is gently lifting me up. It is Billy Spiers.

'What are you doing? one of them asks. 'He's nothing, a cripple, a weakling, him with his twisted arm, useless, no good to anyone.'

'So, you've decided that amongst yourselves, have you?' Billy says.

'Yeah, and what's he to you?'

'He's a thousand times better than all you three dogs put together.'

Three on one. Billy's built like an ox. They weigh up the prospect.

Before they start, I leap on the closest one, biting into his greasy ear. He screams; he tries to shake me off. I bite again, let go, fall and he is gone.

Billy lets rip a great boxing combination on the bigger one. The third runs.

'Good on you, little cobb,' Billy tells me as I catch my breath and spit. 'You're the toughest little bugger.'

'That combination you pulled,' I say, 'that was something; you could line up as a boxer.'

'Why would I want to do that? I don't want to really hurt anyone!' he says, laughing.

'Anyone except those curs. I'd see red if anyone ever tried to hurt you.'

Billy walks close behind me so no-one can see the stains of piss on the back of my trousers and jacket. Once we are underway he goes back to the baggage car and gets me some clean clothes.

* * *

He has said almost nothing this whole journey and yet there was so much to remark upon …

All the stories that were told.

The pandemonium of changing trains.

The pockets of good grazing country we see as we move along.

The mob of kangaroos that kept pace with us.

The pretty young woman and her aunt, who has fallen into flesh and complains loudly of motion sickness, vertigo and prickly heat all at the same time.

The large circle of cockatoos I saw holding council in the grass of a late afternoon hillside.

Mr Sharman spends his time pencilling figures into one of his notebooks. Or stares deep into one of the other notebooks that always he carries.

* * *

The basic rules of boxing, the revised Queensberry Rules, adapted for the tent, are explained to me:

Punches must be above the belt.

Kidney punches are not permitted; these are blows on the back of a boxer, above the hip line. Behind a line from the ear through the shoulder to the ankle, any punch in the area is deemed a foul.

Flicking or hitting with an open glove or 'heeling', as it is known is not allowed, neither is hitting with the inside or butt of the hand, the wrist or elbow is also not permitted, nor is wrestling or roughing at the ropes.

Likewise thumbing, the intentional use of the thumbs into the opponent's eyes, is strictly forbidden.

Should a clinch occur the men are to break away immediately and neither man must deliver a blow without having both hands free.

No seconds or any other person is allowed in the ring during rounds.

A ring shall be roped and twenty-four-foot square.

Points are awarded for attack; direct clean hits with the knuckles on any part of the front of the head or body above the belt.

Points are also awarded for defence; guarding, slipping, ducking, counter-hitting, or getting away.

Where points are equal, consideration is to be given to the man who does the most leading off.

Mr Sharman, as referee, has been known to award extra points for dash … or show … when he needs to … depending on the 'lay of the land'.

If either man shall fall through weakness or otherwise he must get up unassisted; his opponent meanwhile must not stand over him, but step back a distance. When the man is on his legs again, his opponent can advance to attack and continue the onslaught.

Other rules …

Ten count for a boxer knocked down.

Standing eight count for a boxer who is dazed but still standing.

Any competitor failing to come up when 'time' is called shall lose the bout.

The referee has the power to stop a fight if a man is weak or hopelessly beaten.

The decision of Mr Sharman is final.

* * *

Next town the next day, I telegram home. A reply within an hour.

Frank in. Bert too late.

* * *

Twenty thousand recruited in a matter of days. An embarrassment of riches.

* * *

The papers …

Barracks besieged by recruits …

Enthusiasm in all states …

* * *

The troupe interested now. Now that there is a fight on …

A discussion at breakfast.

The Germans have an army of nearly four million; then again, it is reported that the French have the same. And then there's our boys; they say, pound for pound one of ours is worth two or three of them.

'Give the Germans hell!'

* * *

The papers:

Heavy fighting along the River Meuse.

A Mr Cassels-Brown is contributing stationery free of charge to the local patriotic movement.

It is believed that a Mr Wilson has trained several of his horses to remain at a straight line of gallop despite the sound of rapid rifle fire and is now offering to soldiers at premium prices.

The Ladies Hospital Bazaar Fund Committee have very thoughtfully decided to devote the results of next Wednesday nights euchre tournament and dance to the patriotic movement.

There groups of men poring over maps in the papers, importantly discussing unfolding events …

European nations of the Pacific.

A view of the fleets in the North Sea.

The position of forces across Europe.

* * *

Everyone is an expert; there are lectures on the geography of the Rhine and the Austro Hungarian Empire.

There are reputations to be earned for the future.

Everyone wants to go, get amongst it. A chance to see the world. A chance to leave bad jobs and bad bosses. A chance for unhappy husbands to leave unhappy wives.

But they had better hurry; it's going to be all over by Christmas they reckon.

* * *

Temora

A trip down memory lane for Mr Sharman. It was here that he hired the Star Theatre and tried his hand as a promoter of local and visiting fighters. Overheads and a shortage of willing locals saw him change tack and decide to 'have a go at the travelling show'.

We time how long it takes to erect the tent. According to Mr Piggott this time will not be a quick time, with such hard ground and a new troupe.

Frank and Jackie race each other driving in stakes.

Alf lassos guy ropes around stakes and poles.

The others pair up and run canvas out until it snaps taut over poles.

More hauling.

Tightening.

'Done, Mr Piggott.'

'What's the time, Mr P?'

'A good time, boys.'

Mr Piggott begins his inspection. A slack guy rope and a pole out of line disqualify the time.

* * *

Mr Sharman has been busy this morning painting a showground banner. He is a dab hand with both the lettering and the illustrations.

This new banner reads … *For every champion found in the city another six are discovered in the country.*

Mr Piggott broke into a wry smile when he saw it. 'Ah, there is a man who understands his audience.'

* * *

This morning's training …

Stretching.

A short run around the showground perimeter.

Specific training to improve boxers' wind …

Standing and breathing,
full inhalation,
full exhalation.

They have lungs like blacksmith bellows.

A decent turn on the single fixed punching ball, which does wonders for wind as well as vastly improving quickness of the hands and eyes. Running up and down the stairs of the grandstand, sprints, skipping, puff out all but the soundest of wind and limb. Jackie is a stand-out exponent.

* * *

A little different in the tent today. There is a surge of challengers, young men out to prove themselves, preparing to enlist, or proving their courage as if the war has called it into question … and for most of them it has.

* * *

At the next mayoral reception at the next town Billy is over talking with the pianist.

The whiskey-soaked Master of Ceremonies announces, 'Ladies and gentlemen, the Mayor and Mayoress, we have a special treat this evening: William Spiers of Mr Sharman's Boxing Troupe is going to perform a number of popular songs.' I am a little embarrassed for him; how is this giant man going to sing? Then I remember I should not judge people by their appearance.

Billy, so big, wide and tall … begins to sing.

It is truly beautiful.

Mr Sharman turns to me. 'It's a song about our dear old Irish mothers! One of my favourite songs!'

He has diamonds of tears forming in his eyes.

Billy's voice so tender, rising and falling like the sound of starlings calling from the blue sky high above a field.

Then he is finished. Then there is silence, apart from the sniffing of tears, and then the hall is vibrating with clapping and cheers.

* * *

I have a letter from Bert. He has tried to sign up, but he couldn't reach Sydney quick enough … But my brother Frank is in. Got down to the Sydney Recruitment Office as soon as he heard … one hundred and tenth in line! Bert couldn't get up there in time; will look to go in for the next round if there's another one. Whole thing might be over pretty quick. Might have trouble getting in with his poor teeth … he's going to tell them he would much prefer to shoot the Germans than bite them!

* * *

Ardlethan

This is where Mr Sharman first showed; 1911.

'Tough times early on sending off letters and always getting the same reply back again and again … boxing not wanted here … In those early days the boxing showman was like a burglar out of work,' Mr Piggott said. 'Mr Sharman had to prove to the committees he ran a tighter ship than the others … soon, and only after three or four years, on account of his manners and charm as well as the bona fide entertainment, the committees were begging him to show with them.'

Back then, the Temora Show Committee wouldn't let him show there so he tried Ardlethan the week after. Stan, Frank and Tommy were there, and some others who have since moved on. Mr Piggott was there too, remembers it well.

'Mr Sharman was so nervous. Struck down with the worst case of stage fright you have ever seen. Lot of the town wants him to fail. So, he's up there on the boards and I've been giving the drum a fair whack and there's all these mugs hanging around waiting and the cat's got Mr Sharman's tongue.

'He croaks out just one word: "Gents". Then that's it, nothing.

'One of Mr Sharman's friends from Narrandera takes him out the back, chatting to him. Then I see him practising a spiel on a couple of crows on the fence. They didn't much like it so he turns to a tree stump and starts on that. Five minutes later he's back, but this time, he stands on the ladder, halfway, and starts his spiel … who'll take a glove, a round or two for a pound or two … all that stuff. That's how he got started. Lungs of leather, that man.'

* * *

Leeton

It was here Mr Sharman worked as a billy boy, making tea for the workers on the Yanco Irrigation Scheme. Knocked the block off the foreman, a bully twice his age and size, earned some respect. Won a few locally organised fights, backed himself and earned enough money never to be some poor paddy working on a dairy farm.

* * *

Everywhere we go there are new patriotic events.

At Leeton we attend our first Grand Patriotic Concert.

A brass band plays regimental marches and other tunes …

'Rule Britannia' and 'Sons of the Sea'.

The Athenaeum Hall full of flags and flora.

Boer War veterans have polished off old medals and wear them proudly on puffed out chests.

Singing … 'God Save the King' and 'Soldiers of the King'.

Long speeches, hearty cheering, hands sore from applause.

New and old words become well used … Bulldog Breed, Empire's Cause, Courage, Bravery, Defence, King and Country, Kaiser, Kitchener …

* * *

Everywhere, women and girls are busy making comforts for troops … raising funds for the Belgium victims.

* * *

We read war gossip …

A Gunner Bellchambers, an ex-member of the Royal Australian

Garrison, was visiting the Sydney barracks and upon hearing the war news dropped dead.

* * *

Several men who had deserted from the British Army many years ago have appeared in a Dandenong drill hall to offer their experienced services.

* * *

'Surely the Sharman boys will be off soon to get a piece of the action?'

* * *

We do a stocktake of our own:

Jackie says he'd love to go and be a six-bob-a-day tourist … a lark!

Stanley Hill won't … he won't be asked anyway.

Frank's got family to look after.

Jimmy Cowan will weigh up his options at the end of the run.

Alf says nothing.

Tommy Murphy reckons it's too late for any of them; it will be done and dusted by Christmas.

Billy would go if things really turned to custard.

Mr Piggott said he's had his war and it's a young man's game.

Mr Sharman, he's not that old … he says nothing.

* * *

Next morning.

'Alfs gone. He's done a runner,' hisses Jimmy.

Jimmy got up for a leak and saw a pillow under the sheets, wondered why he had tidied up his things so well last night, very unusual for Alfy boy. An envelope addressed 'Strictly Confidential and Personal for Mr James Sharman Only' left on the dresser.

Mr Sharman is trembling with rage when I tell him and hand over the letter.

He angrily tears open the letter and slams the door behind him to read Alf's letter alone.

He never tells anyone about its contents. He never mentions Alf by name again.

* * *

There is a great joy expressed for anyone leaving.

The best leading hands from surrounding properties leave with brand new saddles given to them as farewell gifts by grateful station owners.

Every man on one street in Carlton all enlist together.

Sixty-one 'Old Scotchies' in Melbourne receive a great send-off.

Gifts of the new wristwatches, kisses of promise, smiles from the farewelled and farewellers.

* * *

Les has fouled Fritz Holland, the flying Dutchman, accidental and without malice … Les is in absolute disbelief.

* * *

Lessons in technique:

Guarding a left lead … various options are available …

Duck right leaving your opponent's ribs open or counter with a left to the chin.

Side step or slip away.

Draw back.

Save your energy for your own attack.

Mr Sharman's overall rules for guarding:

Guarding is not to become a habit. The counter, the duck or withdraw are better tactics, the slip is useful in tight corners.

Mr Sharman's advice on leading:

A quick straight left hand lead to the head is the shortest distance between fists and your opponent and will win you more fights than any other. The left hand lead is the best tool in the boxer's tool bag.

There is repeated talk about 'hitting the mark'. Mr Piggott explains that it is the spot below the sternum where the ribs are fastened over the heart.

Mr Sharman's advice on defence and counter:

Counter with a left uppercut as he swings, wait for his head to drop then land one in his face. His momentum and now yours will double the impact.

Divine your opponent's intentions; punch him on the head before he can get his head down.

Right hand leads must only follow a left feint. Although not as safe as a straight left lead it will often meet with considerable success. It is a risk reward move …

Step well in.

Look for the opening just as he swings his left at you.

These are the pure mechanics of fighting and all of Sharman's men are well versed in these. Mr Sharman wants them to dream this in their sleep and I am sure that they do.

The southpaws and the switch stances throw these techniques into reverse, upside down and back to front. Fighters with vision and knowledge of such basic techniques can anticipate, move and outfox their opponents, saving themselves and hitting the mark more often.

Mr Sharman has great enthusiasm for parrying.

The diverting guard will throw the opponent off balance, exposing him to a punishing blow instead of dealing you one.

Parrying is like the sudden slide of a violin bow as the tempo changes.

Counters, time hits and stops are demonstrated and gone over again.

If you have the reach on your opponent employ the stop hit.

Successful countering, particularly left hand head counters, looks a lot like leading.

The right cross counter is an important strike in the boxer's arsenal.

The left cross counter, Mr Sharman's own famous (or infamous) best shot. The hook, arm raised with the shoulder, fist and arm swinging … with weight … into the right side of the head, on the temple.

'Plenty of shots other than that one,' Mr Sharman says. 'There is a tendency to injure … the hitting arm … ' he explains; however, there seems to be more to this than his stated reasons.

Mr Sharman asks them to rehearse at a tertiary level:

Double leads,

the postman's knock,

the rat-tat-tat,

the good old one-two.

Left body and head.

Left body right head.

Left head right body.

Both hands body and head.

Like a musical score … quaver, semiquaver, treble clef.

'What's your bread and butter?' Mr Sharman asks as each boxer pairs up for sparring.

'Jackie, what's your bread and butter?'

'The quick jab.'

'Show me how, quick!'

To Jackie again, 'What's the second bread and butter then, Jackie boy?'

'Great foot work.'

'Show me your one-two; show me the bread and butter! Show me boxing, all of you, show me fighting!'

Like an orchestra they throw themselves into it. The big bass drum hits of Frank and Jimmy Cowan. Bouncing footwork of Jackie on strings and also his bold-as-brass moves. The wind of Stan's fists parting the air. And there in the middle of all of this is Mr Sharman, conducting this great fistic symphony.

* * *

Over the breakfast table Mr Sharman outlines the daily habits he expects of his boxers.

Early rising with walks, running and training before breakfast. The meal times of a normal businessman also suit a boxer although the practice of late dining is not encouraged.

A breakfast of eggs only. Lunch, a few simple sandwiches. Dinner needs to be early, a balance of beef and mutton, vegetables and stewed fruit.

Sleeping should be limited to eight hours, any more will invite lethargy.

The habit of smoking is permitted but not encouraged as it is thought to affect a boxer's wind.

The consumption of alcohol in any of its forms is not permitted as it is the ruin of many a good boxer.

Walking is encouraged ... it is impossible to walk too much ...

* * *

To all these men this sport is a craft, a science, the sweet science, a passion, a minute by minute obsession.

They discuss all aspects of fighting at great length, with great enthusiasm;

in pairs or groups of two or three,
when their mouths are full of toast and marmalade at breakfast,
on windy platforms waiting for trains,
during breaks at training,
on grey morning walks,
taking morning tea, at lunch, after dinner,
they talk and talk about boxing ...
The new transatlantic style.
Rushes, double leads and clinching.
Mr Sharman's opinion on clinching is that it is a coward's hold.

That many a decent fighter has been cheated by an incessant clincher.

In the tent he detests the practice and stamps it out immediately.

Past fights …

Jackie: 'So, he pulls straight back, you can't do that, go to the side, man! Get out of the way! It's like he's running on a train track and the Jackie train is going to keep on coming. Blam!'

Frank: 'Starved for a week to make the weight, lived on orange juice, so weak I couldn't lift my arms into a guard, clinched for three rounds … he propped me up … until, out of the blue, he leans his chin forward, just for me.'

They dissect the fights or progress of others within the troupe …

Suggesting Jimmy Cowan needs a week of skipping to loosen up the feet,

and he should copy some of Jackie's combinations,

that Stan has, weight for weight, the most powerful punch of them all.

Famous fighters …

How Jack Johnson would wrap a piece of gauze tightly around his member. So, under his trunks it looked even bigger than any other white man's … infuriating everyone.

Young Griffo, his amazing headwork, the impenetrable defence, his dazzling feints, the will o' the wisp moves, the rapid two-handed attacks. That fight against Ike 'Spider' Weir. Went missing the night before, found by two Chicago plainclothes policemen in a low dive, drunk as a post.

Taken to a Turkish bathhouse so he might be able to distinguish referee from opponent.

Two hours later he gives the Belfast Spider a sound thrashing.

Joe Grimm, the Italian from the United States who could never be knocked out. Boxers break their hands on his face and he never falls. Came to Australia in 1909 … The fighter who could never lose … but … who could never win either …

He half-walked, half-rode from Melbourne to Perth on a talking goat who swore worse than a sailor. People will still talk about him in a hundred years' time.

Edward Bowes, the great English 'Horizontalist', who despite positive promotion by Australian newspapers never failed to go to ground before the second or third bell in every match of his so-called Triumphant Australasian Tour.

The big stadium fights …

Especially Johnson versus Burns. They turn this over in conversation, daily.

Stanley will often ask Mr Piggott, who was present at Rushcutter's Stadium, to retell the event …

'Punters started lining up at two-thirty in the morning. Two hundred and fifty policemen, twenty thousand spectators inside, thirty thousand outside hanging off trees and telegraph poles.'

'Johnson comes out, the whole crowd booing and hissing calling him all kinds of names. Old Tommy Boy comes out in an old blue suit and refuses to shake Johnson 's hand.'

Listening to Mr Piggott I am there now too. Sitting three rows from the front and I can see everything …

Johnson drinking a mouthful of water and spitting it with great accuracy between the head of one of his seconds and a pressman onto a vacant space the size of a handkerchief.

Checking with a second to make sure if his large bet, on himself, has been placed.

Burns takes off the old blue suit and puts it in an old suitcase.

He's wearing these elastic arm bandages.

Johnson yells to take them off.

Burns says no.

Johnson sits on his stool refusing to fight.

Burns sits too.

Huge Deal McIntosh dressed as the referee (white turtleneck, grey cap, white slacks, white shoes) is in a real flap. Asks Larry Foley to come up and check. Larry rules them illegal and Burns gets really angry tearing them off.

Bell rings, Johnson's talking: 'All right, Tommy, here I am.'

A short right uppercut from Johnson lifts Burns up off the deck. Shocked, Burns is back up off the canvas at the eight count. Johnson counterpunches, taunting Burns, 'Poor little Tommy; thought you were a fighter.'

In their corners, Burns' seconds flap towels and sponge him in champagne but he is already overwhelmed. Johnson sprays water playfully over the pressmen, laughing.

At the bell, Burns rushes and Johnson moves his head ever so slightly, landing an uppercut on the chin. Down again. Groggy but up again by the eight count. Burns shouting at Johnson, 'Come on and fight, nigger, fight like a white man.'

Again and again, Burns rushes in. Johnson hits him on the way in, holds him with a series of uppercuts then punches him three times on the way back out. All the time Jack's talking to him, 'Hit me here, Tommy.' Burns hits him in the stomach and Jack doesn't even wince or cover up. 'Now there, Tommy.' Jack chuckles. 'You punch like a woman, Tommy. Who taught you to fight? Your mother?'

By the fifth round, Jack's saying to Burns, 'This is what they call a left hook.' Burns rushes in and Jack plants a left hook on him.

Sixth round, Jack is chattering to the press. Some of the crowd yelling, 'That's flashness, that is … flash nigger!'

Seventh round, Burns goes down again.

Round ten, a photographer puts his camera under the ropes. Jack stops, smiles, holds the groggy Burns up to the lens, then moves him away asking, 'Did you get that?'

Thirteenth round, Burns has one eye closed, blood drip, drip, dripping. His jaw twice the size it should be, his mouth torn and swollen.

Policemen go to Burns' corner asking if they have permission to stop the fight. Burns – how he even managed to see them is a miracle – waves them away.

Fourteenth round and Jack Johnson is about to lay another one on Burns when the police superintendent signals that the fight must stop. Huge Deal yells out, 'Stop, Johnson!' He announces that Johnson is the winner, the world champion, the first black man to take the title. The crowd screams. Burns is crying, tells everyone later he wasn't beat, that he might have won if he had more time, because 'the big nigger was tiring' …

* * *

On the train there is talk about the specific tactics of tent fighting …

Advice from Mr Sharman …

Size up the opponent, study him … his greatest strength is that you don't know anything about him. Check the length of his torso, the distance between his ribs and his hips, if there is an unusual length this is the place to go for. A jutting chin is another point to aim at.

Overall body composition seems to determine a man's fighting style. According to Mr Sharman, the torso tells everything you will need to know.

A key measure in Mr Sharman's human scale:

A man who is lean around the waist will have less power but move quickly.

A man with long arms and torso will fight like an ungainly praying mantis, telegraphing his intentions. Do not let him determine how long his reach is or he may have you.

A shorter man usually has twice as much anger as a big fellow. Never underestimate them.

A man with a wide girth and fat will have power early then tire quickly … run out of puff.

More advice:

Cultivate quick, slight movements or tricks with the eyes, hands and feet, which will convey the impression of a sudden, rapid movement, which you will not really carry out … These tactics will cause your opponent to make a big lunge or a rapid jerk or spring backwards or sideways. This will take a lot of steam out of him, without having distressed you in any way …

At the bell, throw out a tester … the old one-two, straight left jab then a right. If they see that coming and defend or counter they might have half a clue … there's always more skill and know-how in defending. Wait for them to show their wares and then exploit the weakness. With amateurs there is always a weakness – fitness, character, knowledge, body structure, vision, a gap in training. Find it and answer the questions they didn't know about boxing …

> *Hit a man straight on the nose and it will blind him with tears. One or two square on the mark to distress him.*
>
> *Remain a moving target. Invite him to show his talents, an exchange, that's what people want to see … not someone lying on the ground or wrapped up in clinches.*
>
> *When a man is knocked down don't rush in to finish him up; this is where he often makes his most desperate fight.*

'It's not how hard you hit a fella, it's how tired he gets trying to hit you,' Frank says.

Other peculiarities of showground fighting …

Jimmy Cowan: 'Watch him in the ring; if he scrapes his feet, getting the feel of the grass or sawdust, you will know he has done this before.'

'Watch for the drunk's first big swing then punch him the guts where the beer is sitting,' says Stan.

* * *

We discuss how to best deliver the 'knockout blow'. Frank explains the options …

The solar plexus blow, usually a left hook to the breast bone, right on the mark, is usually the best for this. To execute, first work punches to the head and shoulder, moving his guard up. Step in and aim for the mark.

A more effective punch is the one that lands on the chin. A left or right close-in hook after drawing the opponent in will drop him quickly. The left cross counter is particularly good if timed right.

'Those kinds of moves are not required in the tent,' Mr

Sharman says with a look of sadness moving quietly across his face.

* * *

Snowy Baker is really pushing his correspondence courses for boxing …

> *SOME DAY YOU'LL BE SORRY that you cannot box. When you find yourself facing the bully, your size and strength will not help you _ but SCIENCE _ will. Don't envy others for their coolness and confidence in a scrap _ be envied yourself! Think how humiliating it would be to be beaten by a man smaller than yourself, think of the jeers of the onlookers and the taunts of your pals.*

* * *

Wagga Wagga

We arrive at the train station platform. 'Wagga Wagga … so nice they named it twice,' Mr Piggott jests. He is in fine form today, as many of his people are here.

Mr Piggott mentions that Wagga was the last place Mr Sharman ever fought. I ask Mr Piggott why Mr Sharman stopped fighting. As we hear so often, particularly down in the Riverina, everyone knows about the fierce Jimmy Sharman … the southpaw with the knockout punch, the seventy-seven wins from seventy-eight fights, the man in line for the Australian Lightweight Crown.

'You don't know? Surprised no-one else has told you. Tragedy, it was tragedy that stopped him. The Olympic skating rink hall.

Just down the road there.' Mr Piggott is pointing. 'I was there, I saw it.'

'Fighting Jack Carter, the place packed to the rafters, lots of money riding too. A five hundred pound side bet on Jimmy apparently. Jack's a good mate of Jimmy but he's giving Jack a belting. Jimmy asked the seconds to stop the fight, it was going to be a bloodbath and Jack wasn't up to it. The ref says fight on. Next round Jimmy threw that southpaw punch of his to end it quickly. I tell you, a punch that went around the world. Jack Carter drops to the deck screaming, hands over his face. Jack Carter went blind from that one punch. Jimmy, Mr Sharman I mean, never fought again, couldn't stomach it, the guilt. Stayed beside Carter's bed for weeks. Carter was in hospital for nineteen weeks. That's why we always do the Wagga Hospital fundraiser. Never got over it. You watch him; Mr Sharman lost something of himself that day ... you can see it every day, him living with it.'

I have seen it ...

Making sure none of the troupe are fighting with headaches.

Spells given following injury or heavy knocks.

The money orders to Mrs J Carter of Richmond.

The shaking hands that hold smelling salts under the nose of the fitting boy at Lithgow.

Always picking the exact moment when a fight has run its course, the moment before someone gets seriously hurt.

Instructions to the troupe that ... body blows show more skill than the head shots.

* * *

At the annual picnic sports day Mr Sharman gives self-defence lectures. Fighting at close quarters, how to disarm a man … Good fights and good crowds ensue. Mr Sharman provides, as he always does, a very large donation to the Wagga Wagga District Hospital Trust …

* * *

The war now occupies everything and everyone. Before the talk around town was rain, or crops, or prices; now it is the war.

Fundraising …

Raffles for cakes, paintings, smoking pipes, cushions, fat pigs, fat sheep, more cakes.

Rattling of tins, women moving in packs … 'Cadge, cadge, cadge.'

Assemblies of all kinds …

Fancy dress balls.

Torchlight parades.

Euchre and dance evenings, with a splendid supper provided by the Women's Patriotic league.

Mock battles between the local militia and cadets, rifle fire, the crowd cheering and Mr Piggott looking tense … I see him shiver ...

Promises …

One thousand gallons of port promised for sick and wounded soldiers.

A Perth businessman with South African experience has offered to raise a force of one hundred and twenty.

Huge Deal McIntosh himself has offered to raise a corps of motorcyclists.

Ideas for weapons …

There is a suggestion for the use of stockwhips to rip away weapons from the hands of the enemy.

A man from Hobart has an idea of using boomerang bayonets.

Mr Piggott laughs. 'So, how are you supposed to catch them when they come back?'

Jackie has heard that the Germans have designed and are building a giant aerial battleship.

* * *

Every town has a Patriotic Sewing Guild, a Sandbag Committee, a Women's Red Cross Auxiliary.

* * *

Narrandera

Mr Sharman is greeted warmly by old friends. After Leeton and before moving to Wagga he lived here. Worked for a coal carter that toughened him up … It's where he met his sweetheart and where Young Jimmy, his son, was born. Made firm friends here.

There is a curious number of letters in the paper …

Based on information supplied by the great angel, that this war is our Armageddon, soon all Christian Churches will have fallen and by 1920 we would have seen the second coming.

The war is definitely caused by Martians attempting to communicate with earth.

* * *

Eddie McGoorty smashed his Sunday punch into Les Darcy's jaw and he goes down flat on the floor. Suddenly at the count of seven Les does this flip straight off the canvas back onto his feet and he has that big smile across his face. Les drops Eddie and by the fourteenth the Osh Kosh Terror is done. Les wins.

* * *

More claims made in the papers:

Brave little Belgium and the barbaric Bosh ...

Murderous Hun ... massacres at Dinant.

Babies stolen from mothers' arms and squirming on the end of Hun bayonets. Machine gunning of civilians at Aerschott.

Rape at Tamines.

Bodies of priests thrown into rivers, or worse, killed and hung upside down inside church bells to bang like the bell clapper.

Beautiful Leuven reduced to ashes.

* * *

Confirmation of Belgian Atrocities ...

HORRIBLE STORIES OF GERMAN FIENDISHESS

British war correspondents in Belgium have seen little murdered children with roasted feet. The tiny mites were hung over a fire before they were slain. This done by German troops – men with children of their own at home, or with little brothers and sisters of the same age as the innocents they torture before killing.

The things done to Belgian girls and women, before their

tortured, lifeless bodies with battered faces were thrown into a ditch, are so unspeakably dreadful that details cannot be printed.

Billy and Frank tell me to stop reading out aloud. Tommy clenches his fist and bangs the table. We are sickened by these violations.

* * *

The Bulletin has the headline 'Every Fit Man is Wanted'.

The minimum requirements … eighteen to thirty-five, 5ft 6in 34in chest …

* * *

Smaller men approach Mr Sharman for tips to improve their stature.

* * *

Mr Sharman calls a troupe meeting. Don't think about taking off. Plenty to do here. Enough men have gone to deal with the Germans.

The whole thing will probably be over by Christmas. Moral obligations to the employer, promises to the spectators and each other. Sneaking off makes it harder on those who stay. You have a job to do here, it's not right to leave us in the lurch. If things change you have the summer to consider your options.

* * *

Albury

Mr Sharman can pick out the showground troublemakers, the pickpockets who work the distracted crowds. Mr Sharman can see past their friendly grins. Being pickpocketed in or around the tent is no good for the state of anyone's finances.

Being such a good judge of a man's character has seen Mr Sharman prosper. Matching the best fights helps, battles of wits and wills, but it is more than this; it is the friendly arm around the shoulder of the pickpocket … to move on or be moved … the cheery hello and warm handshake with the show committee men, the mentioning that the show is indeed bigger and better than others in the wider district …

* * *

'Give me a lad from the country,' Mr Sharman tells the Mayor's Luncheon, the Show Committee Soiree … *'Country lad, used to hard work, one who keeps regular hours, is properly fed, he has the foundation upon which to build a good boxer, a much better foundation than any of the city fellows.'*

* * *

I see them all up there on the board, the whole troupe. We are learning more about each other. I delight in the discoveries I find in each of them, I catalogue their habits, their smallest mannerisms …

Mr Piggott. Who always slaps the shoulders of the fighters, asking them if they are 'feeling frisky'.

Billy Spiers. Who smells of slippery goanna oil.

Tommy Woods. His fondness for toffees.

Jimmy Cowan. A foundling. Left in a shoebox outside Scots Church. His kindness to children.

Billy Spiers. How he likes to whisper something funny into the ear of an opponent during a hold to unsettle them.

Jackie Green's attempts at smoking a pipe.

Frank and his early morning humming of band tunes.

Stan's uncomfortable shoes.

Jackie's gullibility.

Frank's special wink and smile he gives to ladies.

The jingling of coins in Tommy's pockets.

Jimmy Cowan who seeks out a hill or rooftop to sit alone and stare off into the distance.

Billy's playing of the spoons.

Stan's shyness or his refusal to reveal anything much of himself.

Billy Spiers who you might need to rouse from his sleep in the back corner of the tent just minutes before his bout.

Mr Piggott, a veteran of the Boer War. His sarcastic raised eyebrow.

Frank's constant efforts to find shade; Stan's complete indifference to the sun.

And Mr Sharman. Mr Sharman has his habits, less revealed and much more difficult to fathom.

Nicknames …

Jackie Green is called 'Twig'; with his surname and being small and thin, the term is an easy leap to make.

Frank Burns likes to be known as 'The Anvil'.

Stan is called 'Snake'.

Jimmy Cowan is called 'Crusher' as a result of his big punches.

Mr Paddy Piggott, the tent boss, is for the most part called

Mr Piggott, as he is a senior man. Sometimes during moments of levity we can get away with 'Mr P'.

Tommy Murphy is called 'Toff' or 'Toffee'.

Billy Spiers is called 'Billy Buckets' on account of his huge hands.

They call me Arch, 'Pencils' or 'Packets', as I am the one who hands out their allowances and sharpens Mr Sharman's grey leads. Frank calls me 'Paperboy' based on my ferocity for reading the news.

Only Mr Piggott calls Mr Sharman by a nickname and never in front of others … 'Squizzy' …

* * *

We see, according to Mr Piggott, the first of many, snake oil merchants. Slightly strange most of them … spend that much time with serpents and become a piece or part of one.

The smaller, out-of-the-way shows usually throw up examples of the less scrupulous types.

They travel alone. Arriving three or four days before a show, with a bag of toffee they get to know the local scallywags, children, especially truants, who know where to find the hiding holes of local snakes.

The 'professional snake catcher' as he touts himself, then catches a few, puts a spade through most others and makes enough money from the town's worried housewives to have a very nice steak dinner show eve.

At the show, he pulls out a drugged taipan or death adder, claiming it to be one of eight he removed from a schoolhouse in Kickatincan or Wheelabarraback. He will show off various snakes he has collected in his travels: a huge diamond python, an Indian cobra, a rattlesnake that ticks in a box. Then he will provide a king brown or tiger snake he claims to have liberated from under one of the town's local landmarks.

Snake season! he will proclaim. Either the start of mating, end of hibernation, warmer weather, the drought, the rain, haymaking, the wheat harvest, lambing season, where there is a plague of rats, an overabundance of frogs.

'Out and about, ladies and gentlemen, they're certainly out and about.'

'Long grass, woodpiles, sheds, every place, where your husband works, where your children play, a snake awaits ...'

'A little reassurance for your family.' He offers snake bite cures, a wee jar to keep above the fireplace. He sells suction cups, various concoctions;

strychnine,

alcohol, benzine and gun powder combinations,

the juice of the coastal pigface plant …

This particular snake oil salesman sells toad urine ...

* * *

We discuss some of the many remedies that can be employed to combat the rigours of boxing …

Boxers who rub their heads and necks twice a day with a concoction of beef brine and borax to pickle the skin and make it impervious to cuts.

Castor oil in the ear with a specially shaped cork to help reduce tinnitus.

Draw a hot bath and have a second bath available nearby

half full of ice and water. Three minutes in the hot bath then three minutes in the ice bath. Repeat twice. This helps overcome muscle soreness.

Champagne and beef tea freshens up an overtrained man.

A treatment for heavy colds … an egg beaten into a bucket of stout and champagne … is a great restorative.

Jackie told us about Jim Jeffries, who once drunk an entire case of whiskey in two days to cure himself of near death pneumonia.

* * *

Each of the troupe has a fighting style, an approach, a method they are known for:

Jackie is all about speed. First, he might throw a few slow short ones out across the bow of the opponent, who might then think he has the measure of Jackie, the range of his punches, only to be surprised when things suddenly speed up … very quickly.

Stan is a circler. Dabs and dabs, waiting for the opponent to be tempted to open up. Or he winds around the fighter; closer, closer, before he suddenly springs in from an unforeseen angle to finish them off.

Tommy is all offence; he takes it right to the opponent. He has a tendency to drop his guard. Mr Sharman warns him about this, to keep his arm up straight not loose and hanging; if outlasted by a good defender, who then counters, he could find himself in a pickle. Not that you tend to find too many quality method boxers challenging at showground fights.

Jimmy relies on a heavy punch regime. He is methodical, stubbornly carrying out a plan he has often discussed with Mr Sharman before the fight.

Frank entertains. A purveyor of punches. He likes to use them all:
one/two/two combinations,
uppercuts,
ones in from around the corner,
a swerve, a duck and a flurry of punches in the guts,
crosscuts on the chin.
A real mixed packet of pugilistic liquorice all sorts is our Frank.

Billy Spiers, as the wrestler, has a specialised fighting technique, employing various holds, approaching things in his unique way. As it is a different discipline from others, it is difficult to make comparisons; most of what Mr Spiers does will remain a mystery to all of us.

Tommy Murphy will play an opponent like a cat with a captured mouse.

According to Mr Piggott, when he was fighting, Mr Sharman had a quick heavy left hook that did all the damage.

* * *

Mr Sharman will let each of the troupe know what kind of fight he wants. Having sized up the challengers' capabilities he will lean in and whisper in his boxers' ears:

'Let him throw a few.'

'Watch for the big swings.'

'Yours has some form.'

'Trade blows.'

'Drag it out, Jimmy.'

'Finish him early.'

Fistic tailoring; fights made to measure.

* * *

There are two aims with fights: 1) try to not let any of the troupe get hurt or overtired, 2) give the crowd what they want.

What does the crowd want?

The local boy to do well.

The town bully to learn a lesson.

To see some of the craft, the fancy, the sweet science.

* * *

Train journey conversations about …

The fairer sex …

What words to write in letters home to sweethearts.

Lucinda the Snake Dancer and occasional friend of Frank's, who was recently arrested by an overzealous constable in Lismore for exposing her midriff.

Repeated soft kissing of the neck can be particularly … persuasive.

Family life …

Jackie: raised by grandmother, mother died in childbirth.

Stanley: born in Victoria raised in by a grazier in Queensland who adopted him after he took a fancy to him.

Frank: the oldest of five, one sister and three brothers, plus him.

Jimmy Cowan: Wollongong Orphanage, number forty-seven. Bastard son of an American whaleboat captain and scullery maid apparently … but aren't all bastards spawned from some romantic tryst? Shifted from one place to the next, beat up, felt up and took off as soon as he could.

Mr Piggott: dad the town drunk, two elder brothers. A wife, two daughters, two of the prettiest girls in all of Wagga Wagga and that's saying something.

Tommy: mother, father, brothers and sisters all very normal. Two boys of his own, another on the way.

Billy: an only son.

Mr Sharman: thirteen brothers and sisters.

* * *

The reputation of Sharman's troupe is extraordinary. Every week people's enthusiasm for us and for boxing seems to double upon itself …

People stare.

People point.

They mill around waiting for the … right moment …

They grab hold of arms to size up strength.

Children approach and wrap themselves around legs or hold up fists in mock stances.

I have never shaken so many hands.

People ask if I am related to the Blackmores of Grafton … or the Blackmores that farm down around Walcha.

There are requests for autographs.

Important men wish to pose important questions.

Men with 'some standing in the community' introduce themselves, their goods, their ideas, passing around their business cards like croupiers.

Others offer promises or make business propositions that Mr Sharman has warned us previously to politely decline.

Women curtsey, offer gloved hands.

People smile, applaud as we enter rooms.

But Mr Piggott says he has noticed a decline in enthusiasm for the troupe since the start of the war. Was it the excitement of the war or was it that we were not going?

* * *

We discuss how a small town works.

Which men hold sway:

the bank manager,

the town veterinarian,

the parson.

The mayor? Usually a fat pompous, irrelevant, grog-soaked buffoon.

Head of the show committee. Yes, important to stay on the right side of him. Hop right inside his pocket …

The town clerk.

The general manager of the local meatworks.

The landed gentry will always have their own point of view.

There will often be a mad Dutchman who lives alone out on the edge of town and who will demand to have his say at all public meetings.

Water diviners will rise in status during droughts.

Undertakers' hands that are never shaken.

Horse whisperers remain peculiar.

A friendly publican who will have his hand more or less permanently attached to the velvet bottom of one or several of his female staff.

A good proportion of the town's drunks must always be Irish.

Storemen must be missing an arm or leg, caught in a thrasher or such like.

Thieves are always the shearers, or show people.

There needs to a group of naughty children and another of older town louts.

There will be a local push. A group of ruffians and ratbags ready to be put in their place.

* * *

We recall how Mr Sharman works the room ... A one-man charm offensive, all five foot four of him, thrusting, smiling, right up into their faces. Whether they are friend or foe he does not leave anyone unimpressed, he does not leave anyone in any doubt that he is the most honest, goodhearted man, you have ever had the pleasure to meet.

With every introduction he gives them exactly what they want or exactly what they need ... whatever needs to be dispensed ... in perfect measure ... not an ounce under or over ...

See him greet mere passing acquaintances as old friends:

'William Morrell, so very good to see you again.'

'James Samson, you are looking in good shape, country life appears to be agreeing with you.'

'Fred Bostock, how's that racehorse of yours? ... Magpie Lad ... how's he going?'

* * *

Superstitions:

Jackie Green's laces, right foot first then left foot, sometimes with a triple knot if the opponent looks especially good.

Stan will always touch the corner post at the sound of the first round bell.

Frank crosses his fingers whenever he sees a black cat, but in the tent, he just gets on with it.

Tommy and his lucky rabbit's foot.

Jimmy Cowan spits into his palms before putting on gloves to fight.

Mr Piggott touches wood.

Tommy Murphy always makes the sign of the cross (spectacles, testicles, wallet and watch).

Billy has worn the same pair of lucky trunks every single one of his bouts

Mr Sharman says he has no superstitions, you make your own luck.

* * *

'Wowsers!' Tommy yells through the tent flap to the others. Now we can see them marching, dour, towards us and the showground publican's booth next door to our site.

I ask whether we should expect any trouble. Mr Piggott says, 'No, we're all right … muscular Christians us lot … they don't mind us this lot … it's the pub they're after.'

A stiff-collared reverend, thin, birdlike, grey, leads a flying wedge of Woman's Christian Temperance Union women. In the middle, two of them, both plump specimens of piety, struggle to hold high a felt banner heavy with embroidery. Others, two dozen of them all up, stick together tightly, lips pursed, brows furrowed.

They halt at the booth, stamping up dust and begin to sing …

'Little drops of whiskey.

Little mugs of beer,

Bring the keenest sorrow,

To the children dear,
'Little drinks of brandy,
Little sips of gin,
Swell the mighty torrents
Of disease and sin.'

The midday drunks and louts, farmhands and rail workers start to boo and hiss, then begin to throw beer over them.

More and more beer is showered on the temperance women until, like it is poisonous acid, the group can stand it no longer and they beat a hasty retreat to the safety of the Country Women's Association tearooms.

* * *

Games on trains:

Cards.

Arm wrestles.

Paper scissors rock decides who gets the window seat and other privileges.

Hand slaps.

I spy.

Similes and metaphors …

Describe the rather large embonpoint gentleman with the colourful waistcoat in the third compartment of first class …

A well-dressed Christmas ham.

A bunyip.

A balloon.

A bank holiday ferry ... covered in streamers …

* * *

At this show there is a bird catcher …

He is walking around the ground. Small rusty wire cages hitched to harnesses hold cages over his shoulders, another set on his chest and a larger shelf around his waist. I hear him coming first. Finches two for a shilling, rainbows for a zak. I buy all the blue welcome swallows he has.

Behind the tent, Mr Sharman sees me release them. 'Back into the wild blue yonder … well done, lad … birds like those need to keep moving. A lot like us.'

* * *

Linseed …

Linseed brings in the admirers of flesh. Young ladies. 'The Linseed Ladies', Mr Piggott likes to call them. Sweat across broad shoulders and down brown strong legs is a powerful aphrodisiac for a certain type of woman. A touch of the exotic. The brave, the young.

Fine samples of manhood.

There are glances held, shared.

Clapping with hands on hearts.

The fanning of their hot, electric, excited necks.

Hellos beside tent corners or near one of the king poles.

There invitations to meet later down by the river.

Addresses held inside handkerchiefs.

The see-you-later winks.

* * *

Mr Piggott asks me to read through a letter he will post to the *Ballarat Courier*. He has written the letter on behalf of the

'Masked Wrestler' …

Dear Citizens of Ballarat,

I, the masked wrestler, a man of mysterious circumstances, whose identity, if revealed would compromise several police investigations in three states, has returned to Ballarat to show Sharman's mob what real wrestling is. I have trained ten hours a day for the last ten weeks and I am now ready to take on one and all. First, I shall wipe the floor with that stinky Billy Spiers, the so-called innovator of the Hammerlock. Tell Mr Spiers I have, for the last year, been under the expert tuition of several Tibetan masters, becoming proficient in the art of single hand paralysis. After I have finished with Spiers, the so-called Australian Wrestling Champion (who couldn't fight his way out of a wet paper bag) I will take on all of Sharman's boxers and any one of Ballarat's young roosters who are man enough to try.

Yours truly,

The Masked Wrestler

I cannot help but smirk. 'What?' Mr Piggott asks. 'We got to do something. Ballarat's the worst site on the tour!'

* * *

The Royal Melbourne Show

Good steady crowds. Some of the better fighters are not back. Gone off to join the greater cause.

The showjumping arena is full of pretty girls from the Western Districts with double-barrelled surnames … Elizabeth

Carlton-West riding Sir Robin and Anne Holdsworth-Bushmere riding Red Jester.

* * *

We see signs in shops … *'Hannan Groceries declare war on prices'.*

Yet the price of meat, sugar and other goods has risen sharply … butter threepence a pound.

'Profit and war,' Mr Piggott says bitterly, 'are happy bedfellows.'

* * *

A flyer left behind on a seat …

Soldiers Tea Rooms, Rear of Adams' Butcher Shop.

The takings of these rooms will be used to send parcels to our local boys at the front. Have you joined the committee and placed your boy's name on the list?

* * *

An advertisement …

Are you drinking German Waters? Apollinaris, Johannis, Camrunnen, etc. These come from Germany. Perrier, the greatest of all table waters, comes from France. Perrier. The table water of the allies.

* * *

Little girls and little boys,
Never suck your German toys;
German soldiers licked will make
Darling Baby's tummy ache.
Parents, you should always try

Only British toys to buy;
Though to pieces they be picked,
British soldiers can't be licked.

* * *

Port Fairy

An evening walk out to Mutton Bird Island. As we cross the isthmus we leave the war behind us. Talk returns to boxing. Mr Sharman is asked his opinion on countering.

The old adage 'The best form of defence is attack'.

Many fighters never learn to properly counter. There are men who are fast, firm hitters, good guarders, movers, but never counter … personal error is the key … the ability to anticipate the intentions of your opponent and choose your counter … all this in a split second as the opponent fist starts to land your blow needs to have landed on him!

The best counters:

Jack Johnson,

best in the troupe, Jackie,

best in the country, best in weight and inches, Les Darcy, the Maitland Wonder.

'The best of everything has young Les,' says Mr Sharman.

We stare out into the ocean, the horizon swirls like cordial.

Mutton birds, dark twisting clouds of them, return, the sunset crimson on their swift black wings.

Briefly they hover above their burrows, take aim, and dive straight in like icy hands stuffed right back into warm pockets.

* * *

The newspapers, a report from Sydney …

Splendid in physique, courage and patriotism, the first draft of the Australian Imperial Expeditionary Force for military service showed itself to the citizens of Sydney yesterday. The troops, whose very appearance carried conviction that they will account themselves well wherever employed, were a fine, vigorous body of men, and as, to the accompaniment of rousing martial music, they steadily advanced from Moore Park to Fort Macquarie, for embarkation to Cockatoo Island the citizens of Sydney poured forth in thousands to cheer them on their way and wish them 'God speed' in the enterprise which they have undertaken.

There was a great deal of rushing forward on the part of the crowd to say goodbye, but, quite properly no-one frowned upon it as a breach of discipline. Here were 'our boys' marching to the defence of the Empire, and everyone felt like shaking them by the hands.

We are flush with excitement, such a stirring scene!

* * *

Sunday in Daylesford. A game of ducks and drakes in rowboats on the lake. We visit the spa and drink the waters.

Again, there is a stream of smaller fellows who ask Mr Sharman ways they can increase their chest size or height so they can be accepted.

* * *

A local correspondent to the local paper suggests that

All Germans and enemy sympathisers should be interned until the crops were harvested and safe at the railways because of the danger of the Germans setting the wheat alight as it stood in the fields.

* * *

Ballarat

The masked wrestler never appears; Billy had read the letter and swallowed the story, hook, line and sinker. Telling me how he had really been looking forward to seeing how double hand fighting was executed as he had heard about the Tibetan monks' perfection of this technique.

The crowds, as usual stay away too. We hear, however, that the local lads haven't shied away from the big fight; record numbers of them have enlisted.

* * *

There are two classes of Australians in this war: those who go to it and those who stay behind.

* * *

A few bad eggs in Dandenong who really give it to Stanley …

Names for Stan:

coon,
golliwog,
nigger,
the stove,
abo,
big gobby coon,
dark meat,
boy,

darky,
big smoke,
boong,
the dinge.

* * *

A recent article in a certain sporting magazine that might have caused the trouble …

It is recognised that your coloured man, your aborigine, are harder headed than the white man. The nigger is usually a child in his temperament, the child's bad points as well as their good ones, the black man's head is easily turned and when his personal success over a white man is manifest he behaves like the worst kind of spoiled child. He turns from primitive man into a fiend, and his insolence is appalling.

'Bollocks that is.' Tommy shakes his head after reading the article.

'Never seen him gloating; real grafter is Stan. Toughest and most humble bloke you will ever meet. Pride that's what he's got, pride about who he is.'

'Fighting out at Peak Hill once, Stan up against a real mongrel. This cur had made his feelings known about having to fight a black, so he starts using the sly elbow, heeling, he's a real bag of dirty tricks. Stan cops an elbow in the face and gets two of his teeth snapped off. Stan doesn't want to let the mongrel or any of his mates see the damage so he swallows his own two front teeth.'

* * *

Les, with a heavy dose of the flu, beats Clabby then spends the next four days in bed.

Les has told Huge Deal McIntosh thanks but no thanks … HD all ready to set up fights at the stadium … not the kind of man you really want to say no to …

* * *

Melbourne

The tour is over, no more fighting. We stay at the Golden Fleece Hotel. Mr Sharman's favourite. A few days tidying up business matters, seeing the sights, the Melbourne Cup, then we break off.

We visit Luna Park and ride the Scenic Railway. Tommy bends the steel handlebar in fear as we roar into the sky, the brakeman ducking at the very last second as we barrel through a tunnel … the speed … the turns … the thrills of ascending and descending … swooping like shallows … we are alive!

We watch the remarkable Miss Thelin, the Swedish high diver, who dives sixty feet into a blazing pool.

Across to the Palais De Folies, a 'while you wait, photography shop'. We get postcards of us, in ones and twos, some sitting in the moon seat, a ghostish face on a crescent moon, with stars behind, and it looks just like you are sitting in the moon. Hanging up there in the sky. Others where you put your head in a particular wooden hole and then there is a photograph of you flying a plane, being a baby getting a bath, being a cowboy or an Indian. We get a group photograph of all of us, even Stan, paddling a Māori canoe … Who knows after Cup Day whether all of us will ever be together again.

* * *

A stroll along Bourke Street; it is khaki green with recruits and trainees. Photography studios are doing a roaring trade.

* * *

We visit Cole's Book Arcade. A million books under the rainbow. I am in heaven! At the entrance, a giant rainbow; inside, an aviary, a fernery, a symphonia playing. Some miniature mechanical men, two sailors perhaps two inches high who winch a handle that turns and flips down signs advertising the store or offering sage advice, prophecies …

Let prejudice perish, let justice and charity extend to men of every creed.

Flying machines may materially assist in world peace.

Read as long as you want – no-one asked to buy.

Inside the long room are books from floor to ceiling.

Above us the Cole family's washing is drying on lines under the wide glass ceiling.

Stanley's attention is drawn to the metal replica of a hen that, with a penny, lays a golden egg. Inside each egg a child's toy or a small bag of boiled sweets.

This is where ideas are kept, explored, made real.

I buy so many books Billy and Stan have to carry the boxes of them. Frank buys some American penny dreadfuls.

Mr Cole is there, a whiskery marmoset anxiously crouching over his shoulder.

* * *

At dawn we walk along the banks of the Yarra; in the cold, the brown river steams like a broth.

Early morning, scullers a glide.

With their minds always on fighting, they ask for Mr Sharman's opinion on ducking.

The smaller man will often favour the duck. Pedlar Palmer an example of the ducking fighter. Many small men, particularly a proud small man, like Palmer, will resort to this tactic too often. While this may gain applause, it will not gain any points. Many a skilful boxer has spoiled his career by the overuse of the duck.

* * *

We see Stiffy and Mo's vaudeville at the Athethum and laugh at its foolishness until our cheeks go numb.

* * *

Word is that Les Darcy is talking to the American promoter Jack Kearns. Les has run out of fighters here and the Yanks won't travel. A fight with Jack Dempsey is promised. Mr Sharman doesn't care much for this Mr Kearns … blunt as a spoon … full of flapdoodle … a mug-twicer …

He tips one hundred dollar bills in restaurants … calls himself 'Mogul of the Pugs'.

Les decides not to go.

* * *

We dress up in our best and pack into trains out to Flemington, the Melbourne Cup. Close together in packed carriages I smell the perfume off pretty girls' necks.

We stand and watch the jockeys come and go in the birdcage.

'God's little punchlines,' Mr Piggott calls them.

We laugh. Little men for hire, little sports, just like us. There are many similarities; our own knowledge and terms, sweating flesh and rippling muscle, strength and courage. Like them we don't make anything or look after things. We are just there to amuse people, to distract them; up on the boards or out on the track we are very separate from everyone else.

Kingsburgh wins. Having studied the form guide in detail I take away a tidy sum.

* * *

I, Mr Sharman and the others heading back to Sydney decide to wait for the night train so we can see ten thousand of the next deployment march down Collins Street.

It is the shift of ten thousand pairs of boots, all in unison, in exact timing, that strikes me the most. So many of them, but marching as one determined group. The crunch of hobnail boots, arms swinging from proud chests.

The boys recognise the odd hard nut scrapper from the tent amongst the marching rows of packs and clean rifles. 'Good on you!' we cheer! Even I with my bad leg feel like joining them. The others must feel it too; it would be impossible to resist.

A bystander tells us that they are much bigger than the men who went in the first contingent; more hardy as well as more freckled.

'Country boys,' Mr Sharman says. 'Those who lived out too far to make it in quick enough.'

They are fine men. So determined, tall, their chins forward and bright gleaming eyes. I am proud of them, this fine collective, this group, representative of all the men I have come to know over the last year travelling. So many of them … The column seems to march on and on, disappearing through a tunnel of the crowd's cheers and best wishes.

1915

CHAPTER THREE

A race of athletes

This year's troupe:

Jackie Green

Stanley Hill

Frank Burns

Young Eddie, who Mr Sharman found courtesy of the Aboriginal Boys Home

Mr Piggott

Billy Spiers

Herbert Townsend, the new heavyweight

Mr Sharman.

Tom and Jimmy have decided not to tour. Both have joined up. Mr Sharman reckons it was going to the Collins Street send-off that did it.

'We won't be going to watch any more parades,' he says.

Couldn't stop them joining up outside of the season. So, we

lose three if you count Alf's bunk last year. Tommy joined up after his brother did and his mother told him to go look after him. Jimmy Cowan told Jackie he wants to fire the big guns and attested the first chance he could after seeing the second deployment march past us in Melbourne last year.

* * *

We will leave Narellan mid-morning. I drag myself up the main street. I see lots of lads I went to school with or knew growing up.

Frank Cashmere at the blacksmiths, swinging a violent hammer across steel that bends as he wants it across a noisy anvil.

I see Stanley Columbine at the Bank of New South Wales filling in a giant ledger book that spreads over an entire desk; he looks bored.

Eddy Creese gives a friendly handshake and asks what I am up to.

The school bully, James Dixon, drives his team of horses through the street at high speed and swerves at me. 'Get off the road, cripple.'

I speak to Jack Scott at his father's greengrocers; he says that William Sinclair has signed up and already gone and that he will be going too when he is of age.

Gordon Fife has delivered the farm milk and asks about my brother; he tells me that he and Amy Fairburn are stepping out and what a handsome couple they make.

I see Thomas Woodward at the printer's and Billy O'Shea at the baker's. Arthur Morrison at the telegraph office tells me that he is signing on soon with his best cobbers, Roy Shennan and John Morrow. He is keen to get over there before the whole thing blows over.

* * *

Over the summer great numbers of men have been marching, walking from town to town … recruitment marches ... the snowball marches … from all over ...

The South West Waratahs.

The Wagga Kangaroos.

The North West Wallabies march over wheat fields after farmers cut their own fences to allow them a more direct route.

The Men from the Snowy River start out from Delegate.

The Tooraweenahs.

The Kookaburras receive a rump steak and eggs dinner at a Singleton mayoral welcome.

The North Coasters.

The Middle West Boomerangs.

The 'Cooees', 'Hitchin's Moving Army', march the furthest, from Gilgandra to Sydney. At Eumungere they were treated to a turkey dinner and each received a harvest hat from a Mr Wheaton.

At Dubbo they are issued fifty overcoats.

Reportedly there was no need for the Cooees to kiss themselves goodbye as the local girls attended to that.

* * *

'We are a moving army,' Billy says. 'Mr Sharman's Moving Army.'

'B Company,' Mr Piggott adds. 'Be here when they go, be here when they don't all come back.'

Sharman's Soldiers.

* * *

Mr Sharman gives me this year's itinerary, which I take straight to the lads who wait nearby. Broadly similar to last year. The alternate route, Mr Piggott tells me, the same every second or fourth year. Starting in Goulburn, up to Newcastle, the New England run with a few new towns – Tamworth, Armidale, Grafton, Lismore, Tenterfield, Maitland.

The Royal Easter Show, Camden, Campbelltown, the Central West, Wellington, Dubbo, Narromine and Gilgandra.

The show train up and down Queensland.

The Brisbane Exhibition.

The Riverina, Canowindra, Forbes, Parkes, Cowra, Harden, Albury.

Western Victoria, Hamilton, Casterton, Warrnambool.

Bendigo and districts, Ballarat (having another crack at it … goodness knows why). The Royal Melbourne Show, Eastern Victoria.

I realise that until now that the troupe didn't know where they would be travelling for the next ten months, what they might be asked to do … but they still follow him willingly. There is a deep respect for him. There may be a war on, men doing the same thing off into the unknown, but these ones aren't going, at least for now.

'They follow,' as Mr Piggott had once said, 'the beat of a different drum,' pointing to the yellow bass drum resting nearby.

Mr Sharman has decided this year to pair us up, getting us to share rooms. Stanley and Eddie, Jackie and Frank, Mr Piggott and Herbert Townsend. I share with Billy. Good old Billy, my best chum. Although he could do with a wash a little more often, he is my favourite. Gentle, polite, a keen observer of things, knowledgeable, always looking out for the others, honest, trusting and trustworthy. Mr Sharman has paired us up after some thought; this isn't just to save money, it is to mould and improve us, bumping up against each other, sharing the same air, talking. It is a chance to learn from one another. Stanley and Frank are mentors to the young ones; Mr Piggott and Herbert, both older and a chance for Mr Piggott to help Herbert stay off the sauce. Mr Sharman still has his own room. He must have his reasons; he is the boss, his need to be separate, to plan, to brood, to hide, to contain certain things just to himself.

* * *

Crossing a river we see beneath the rail viaduct a new battalion wading in to soften up their boots.

* * *

Goulburn

As promised, a few of Mr Chipford's young fit lads are present to fight but a lot of them must have joined up and gone away.

* * *

As instructed, I have given out the contract Mr Sharman wishes each of us to sign. He has made his marks. We had a few hours to chew it over. I peruse mine carefully.

Again, it's clauses four and five that the others grumble about the most.

But we all sign.

* * *

A discussion with Mr Piggott, myself and Mr Sharman. Maybe they are affronted by the legality, maybe they trust him and thought he would regard them in the same way. The grumblings about the bond are more of a signpost of those thinking about enlisting or those who might be getting a few whispers from the stadium. Jackie is getting too good to go unnoticed. Billy and Frank are the ones grumbling the most. Mr Sharman tells me the contract is watertight and crystal clear. It will make the boys think twice before taking off …

I think it's more about saving them from going rather than making them stay.

* * *

Sheffield Shield Cricket is in the paper …

Eight from New South Wales have enlisted.

Six from South Australia.

Only one from Victoria has joined.

* * *

We invited to attend a mayor's salon.

Mr Sharman's advice on the buttoning of a jacket:

Top. Sometimes.

Middle. Always.

Bottom. Never.

Billy sings the sad song about leaving Ireland and we all think of our mothers. Billy sings so beautifully, with so much love. As he lifts toward the finish, his voice fills the hall with warmth. As he finishes, people rush towards the stage and embrace him.

* * *

We listen to Nellie Melba on an Edison portable gramophone.

Herbert says some of the notes she reaches sound just like rubbing of a wet finger round and round the best crystal glasses. I think her voice is like poetry – portrait and sculpture stirred, poured and mingling in my ears.

I tell Billy that he could sing duets with her. He smiles.

'Do you really think so, Nipper? I would love that, if I was good enough.'

'You are certainly good enough, Billy,' I say.

* * *

Mr Sharman has his first occasion to use the smelling salts this season. A bootmaker called Roly has walked into Stan's left hook as it was heading out … a blow to the side of the head and another as he hit the ground. Stan was just planning to put one out there for show, one across the bow. The boy is fitting, eyes rolling. Flapping like a fish.

Mr Sharman looks terrified.

Roly is doing a merry jig. The salts kick in … he stirs and comes around. Mr Sharman gives Stan that look.

* * *

A self-important local government official of some kind approaches. 'Hello, gentlemen, are you not members of Mr Jimmy Sharman's Boxing Troupe?

'Yes.'

'Well, a very warm welcome to town. What are your intentions with the war?'

Mr Piggott replies on behalf of all of us: 'We hope to continue to tour and pass on the hand-to-hand combat skills to those enlisting.'

'But surely others could do that. I mean, I used to box back in the day. It's just that when I look at you lot I think some of our best is not being used. Apart from you, boy, I suppose you couldn't shoot a light pistol with a twisted and useless arm like that. But you there, the big fellow, you are worth twenty Germans.'

* * *

Newcastle

The wharfies have made some heavy betting on their man Sam to win.

Mr Sharman usually gets wind of a plunge on a particular fight, an overheard whisper from a punter, or he sees the money swapping from hand to hand, hearing a challenger's name once too often.

In such situations Mr Sharman plays it straight, everything by the book. Frank is told to not hold anything back … to play it fair and square …

Frank drops the wharfie quick-sticks. He's stunned.

His second is over him as soon as Mr Sharman starts the count.

'One!'

'Get up, Sam!' the wharfies shout.

'Two!'

'Will you get up, Sam!'

'Three!'

'If you don't you won't get a penny.'

'Four!'

'You better get up before he counts you out.'

'Five!'

'Get up or you'll never fight again,' the second snaps.

Sam looks up, 'You can count to hundred thousand, but you won't get me off this floor.'

* * *

Tamworth

The temperance group's back again, the Band of Hope, the Mayflower Lodge, the Junior Rechabites. All of them banding together into one long, grey-skinned morose platoon. We hear them shouting from a safe distance …

'Take the pledge … Abstain for a month … we will drink no wine.'

We read their carefully embroidered signs …

'Liquor bad for everybody … good for nobody.'

The louts toss a bottle at them to keep them away but that is about it.

* * *

Today the papers describe the weekend's events at Freshwater Beach. A Hawaiian, Duke Kahanamoku, stood on a piece of fashioned sugarpine board and rode it skilfully along a wave to shore. *The newspaper recounts how he rode the surfboard, as the craft was known, towards the beach at thrilling speeds, then made his way back out through the waves again, stroking powerfully, refusing all offers from the local surf boat crews to be towed out. Later a young girl ... Isobel Latham ... rode at the front of the board.*

What an interesting sensation that must have been! To be pushed along by the ocean ...

Like walking on water, Billy said,

or like standing on the back of a dolphin, said Tom,

or leaning out over the bow of a ship.

* * *

Fights, bare-knuckle fights and street fights the lads have had or seen outside the tent:

Frank Burns ... an all-in brawl in Penrith.

Stanley ... a fight in a police cell in Perth.

Eddie in trouble with the police also. Five on one ...

Frank again ... a fight with a bloke holding two smashed beer bottles in his hands at a Watersiders pub at Victor Harbour.

Herbert ... a brawl in the Australian Hotel in Cowra. Saw blokes going through windows. Fought a forty-year-old man and him only just twelve.

Billy tells us about New Orleans in the United States of America where wrestlers team up in groups of four and 'tag' in 'Battle Royals' that last four to five hours. He's not had a real fight, like a fight in the street. 'Always got on with most people,' he said.

I tell them about my on-the-ground wrestle with James

Dixon, grabbing and then twisting his balls until he yelped and staggered away.

Herbert demonstrates how he once took on five Portuguese sailors with knives.

Jackie Green hasn't had any real ding-dongs beyond a bit of school-ground push and shove, so he and Eddie imagine that Eddie is a wheat carter who is stepping out with his girl; they playfight a pretend duel for her affections. Jackie pretending to punch Eddie in the head and Eddie throwing back slow punches into his stomach, before Jackie slowly throws a pretend left hook tapping Eddie's jaw, whispering, 'Ha ha, never saw it coming, did ya?' Eddie acting beautifully, going down, pretending to spit out a tooth.

Billy pretends to be the girl, telling Jackie he's 'no good at lying down' and that Eddie's really her best boy, delivering a woman's best punch … honest words about the bedroom … Billy is only half-joking.

* * *

I have a letter from my brother Frank in Cairo and it sounds like he's having quite an adventure …

Visits to the local amusements and unamusements.

Making some good cobbers especially with the New Zealanders.

Donkey races.

Route marches through the desert.

A felucca ride down the smooth wide Nile.

More route marches.

Sitting cross-legged on a camel.

An entire column marched past a kangaroo at the Cairo Zoo cheering from end to end.

Climbing up the pyramids, then climbing down into the pyramid underground crypts. Smellier than a shearer's armpit!

A two-day riot at the 'Wazzer'.

He cannot wait to get into the scrap. He hopes that Bert gets in soon. He is sorry I can't be there as well, but then knows that I am usefully employed where I am. He has met a lot of blokes who know Sharman's mob … hard nuts, that lot … could do with some of them when the scrapping starts. He asks if any of them have joined up yet. He sends his love to me and of course to Mum and Dad.

* * *

Mr Sharman's advice if cornered by a gang of thugs:

Pick out the leader, the one talking the most. He will often be the biggest, or the one the others seem to follow. Take out the leader, take him out good and proper … the others will scatter.

'What if you don't beat the leader?'

Mr Sharman considers this for a while, replaying the scenario in a dimly lit alleyway from his past. 'Well, if you can't beat the ringleader … well … then you're pretty much stuffed.'

* * *

Armidale

A burly blacksmith bursts into tears. He had received a few blows to the stomach and a knock on the nose, but is sobbing. Most men take the knocks and swallow the pain. Some, like this one, turn to tears; the pain triggers a despair that must have been sitting under the surface for a while.

* * *

From the newspaper …

A plea from small men

The 'Bantams', those brave little men under five foot six, can fight just as well and want to play their part.

A Bantam can shoot just as straight as any other fellow. There are many advantages with the use of the smaller soldier; they eat less, they are lighter on a horse and they offer a much smaller target to the enemy. The authorities need to reconsider the opportunity they have before them, the lost potential of hundreds of brave little men, eager to defend their King and Country.

* * *

'See, Billy, you don't need to go. Let the smaller fellows have a go; they are always so much angrier than the big fellows,' Mr Piggott says.

'I reckon it's going to take more than a battalion of angry dwarfs to win this silly war.'

* * *

Sydney Royal Easter Show

The big one. The tipping point. Go well here and the rest of the year falls into place. We set up two days early; there are crowds of men and animals and tents everywhere. Shouting and hauling, the clang, clang, clang of sledgehammers on pegs.

We hear that Snowy Flynn and his boxing troupe have also set up.

Mr Sharman seems more determined when he hears this news.

Prudently, he gives us all a half-day off so we can look around now and not disappear. We go 'amastering' free rides and toffee apples.

The showground is our playground. In the distance we see Jacob's Ladder. The high ladder act … 'the world's greatest aerial extravagance' … A single ladder with added extensions supported by side stays rising so high that staring too long at its summit makes you dizzy.

We go over and watch the 'Fabulous Phelans' up on their ladder practising.

'The fruit bat', where they hang upside down by the ankles crossing their arms,

'The inchworm'.

'The double dangle'.

'The death drop', where, wearing gloves and holding the sides of the ladder, they slide downward, down a few sections of the more oiled part of the ladder until they hear a scream from onlookers, then they grab the edges tighter, brake and stop.

The death drop reminds us all about the physics of things.

Every sideshow stand has a trick or two, a lie, a deception …

The Flying Flea Circus with their string pulling.

The half-man–half-woman show.

The glue at the coconut shy.

The twisted gun sights at the shooting tent so the country boys will leave with nothing.

By far the best trick was the Merman in 'Dr Worthing's Tent of the Bizarre'.

A monkey's head sewn onto the body of a lizard and the tail of a fish, it looked real enough in the half-light of the tent. 'Caught in a fisherman's net off the coast of Madagascar', the sign said. 'Known to live on a diet of seahorses, crabs and dead men's tongues'.

I watched how the boys argued amongst themselves about it. Some believing all of it, defending its existence quite logically: 'People swear on the good book that they have seen mermaids at sea, so it follows there should be a male of the species.'

Some hold their faith in Dr Worthing's qualifications as a man of science: 'A doctor can be relied upon to tell the absolute truth however ghastly it may be.'

'Science isn't pretty but more than often it's right.'

The others ask the believers questions, debating various points (to which they themselves do not know the answers) and use their quick wit to gently ridicule them.

Jackie's entire day is ruined because of the Merman.

The livestock pavilion …

Sheep, the Melrose trophy for three prime lambs by long wool rams dropped prior to show.

Poultry, best Rhode Island Red, best box of chicks, best half-dozen eggs hen (white, cream and brown), duck eggs.

The general exhibition …

Dioramas of regional produce.

From the Riverina, a giant horse made of watermelons pulling a wagon of fruit, heavy with apples, oranges, grapefruit, lemons.

From New England, cured meats, of various cuts around a massive taxidermy Hereford bull.

A home set in among rolling dairy hills, all made from cheeses and butter from the South Coast.

A map of Australia showing rivers, mountains, deserts in various shades using the grains from the inland slopes.

Blends of wool from the faraway West is used to build clouds coming from a puffing stream train.

Farm produce …

Wool, prizes for merino (fine, medium and strong) as well as crossbred fleeces.

Wheat, (sample of hards and softs), oats (milling and feed), barleys (malting, triticale, pea and lupin), fodder (lupins, canola, cereal chaff, sheafs of green clover, green lucerne and bales of conserved fodder hay).

Massive vegetables. All kinds. Ready to roll onto a giant's dinner plate.

Fruit, shiny and sweet. All types. Collections of six types of oranges, lemons, grapefruit, mandarins exhibited with twig on which it is grown.

We move into the food and produce pavilion …

Home crafts …

Crochet, hardanger, candlewick, embroidery, counted thread, patchwork, knitting, needlepoint.

Home produce ...

Honeys, the sunlight sucked up by bees from a hundred thousand flowers, now the sunlight captured inside glass. The bitter dusky hue of stringy bark, the orange sunset of red gum, the white clouds of clover.

Cakes … date cake, plum pudding, scones. Combined afternoon tea trays.

Preservatives …

Jams; strawberry, blackberry, cranberry, boysenberry, strawberry, blueberry and fig.

And plum jams, light and dark. Cherries, tomato sauces, mayonnaise, relishes and chutneys.

There are at least a hundred varieties of quince jam.

Then various blends and combinations of both the former and the latter. The jars spread out like a rainbow of colour across tables.

We don't have the time to consider the infinity of marmalades that stack high along the long row of straining trestle tables.

Free rides on the chamber of horrors, the giggle palace, the scenic railroad, the Ferris wheel.

Back to sideshow alley.

Mr Piggott places several coins into 'The Electro'. He grabs the two brass handles that provide electric current through the body and holds on … dials go to surely dangerous levels until he can stand it no longer …

What is it like?

We all try it and then discuss:

A feeling like drinking freezing lemonade on a hot day; that shiver that runs down through the spine.

Stanley … Pins and needles.

Billy … A strange feeling to the tongue and the possibility of speaking fifteen hundred different languages.

Mr Piggott said it was like a spirit walking over him.

'Or a cold hairy spider,' said Jackie.

My leg and arm straightened, for a moment, rigid with a strength I had never felt before. For a minute after, I walked normally until the charge dissipated and my limbs returned to their old twisted unhappiness.

Across to the Freak Tent. 'Alright if the Sharman boys call in?'

'Yes!' A chorus of strange voices from inside the deep dark tent.

Inside now. Dark. Two Siamese twins whisper to themselves.

Pinheads laugh.

Dwarfs waddle.

An armless lady eats with her feet.

Introductions …

The beautiful Gertrude from Hobart … eight hundred and eighty-five pounds of fabulous fatness …

Mr Piggott tells me, with some authority, that Tasmania, Gippsland and New Zealand, particularly the township of Gore near Invercargill, never fail to provide a plentiful supply of particularly fat ladies.

I shake hands with the tattooed man, who Mr Piggott tells me once lived with cannibals in the dense jungles of Siam, adopting all their shocking customs and the crudest of full body arts.

We watch the Human Emu practise his eating …

An entrée of nails.

A main meal of spectacles, watches, pens, pencils, a light bulb.

Finishes with a pudding of small pebbles.

Over to the big top just in time to see the final full dress rehearsal put on just for us 'showies'.

First, a long line of bandsmen crashing through the usual marches, big bass drums strapped either side of an enormous Clydesdale.

Then, the circus menagerie parades into the ring:

gleaming Arabians,

indignant giraffes,

a hot polar bear dancing in time with the band, hugging a block of ice,
lions pacing in cages,
the enormous bulk and gentle nature of elephants,
chimpanzees blowing kisses,
rabbits, guinea pigs, hopping along on leads,
buffalo, a rhino. It is as if Noah's Ark is setting sail from Sydney.
Next the performers;
high angle aerialists,
the flying Gordons
equestriennes,
Chinese contortionists,
perch and balance performers,
dental aerialists,
Mexican knife throwers,
a giggle of clowns,
rough riders, Salome dancers, jugglers.
Indian fire eaters Chirgwin and the White Kumar of Rajasthan,
who tongue and then swallow lumps of red hot coal.

Finally, the ringmaster high up on a carriage drawn by white tigers.

* * *

It is the longest line-up board I have ever seen.

Mr Sharman has called in a few favours … old pugs a little fatter but still crafty … prelim boys from the stadiums, kids he had found training in gyms and police clubs. As the bass drum starts, Mr Sharman calls out over thirty boxers: 'Is any boxer worth his salt in Australia not standing up here?' Word spreads. Mr Sharman has three times more than Flynn, more variety more choices, more fights at half the price. I sneak over to Flynn's tent; they don't strike even a half full house by noon and start packing up.

Hundreds of challengers wait their turn to weigh in. The scales are an unnecessary formality. Mr Sharman gets each of the fighters to stand on them before bouts so the challenger feels comfortable he is in the right class. Mr Sharman can pick the fighters' weight right down to the ounce just by watching how they walk. He will shout out the correct weight just as the challenger steps up to the scales. He studies and catalogues them. He writes down details in his notebook. He knows men so well. Their weight, their boxing ability, their fighting spirit. Mr Sharman's scales measure much more than just the weight of a fighting man …

Fights run continually with full houses from ten until ten thirty at night. I have never seen so much money.

Mr Sharman has scared away the competition. We hear Snowy Flynn has decided never to show at the Royal Easter ever again. I hear that Mr Sharman and Mr Flynn have struck a deal in a secret restaurant meeting. Flynn gets South Australia, Western Australia, the Northern Territory and New Zealand; Mr Sharman gets the rest.

* * *

The number of tickets sold does not reconcile with the cashbox.

I look up and Mr Sharman's eyes meet mine. It is as if he has reached into me and ripped out my innards.

We count again and it is still out.

Then I see the small roll of notes that has fallen under the chair and Mr Sharman's demeanour returns to normality.

* * *

Mr Sharman …

Your best friend is your bank book …

* * *

Mr Darcy shakes my hand very gently, the way a man would when they have nothing to prove.

He strips down. He is so beautifully balanced: arms and shoulders like cannons, muscles wrapping themselves around him, a broad tight chest, tapering to the waist, with wide muscular legs. The blacksmith striker's forearms and wrists. A mix of fluidity and power.

We are both jealous and in awe. Mr Sharman had said to us many times that the boxing gods had arranged only one boxer perfectly and that boxer was Les Darcy and we all agree.

He spars with Frank, then with Jackie. It is like he has three arms, even four.

Later they tell me, 'First, he'll hit you with a jawbreaker, then another, following four inches after that one on the mark, then a third, following up behind quick smart.'

'The boxer's yardstick, that's Les. The best you will ever see: physique, fitness, ability, speed, toughness, courage, how he reads the situation,' said Mr Sharman.

'There's boxers, good boxers, great boxers, then there's Les,' Mr Piggott added. They marvel how he excels in every aspect of the craft.

'Once in a lifetime you come across one like him,' Mr Sharman said.

It is the gentle handshake that I remember. So gentle. Handshakes are bridges or gateways to the soul. As I take his hand I look into Les's face, his friendly smile … a remarkable store of patience, kindness and strength …

* * *

After again seeing Dr Worthing's Tent of the Bizarre and his new exhibit, 'The Catboy of Panama', we try to outdo each other with farfetched tales ...

Frank has a cousin at Mole Creek in Tasmania who late one night caught a Tasmania tiger drinking from a milk pail. It turned, stood up on its hind legs and tail, all six foot three of it, and began hissing at her.

Stanley has seen a moonlight catfight on a nearby stable roof. Two cats going toe to toe and around them twelve others in a perfect circle, evenly spaced out like marks on a clock, all quietly watching until they are finished.

Last Christmas Day, one of the hottest on record, Frank saw thousands of snakes swimming at the beach. 'Fair dinkum … Hot! So hot birds dropped dead straight out of the sky.'

'If the tide is right you can throw a beer bottle over the side of the Manly ferry and sharks will jump out of the water and swallow them,' Mr Piggott tells us.

Later Jackie asks Mr Piggott what kind of beer it was, and what tide he should go across on.

* * *

Mr Sharman tells me more about Les. He is very enthusiastic …

Such a pleasure to watch … A blacksmith by trade. A good Catholic who goes to Mass every morning at six. A good trainer too … runs everywhere ... early Mass … to work ... to training ... home again.

Started boxing under Father Coady around the back of the church hall.

Worked as a rail navvy on the cuttings between Newcastle and Maitland before being apprenticed as a blacksmith.

On the railway he fought an ex-jockey called 'Guvnor Balser' for bets … took fifteen shillings home. Changed it all into one penny pieces to throw over his mother's bed … she bought a second-hand stove with that. Every bit of prize money he wins he gives to his mum and family. Poor as dormice, those Darcys. Dad … old Ned, a lovely man, very good on a horse, very polite, but likes to get on the sauce. Les, the second oldest, lots of younger brothers and sisters to look after, one brother with a turned-in foot like you, he works as a bootmaker. Les always doing his best to look after all eleven of them …

Trained at the house of stoush in East Maitland and still working at the smithy.

On to bigger fights in Newcastle.

Big hands, biggest you have ever seen … a tough jaw … the number of times he has copped one smack-on and just got up and walked away …

Then training under 'Gentleman' Dave Smith, learning how to ballroom dance and to fight.

Les is always smiling in the ring. Very unnerving to see someone smiling as you are trying to knock their block off.

Took care of the classy Dave Depena.

Saw his puffy hands after his fight with Billy McNabb's steel jawbone.

Lost on points to Whitelaw, but by then on the up and up.

Fell into the clutches of Snowy Baker and McIntosh …

Knocked out Whitelaw and got McNabb on TKO …

* * *

A headline in the paper.

Sportsmen and the War

Reports have been provided by various New South Wales sporting association as to enlistment numbers of their members.

Rugby Union over 400.

Rugby League 235.

Cricket 306 approximately.

Lawn Tennis over 200.

Manly Swimming Club 56 out of a total of 90.

'No boxers.'

'Not yet.'

* * *

Camden

My cousins Horace and Fred Lewis are out on the ground, standing out front watching proceedings with interest.

'I see two brothers there, the Lewis brothers! Their cousin Archie is part of my troupe and he works for me. Fine boys and a fine local family. I bet that if they are as brave as their little cousin they will climb the ladder and take a glove.'

I am full of pride.

They are smiling too. They were never afraid of a fight, looking out for me or defending schoolyard injustices.

Horace is matched with Stan.

Fred gets paired with Jackie.

Now I am nervous. I have seen these men fight. I love my cousins and I do not want to see them hurt or embarrassed.

I act as their seconder, so I do not hear Mr Sharman's instructions to his fighters.

Jackie throws out a few slow. Fred doesn't fall for it – I have briefed him. Of course, he's never going to be a match for Jackie, no-one is. Jackie goes easy on him, let's him get a few away then adopts a point-scoring approach, picking off the body. Fred knows he's done in … outclassed.

'Christ, Nipper, this bloke is all over me!' He laughs. 'What do I do?'

'Dunno … can I have your stamp collection?' I reply.

* * *

Horace starts well, putting a few away until he gets caught in Stan's infamous circle. He leaves his chest too open and it is obvious that Stan needs to go for the mark. Horace drops, the air gone from his lungs. Stan looks over at me apologetically. Saved by the bell. I freshen him up using Mr Piggott's special methods. I tell him to keep his guard up and stay out of the way. Horace never gives up, trying his very best. Stan keeps him honest. Stan wins on points.

Afterwards my mother and father meet the entire troupe, and Mr Piggott and Mr Sharman. Later they tell me how impressed they were with the whole enterprise, how they very much enjoyed the spectacle, that Mr Piggott seemed like a wag and how pleasant they all were, even that Stanley Hill, who whacked Horace so hard he will be off farm duties tomorrow.

* * *

A young kid boxer asks Mr Sharman for a few tips.

Stay hungry.

* * *

Campbelltown

'First time I came to the show here I was seven or eight,' Mr Sharman tells me in an unusual moment of familiarity.

'I volunteered as the dummy in a William Tell act, with a sharp shooter leaning over a bass drum firing a pea rifle at an apple on top of my head. I didn't think my mother was at the show and when she sees me she comes right up on stage and whacks me with her umbrella. I took off and hid under a tent flap. Turned out to be a tent full of monkeys and I got bitten on my leg.' He shows me the small semicircular scar.

* * *

The Campbelltown Races. This is where Mr Sharman started boxing, Mr Piggott tells me.

Won a local bout. Won eleven pounds, sixteen shillings, went home to show them all and got a solid thrashing with a belt. Mother had thought he had robbed a bank. Worked as a bread carter, woodchopper. The Reverend Lionel Fletcher taught him a few boxing tricks behind the vestry. The Reverend had to give it away after sporting a few too many black eyes at sermon time. Jumped the train to Cowra, to make his fortune, fighting shearers, called himself 'The Shadow'. Twelve years old.

Skinny little kid looking for professional fights … as about as much meat on him as a butcher's pencil …

Caught by the local constable at the Bread and Roses Café. Sent home on the next train for another walloping.

Worked as a water joey at the Cataract Dam, smart enough to end up the paymaster.

* * *

Although it is easy to tell that these men are not bookish types and left school early, each of them have interests, a range of topics they know a great deal about …

Jackie is a great fan of Gilbert and Sullivan and can recite verbatim.

Strangely, Stanley knows all about whales.

Frank once told me how when a giraffe eats leaves from a savannah tree other trees within a mile will all retract and turn bitter.

Herbert knows a lot about England's kings and queens.

Mr Piggott an expert on proteas.

Herbert … the French Revolution.

Eddie … Sheriffs and outlaws of the Wild West.

Billy … Birds and the scientific names of clouds and his beautiful singing voice.

Mr Sharman … The history of bare-knuckle boxing.

* * *

Mr Sharman likes to always tell me that he went to the University of Hard Knocks.

* * *

It is always Billy Spiers who playfully tweaks the noses of the laughing children who follow us.

It is always Billy first to his feet to offer up his seat to another, first to carry parcels or open doors. The last to say, if ever at all, an unkind word about anyone.

* * *

Early reports and rumours of fighting in the Dardanelles.

* * *

Today for some reason Stan has decided to chat to his opponents …

'You're a boxer? What kind of boxes do you make?'

'Once I finish with you you'll need a shoehorn to put your hat back on.'

* * *

Later a young greengrocer's assistant is … on his bicycle … running away from Stan. Arms down, back turned, running around and around in a giant circle.

'Hey!' Stan shouts, 'get back here, Captain Cook!'

* * *

I have come to know very well the various mannerisms of the challengers. Each a particular trait a signpost of their occupation, their background, their stories. Each kind of man has a certain type of walk. Shearers move with a certain economy of movement one learns when you are bent over nearly two hundred sheep a day. Blacksmiths plant their feet deliberately. The way a man speaks also differs. The further out you go the slower people talk. Shepherds in from the outer stations have louder booming voices; a storekeeper or clerk from one of the bigger towns will have a curt politeness.

* * *

At a mayoral reception Billy sings a song about sweethearts and all the women in the hall look longingly at him.

* * *

Wellington

Mr Piggott, Jackie and I have a look at around, wandering around aimlessly while Mr Sharman is out calling in on a few fighters from his little 'Book of Men' as Mr Piggott calls it.

Three young boys aged somewhere between six and eight run towards us.

'Here, take … take!'

Their hot little hands plant white feathers in ours.

They are smiling, laughing. I put mine in a pocket. Jackie drops his.

Mr Piggott removes his hat and fits the feather into his hat band. The boys laugh. He puts his hand up to his mouth and makes a Red Indian dance and noises. The young boys think it is a fine game; they have no malice or understanding as to what the feather might mean.

A woman, probably one of the little dukes' mothers, from a

distance, stands with hands on hips, watching. She sees how her plan hasn't produced the desired effect and beckons one of the older boys over, instructions are given and the boy runs back.

'Aren't you brave enough to …'

The boy has forgotten his line.

Mr Piggott smiles and pats the boy on the head. 'Tell your mum we're plainclothes soldiers.'

He doesn't understand and they skip off to find a nearby puddle. The woman has gone. Mr Piggott removes the feather. None of us needs be upset; the delivery of the feathers from the little mites is more comical than anything else. As I said later, they got the wrong crowd: 'Jackie's too young, Mr Piggott's too old and I am too bung.'

My white feather is from a cockatoo … this would have to be an accuser's first choice. Big and white with a streak of yellow running right through it.

* * *

New reports in the papers …

Australians fighting in the Dardanelles.

Much of the splendid work undertaken by the colonials.

A determined attack.

Brilliant achievements.

High praise.

* * *

A nation breathes a collective sigh of relief as the boys have done us proud … They certainly haven't let us down …

The fortune of war has at last given the Australians and New

Zealanders their turn. The Turks hurled back at Gaba Tepe, the landing a race of athletes …

It will not be long before the troops will be marching all the way to Constantinople …

* * *

Now there are the first lists of causalities …

'Heroic in action, gave their hearts blood.'

I think about my brother.

There are photos. Frozen men staring off into the distance, portraits of them in uniform, dinner suits and their Sunday best. Now peering at us from the past and not the future.

Billy stares hard at each photo as if trying to commit them to memory or save them. It doesn't pay to dwell on these things, it cannot be good, but we all find ourselves doing this; there is too much anger and lust to avenge, too many opportunities to make rash decisions.

* * *

Today I start a dark, unpleasant habit. Today I start to read through the lists of the dead and wounded, hoping not to see any names I know. I start a macabre habit that I wish I had not; as every day of this war will find me searching these lists. I note every name. I am the grim reaper's clerk … making my own detailed and tragic inventory …

* * *

A.J. Onslow-Thompson, Camden's Show Society President, has

been killed in action at Gallipoli. Mr Sharman knew him well. He is the first we know that we lose.

* * *

Letters about Les in the *Sunday Times* …

> *It is well known that a strong movement is set on foot to send him to America. Is he prepared to go to America to hunt for money at this time? Is he so devoid of manhood as to lend his support to any attempt that may be made to get him out of the country, whilst all around him thousands and thousands of men with far greater ties in the world are gladly offering themselves as sacrifices on the altar of liberty? Will the Commonwealth Government offer this great 'sport' a passport to enable him to run away from his obligations? I hope you will publish this letter or at least make public reference to this cold-footed lot who are staying home and sham-fighting and making money at the expense of the lives of true men.*
>
> *Les will surely soon join the sterner fight where the gloves are off and there is no call to corners.*

'They want Les as a star recruit,' Mr Piggott says, 'to strut around like a prize peacock, acting as bullet bait for the cream of the country.'

'And we are next, I reckon,' Mr Sharman says.

* * *

Dubbo

At Dubbo, the mayor welcomes us to God's own country.

* * *

There are two kinds of temperature on this tour: hot and bloody hot. Dubbo is very much the latter.

Across the town I overhear the drought stories …

Wooden pegs on washing lines, so dried out, brittle and snapping in half.

A whispered tale about the vicarage hedge and its spontaneous self-combustion.

Third-hand rumours of locust plaques in the Far West occurring in Old Testament proportions.

A woman complains to a friend about a flock of cockatoos that have flown in to find food and water and is working its way around the town's front gardens.

'They're like well-paid mercenaries. Destroyed every one of my poppies, each of them bitten off right at the top of the stem. Couldn't do a better job myself with a pair of secateurs … Why? Why?' she mourns.

* * *

Some Russian gypsies towing a brightly coloured caravan have kaleidoscopes for sale. Jackie buys two. One views like two thousand church windows, the other like fruit salad in a giant glass bowl. Behind the caravan curtain Billy and Jackie hold out their hands and get their futures told.

Dark times … dark times approaching …

* * *

On the last day of the show we attend the Annual Dubbo Harvest Dance. I sit among the wallflowers, the shy crimson-faced girls, the myopic clerks, the farmer who can repair the knock in a header machine in seconds but has sweaty palms and clumsy feet anytime he is forced up to dance.

We sit, the meek and the mild, and watch the bold and the beautiful dance the latest dancehall crazes … the 'Turkey Trot', the 'Chicago Hug' and the 'Romping Rooster'.

* * *

Every town is the same. The layout of one matches another. We carry a map in our heads; it is difficult to get lost. Town after town we can almost overlay the characteristics of one upon another …

All will have a wide, hot, dusty main street, banks three, hotels six, usually one called the Railway Hotel or the Criterion Hotel, one hotel at one end of the main street is known as the upper while another at the other end is known as the lower.

A Church of England and a Catholic church hold any hill or highpoint.

There is likely to be an odd fellows hall, a Freemasons temple, a hall for the Rechabites. A mechanics institute.

There will be bakers, butchers and blacksmiths on or near the main street. Verandahs will lean over dress shops and haberdasheries.

A large family-owned draper's and milliner store. Tearooms next door where local women gather to gossip.

A large shire hall, its Corinthian pillar aspirations out of scale with the rest of the town's more modest achievements.

A chessboard of wide streets running open with the prevailing winds to allow the stinking malaise of nearby abattoirs or tanneries to blow straight through each street, door or window.

A busy post office.

A Queen Victoria Garden, a band rotunda, a riverbank or promenade of young trees. A railway station with long platforms.

A stockyard, a meatworks.

The showground on the edge of town.

The worst pub for fights, the town bloodhouse, is usually the Railway Hotel.

I wonder why.

Billy reckons it's because it is near the railway line, closer to where those from the wrong side of the tracks can come to fight.

Mr Sharman reminds us again that our contractual obligations did not include fights in public houses.

* * *

Rain is coming, the drought will break, Billy says, as the ants are busy and moving faster and faster.

* * *

It did come a week later.

Rain.

The word 'rain' is in every conversation we hear.

People expressing their amazement and gratitude as they talked of full tanks, the re-emergence of ducks, puddles on lawns, the lovely noise of it on roofs. Wet grass now combed neatly by wet sheep. There is hope for new crops, fat sheep, heavy bags of wheat, new clothes, the repaying of debts to polite but impatient lenders.

* * *

We attend the final night of the local eisteddfod.

The usual meet and greet. The masons, the odd fellows, the loyal orange lodge and the Hibernians are almost lined up in columns. Other assorted townspeople, bank managers, town clerks, headmasters, all patiently waiting to tell us their best joke or amusing antidote.

Mr Sharman is asked to hand out the prizes for girls deportment and boys poetry recital; he also announces a sizeable donation to the Ladies Benevolent Society.

***

Mr Sharman says, 'You can never trust a man who doesn't wear a belt.'

***

'There are as many types of men as there are types of dogs,' Mr Piggott says. 'Men all are all like dogs, and there are many different breeds of dogs …'

Small yappy ones, terriers, big ones who are roly-poly happy and gentle until they get one square on the nose. Sometimes the big ones are often the weaker in temperament … the bark always far worse that the bite.

The meaner men are like mean dogs, raised on daily beatings.

Some men have a stubbornness, a hardness about them, a certain composition … a grip like a bulldog.

Some are light but as quick as whippets.

Others more like sheepdogs, faithful and never give up, like the big New Zealand huntaways striding up hills … chasing … or like the eye dog … they are cunning … staring … confusing their opposition ...

Others are timid, young and naughty like puppies.

* * *

Frank says that taking a blow on the right part of the head can produce a strange epiphany … he had experienced this several times. Like a strong sniff of smelling salts …

the sudden clarity,

the rush of ideas,

an awakening,

a restfulness like waking from a long sleep.

A good knock was something, he said, he actually quite looked forward to.

The others have different opinions about knocks.

Plenty of mad old pugs out there, old champs, prize fighters who have gone soft in the head, gone punchy …

The ones that take on a sudden uncontrollable liking for the drink.

Those who start slapping their missus about on a daily basis.

Others who become as gentle and as meek as lambs.

The ones who have gone so silly they forget to put on their trousers and stroll bare-arsed up the main street.

The one who rides on Melbourne tramcars standing up to fight every time the tram bell rings. The same one you will see ducking and weaving at the corner of Clarendon and Dorcas Streets every morning.

The ones who develop a queer look, go and crouch in corners, ones who lose control of their limbs, bladder, tongue, saliva. Others who suddenly stop talking and just sit.

'Is there any cure for such injuries?'

'Just keep dodging.'

* * *

We visit another photographer. Boxers! They seem to always want their photographs taken. We visited a studio no less than a month ago!

Jackie likes to pose in his southpaw stance, fists out, ready for his trademark quick one-two.

Billy, his big hands open and up close, looking like he is about to grab, swing and lock down someone firmly into place.

Mr Piggott cocks an eyebrow and tilts his hat.

They all want to pose with Mr Sharman. As he sits in a stiff jacket and waistcoat beside a desk, only just tolerating the flash of photographs. Him staring to the back of the camera's eye and his fighters standing there, ready for instruction.

Employee and employer.

Teacher and student.

Father and son.

Friend.

* * *

At Narromine, Mr Sharman tells the crowd that the town and district is truly God's own country.

* * *

A call for more country lads, good riders and good marksmen.

'What's wrong with the city blokes?' Billy asks.

* * *

Gilgandra is a town of windmills. For years there were heated arguments about the location of the town's water supply. In the end the townspeople gave up and put in windmills, one for each house, each a signpost of the town's bitterness and lack of cooperation.

The welcome here is restrained; eventually one of the townspeople lets it slip – we should not think ourselves as half as good replacements for the men who have walked their way to the war last year.

* * *

Ted Larkin the Rugby League player has been killed at the landing of Gallipoli.

* * *

More often these days my mind turns to a dark corner and starts thinking the worst ... Dreams of my brother Frank, lying in dirt, dumped off a bloody stretcher, spadefuls of soil heaped on him.

* * *

Headlines ... Sinking of the SS *Lusitania* ... A passenger liner. A United States vessel, a neutral ship, carrying civilians, women and children. Fourteen hundred lost, killed, murdered. Sunk by a German U-boat torpedo. Sunk off Kinsale Head, Ireland. An act of cold-blooded piracy and murder. A very low act ... A very low act that needs to be avenged. Even the most mild of men snarls at the news.

* * *

'I don't think I can stand by with all of this. I need to get a move on,' says Billy.

Mr Piggott turns to Billy: 'Winning this war will not be up to you. There are thousand, millions of men in this thing, they can avenge all of this.'

'We all contribute in different ways … we fundraise, we teach, we entertain in hard times. We need you here, your parents need you here,' says Mr Sharman.

'But I would feel a lot better if I could avenge this terrible travesty myself. Right some of the wrongs.'

'Billy, that's not you killing someone and you know this,' Mr Sharman says.

'The thing is Billy,' says Mr Piggott, 'the bullets and the bombs don't care a jot about any of your honourable intentions.'

'If I stay here I am a coward; if I go I am courageous; if I go I am going to have to kill people.'

Mr Piggott sighs. 'Going to war is not the best way to sum up a man, his courage or his cowardice. Take it from me, you see the same man at a war at different times be a mix of both cowardice and courage. There is no referee, no spectators, it's not a fair contest, not a clean fight, the best man doesn't win, no-one does, except death and the general who sleeps soundly in his bed at night. War is not a test or measure of a man.'

'I wish you could tell that to a few more people around here,' Mr Sharman says.

'Well, I have learnt the truth of it the hard way. People will always apply their clumsy labels to others no matter how poorly that might fit.'

* * *

Words to describe new recruits …

Hale and vigorous.
Formidable adversaries.
Young men with ardour and dash.

* * *

A British nurse, Edith Cavell, has been executed by a German firing squad. Accused of aiding British prisoners to escape and after a one-sided military trial, without representation, she is killed in cold blood.

Outrage! A woman, a nurse, a non-combatant – these Germans have no limits. Even Mr Piggott is appalled. For many men this is the last straw.

* * *

According to a man recently from Melbourne, The Prahran and Malvern Tramways Trust now has an illuminated recruitment tramcar that tours the shopping areas. It carries a brass band, a tableau of Britannia, supported by its sea and land forces, the driver dressed as John Bull accompanied by a real British bulldog.

* * *

The minimum height for recruits has changed from five foot, six inches to five foot, five inches. Mr Sharman looks through his Book of Men, checking to see how many of his angry little men he is likely to lose.

* * *

'Maybe it's time to go; here is the idea then,' Jackie says. 'Get hold of a rifle, learn to shoot a bit, proceed to Gallipoli or France at the earliest, kill vast quantities of Turks or Germans, maybe get wounded in some artistic place, win the war and march back to town colours flying band a playing and the girls hanging off your necks. How's that for a plan?'

'You're too young!' Mr Piggott grumps.

'Plenty of lads younger than me joining up.'

* * *

The Council for Civic and Moral Advancement has called for all boxing stadiums across Australia to be shut down for the duration of the war as they represent *'A serious hindrance to recruiting'*.

* * *

The Very Reverend Professor McMillian has suggested boxing is …

A moral blot on Sydney and on the state as a whole … If there is any fighting to be done today, the proper place for it is in trenches in France where Georges Carpentier, France's greatest boxer, is giving his lifeblood for his country …

'It all feels like it's getting even closer to us now, Mr Piggott,' Mr Sharman whispers.

* * *

Brisbane Exhibition

A warning from Mr Sharman to watch ourselves ...

Different mob in this year … A lot more thimbleriggers and

three card men here ready to help you part with your cash.

* * *

The Brisbane Exhibition's Grand Parade:

Saltbush Bill and his accurate stockwhip, physical drills and callisthenics.

All the winning animals from every class proudly displayed, even the champion fish are paraded carefully inside their glass bowls.

Sideshow acts …

The invisible man.

The X-ray woman.

The rooster trained to walk like Charlie Chaplin.

The pig-a-dilly show. Dinny the biggest pig on earth.

The bulletproof lady.

The spruikers calls … hurry on, hurry on … hurry, hurry, hurry. Kno'k'em over, kno'k'em over.

The Fiery Phoenix who asks people to concoct their own poisonous mixtures and then bring them along on show day for him to drink. He sips politely from a crystal glass that rests on a nearby card table covered in white linen and flowers.

The Slapping Man. A queer-looking man with an oversized jaw who you can slap as hard and as long as you want for a pound. There is a long line of people seeking revenge. Mr Sharman tries in vain to recruit him to the tent.

The Artful Dodger, who avoids hard wooden balls thrown at him by punters in time to music.

A midget pulled along in a tiny cart by a whippet.

The one-hundred-and-sixty-one-year-old woman.

Rumours that Harry Houdini the 'Handcuff King' will attend …

* * *

Billy is teaching Eddie how to read and write. Hour after hour, they knit the sounds and letters and words and sentences together. 'Bit by bit,' Billy says softly, 'bit by bit.' Billy is so patient, gently picking Eddie up every time as he stumbles.

* * *

Bill Squires, the ex-heavyweight contender, is here to referee. A big balding man, he draws in the crowd; he is famous for stopping a Tommy Burns right hander on the chin and living to tell the tale. Stanley is particularly keen to meet him.

We come across our first take of the season. A surprisingly quick Brisbane boy drops Eddie when he leaves his guard down. Eddie stops one right on the chin. He feels like he has been on the booze for a week. Mr Sharman is not happy … having to shell out good money to the take because Eddie hasn't done his job.

* * *

It is here in the cities that, Mr Piggott says, a young fella is more likely to get carried away by war fever. A lot more pressure there. More men walking around in their nice smart new uniforms. More girls with their staring at you still stuck in civvies. More posters and flyers to prick your conscience. More recruiting centres and speeches that a young fella could see and suddenly get carried away with. A band to whip things up, a close quarter chat with a recruiting sergeant or someone from the women's patriotic league, a few returned servicemen speeches from a platform and before you know it you've got yourself a nasty case of war fever and you're off to barracks.

* * *

Our favourite meals:

Jackie … Sausages and mashed potato with peas and gravy.

Stanley … Prawns and crabs cooked on a hot plate.

Frank … Bacon sandwiches.

Eddie … Steak.

Herbert … Pies and lots of them.

Mr Piggott … A roasted rack of lamb.

Billy … Poached pears and custard and also … sago, tapioca pudding with golden syrup. Typical Billy; two favourite meals instead of just one!

Mr Sharman … Pork flaps, bread and dripping, wild rabbit.

* * *

Annoyances:

Mr Piggott and his range of loud and often violent profanities.

The pigheadedness of Frank.

Eddie's constant chattering.

Herbert's occasional petty thievery.

Jackie Green's 'roughing up'.

Frank and his snoring.

Stanley's self-imposed separation, his resistance to reveal too much of himself to any of us.

Mr Sharman's constant checking and smoothing down of my collar.

Mr Sharman's insistence that his way is always the right way. (But it usually is.)

* * *

We have arrived to join the show train that will take us north for the next three months.

Huge signs painted along the carriages shout out …

Ringling Brothers and Barnum Bailey Combined Circus.

You would need to travel the entire world twice to find another show half as good as this.

All new daredevil circus acts.

Boasting more than one hundred novelties …

Jandy the Clown.

The (absolutely unique) Mi Re Do with his medals and diploma awarded to him by his Majesty the King of Cambodia.

Lion tamer – the incomparable Captain Fitzsimmons.

The Flying Astons.

Michelago Cozmelli – the dancing, tumbling, somersaulting wizard of the wire.

The Three Amazing Brittons – sensational jugglers and trick cyclists.

The death-defying bareback riding of Madame Garcia.

Madame Duisans … fortune teller … your future told right down to the minute.

Aerial bicycle riding. A penny farthing, its wheel riding the thin high wire eighty feet up, two acrobats dangling on a trapeze attached to the axle.

'It's not the long way down that hurts, it's the bump at the end,' Mr Piggott jokes ...

We walk past the menagerie cages …

Abu the elephant and his harem.

Giraffes, horses.

Smooth armadillos whose sweaty skin reminds me of old men's bald heads.

Monkeys, cages of snakes, baskets of frogs.

Lions, tigers.

Troupes of jumping fox terriers.

Birds and bears.

Every species, every genus of creature on Noah's Ark on tracks and the wheels of a steam train heading to the far far north.

* * *

Mr Sharman gives me his ups and downs.

Jackie Green is on the up and up. Young and fit. Likely to lose him to the stadiums soon; need to watch him and try to head this off.

Eddie a good performer for the crowd.

Stanley Hill is steady. Older but a real journeyman boxer.

Frank Burns a bit long in the tooth but still trains hard. Useful.

Mr Sharman keeps a close eye on Herbert. Rumours that he has a few problems with the drink, that's why he's here, looking for a little boxing redemption, a way back.

Billy is on the wane, a lazy trainer and eating too much. But he is such a lovely fellow, he is the glue that holds the troupe together and wrestlers are hard to come by, so any slack training will be tolerated.

* * *

A letter in the Brisbane *Sun* attracts our attention:

Osh Kosh of the North … Frater is the answer to Sharman

The following letter from a reader in the Burnett district is given in its original form. It speaks for itself…

The sun was of hinterst last week becawse it let hus no that sharman the show man is comin this way agin with the intenshion of metting our champ Frater. Well, you can let this loud speaker from the south no that he his goin to mett a 'ot propusishion in the 'Osk Kosh of the North' this time. Sharman forgot to tell you that Frater hallways gives his blokes a doin and he will do it agin if sharman has any money to spear when he blow in 'ere. Frater is the best nataral fiter in Australia, and sharman nos it to be-cawse he would gives pots of money to get Frater squared for his blokes, but Frater is a dinkum fiter and he always gos in the tent with the intent of knockin spots hoff sharman's blokes. Sharman talks about havin a bloke who can knock hout Frater. Well tell him I will be at the show when he comes hear and I'll bet him me year's savin's that Frater will stop the best bloke he can bring from the south or anywhere else. Fraters game is dairying, but when it comes to fitin he's the bloke to take the starch out of the city pugs. He has never been nocked out, and he is not likely to be skittled by any man in Queensland. You sign me up for putting in the paper as 'Ayseed' but you can give Sharman me address if he wants it as I would like to meet im in person.

* * *

Enlistment numbers are up. Thousands join to avenge Edith Cavell, lost brothers or friends at Gallipoli.

For now, we all are still staying. Jackie's too young, Paddy won't say, Frank's putting his family first, Eddie's too wild, Mr Piggott's too old, Billy's needed here, Herbert has things to sort out in himself first, Mr Sharman says he is yet to be sold on the idea. Anyway, they have all signed contracts so any notions to go are just ideas and that is all.

* * *

An elephant at Bundaberg sets three other elephants on a rampage after being spooked by seeing a travelling waxworks exhibition. It destroys twelve wax figures including Kitchener and the Kaiser before leading the others through the town, smashing in the windows of five shops.

* * *

At the Gladstone stockyards, fifty patriotic rams are donated for sale. All proceeds going to the cause with Dalgety and Company foregoing all commissions.

'Even the bloody sheep are enlisting!' says Mr Piggott.

* * *

There are long lines outside the travelling dental pavilion. It is busy with men getting themselves fixed up so they can try to enlist again. They leave this place of horrors with swollen faces and spitting blood from their mouths.

* * *

Reasons why men are enlisting …

Want to be in something a bit more than just earning a living.

All my best pals were in it.

The *Lusitania*.

Dodging a Tobley.

For King and Country.

To stop the Prussian jackboot crushing the world.

Edith Carvel.

Had enough of the missus.

To see the world.

A few sling-offs that got under my skin.

Better than starving without work. Unemployment is a popular recruiting sergeant.

My action is purely my own decision.

* * *

The *War Census Act* has been passed. There is to be a census of all males aged eighteen to sixty.

There are also to be state enlistment targets. At least eighty a day in Victoria similar elsewhere …

'It's the start of a bloody stocktake,' Mr Piggott said in an overheard conversation with Mr Sharman.

* * *

Rockhampton

There are discussions overheard about who should go first; the single men first before the married men? Discussions about who should be allowed to stay and not be tormented for it, married men, those supporting family, those in reserved industries, those whose beliefs prevent them from fighting … they could still go … stretcher-bearers, labourers, drivers, why should they see themselves as beyond reproach in God's eyes?

* * *

Eddie has had a bare-knuckle fist fight with one of the warbs over some half-inched bottles of beer and the labourer is badly hurt. A showmen's court hears the matter. Local police are not involved – it is showmen's business. Eddie is made to scrub out and lime the various showground long drops of Queensland for the rest of the circus train run. He has his tail well and truly between his legs for weeks.

* * *

Herbert Townsend has to fight the biggest man we have ever seen. Mr Sharman agrees that he is the biggest man he has ever seen in the tent – six foot six, twenty-five stone, all muscle. Too nice a fellow for the ring. There is heavy waging, but the big fellow is too afraid to hurt anyone.

'Carn, ya big pudding, get into it,' someone yells.

Mr Sharman, like in other big betting fights, plays it straight and has told Herbert to hurt him into retirement by working around the guts. Herbert protests: 'He's a nice bloke, I dunno.' Nevertheless, he follows instructions. The big fella is stoic and hangs in there. Herbert accidentally whacks the big man on the nose. As what often happens with a placid big fellow who cops one on the snotbox, he gets angrier and angrier like a bull stung on the nose. He swings wildly, the crowd cheer, until Herbert dispatches him with a quick tap on the chin.

In Herbert's next fight, a giant Black in from the missions is shaping up. There's a shout from somewhere in the crowd, 'Hey, boss, don't let her have a go, dat's me missus!'

* * *

Tropical climes bring new things. Fireflies shape out loops and letters in dank ferneries that grow thick between buildings. Bats are wheeling up and away to gorge on mangoes or pawpaw and eat out the soft parts of coconuts. Clouds that puff up over the day swell dark with rain then burst at four o'clock each afternoon; you can set your watch by it.

* * *

Bowen

Someone has undone bolts to several of the animal cages.

The town clerk awakes to find an eight tonne elephant in his vegetable patch enjoying the last of his prize lettuces.

Spider monkeys are caught swinging among the rafters in the Anglican church.

It takes three to four hours to recover all the animals.

A lion is found in the cellar of the Club Hotel; the barman is discovered shortly after hiding in a nearby cupboard.

* * *

News of fierce battles at strange places … Gaba Tepe, Baby 700. No news of my brother.

* * *

A Lance Corporal Jacka has perfected an efficient way to kill Turks …

Lance Corporal Jacka, a timber worker from Victoria, has won the Victoria Cross at Courtney's Post on the Gallipoli Peninsula.

Lance Corporal Jacka, while holding a portion of our trench with four other men, was heavily attacked. When all except himself were killed or wounded, the trench was rushed and occupied by seven Turks. Lance Corporal Jacka at once most gallantly attacked them single handed and killed the whole party, five by rifle fire and two with the bayonet.

Now the first Australian has been awarded the Victoria Cross it seems as if everyone wants to head off and win one.

* * *

More battles on Gallipoli. No news of my brother Frank.

'No news is good news,' Herbert says.

Fresh papers as we disembark in Sydney. Reports of a battle at the Nek …

Sheer Heroism, Australian Light Horse Attempt the Impossible

Tornado of Fire Defends Eight Fold Turkish Trenches. Soldiers Fight Over Bodies Three Deep.

* * *

An account by CEW Bean, War Correspondent of Gallipoli. August 15th

The attack on Lonesome Pine had already forced the Turks to rush brigades of reinforcements South …

Our men were ordered to wear only shirt-sleeves and carry only bayonets and grenades, and change an amphitheatre of tiered Turkish trenches which gave clear fire from up to seven tiers, onto defenceless men. It was clearly suicidal to the lowest mentality …

The attacking party was divided into four lines of 150 men in each.

The Victorian 8th Light Horse led the charge. No trenches were gained in this fight, but for sheer self-sacrifice and heroism, this charge of the Australian Light horse is unsurpassed in history.

A cable message received yesterday stated that the 8th and 10th (Western Australian) Light Horse were practically wiped out in the fighting on August 7th.

Frank isn't in the Light Horse but this doesn't make me feel any better reading this news. Anyone there will be in it. I fret; every telegraph boy, every new newspaper, makes me jump. Is it the fear of loss or the strength of love?

* * *

Townsville

Herbert cops the punch of the year from a watersider. Mr Sharman spends two nights up all hours tending to his concussion. Waking and walking him about, inhalations, gentle damp cloths across his brow and neck soothing whispers and holding of hands.

We wait and wait, peering through the tent flap, but Frater does not show.

* * *

Ingham

Mr Sharman organises fights between the Italian sugar workers … The Umbrians from the Gairlock Sugar Mill versus the Naples workers at the Macknade Mill versus the Sicilians from Victoria Sugar Mill.

* * *

Overheard in the tearooms at the Ingham show …

> *'The danger? Oh no, my dear. Our boys need not be afraid of heading off. Why, every Saturday in summer they face, up close, the furious crack of willow on leather.'*

* * *

Billy is asked to sing another popular Irish song …

Mr Sharman is swaying to Billy's waltzing voice. He sees us watching him enjoying all this. Are we going to be in trouble for seeing past the wall that is Jimmy Sharman? No. His eyes are smiling. It is so beautiful. Like the song says, Billy has stolen all our hearts away.

Mr Sharman is clapping with excitement and pride.

'Archie! I think I should just tour Billy, he's so very good!'

'I think he could make a professional living from singing. After the war he could study and then perform around the country, around the world.'

'Yes, indeed … he's wasted as a wrestler.'

* * *

Tully

Dante's inferno. Out in the dark we see a line of fire loop and gather, loop and gather as the show train glides past burning cane fields.

* * *

Cairns Agricultural Show

I watch out over the ground, a group of Afghans who work as canecutters are dressed smartly in starched coats and crisp turbans. Chinese are here too, with their thin tricky eyes, square hats and long pony tails.

A man is selling a mass of twisting pythons that curl up one of three large poles inside a tent, forever trying to reach the canvas roof above them. A swarm of small boys crowd in, daring each other to let a snake coil around them. Some of the boys are small enough and the snakes large enough that if the snake seller was not present one of the little darlings could easily become dinner.

The boys' games are interrupted by cane farmers who push their way through to buy a 'couple of lengths' of snake. The snake is used to control vermin; the snake seller at this tent is well known for providing a particularly 'active snake' so his sell at a premium of five shillings a yard.

There are the usual discussions between farmers about farming, but here they debate topical farming. Which is the better variety … Trogan or Badilla Cane? They argue about the life cycle of the Hairy Mary Pest and the best time of year to light it up. How to best grow bananas, pineapples.

There is a competition to guess the weight of a stack of sugarcane heaped on a cane train.

* * *

After six months the fights and the travelling are taking their toll.

Ailments …

Of all the troupe, Frank has the oldest hands. Every evening you will see him soaking his hands in cold water or holding ice from the ice chest. He says his knuckles feel like they are full of broken glass marbles.

Mr Piggott. Lately a head cold. Bunions. Night dreams … a strange sense of things repeating themselves …

Billy Spiers. A shoulder that grinds like pestle and mortar. A neck that aches every time he sneezes.

Eddie. A foggy head from an earlier knock. But not a knock worth Mr Sharman finding out about.

Jackie Green's weak ankle.

Herbert out for one more week under Mr Sharman's concussion rule.

Stanley Hill still tip-top at this stage.

Mr Sharman's voice is hoarse. He sleeps longer.

* * *

After Cairns, the show train starts its return south. We have come across to Magnetic Island for the showmen's annual picnic, a traditional break-up before showies and circuses head their separate ways to do their own small town tours. On Hayle's ferry the sea is a thousand lights; everyone has a joke or easy laugh.

We make a camp over the hill at Nelly Bay. Huge knuckles of rock are beside us as we lie across a lawn of rugs. What a beano! A real feast … Tropical fruits … mangos, bananas, sweet pineapples that make mouths drip. A roast pig, trifles, puddings! Wine and beer that Mr Sharman allows us to drink in moderation. Plenty of other refreshments, iced fruit juice, punches, coconuts, a range of fruit vinegars, iced tea, more than enough lemonade to guzzle.

We lie bellies full, too full to move, stuck on our backs … upside-down turtles! The giant stones like sundials. The sun tracks across the tumbledown hills and rock ridges that surround us. We take turns in describing what we see in their forms ...

Eddie sees fists.

Stanley sees whales and ships.

Billy … loaves of bread. Of course he does!

Eddie sees vampire teeth and dinosaur eggs.

I say that the hills are like the claws of tigers.

Darker now, the sun's last brightness backlights the ridge, the jagged hillside silhouettes the very last of the light like a torn piece of curtain.

Rock wallabies, clumsy in nearby bushes, eat the smooth yellow blossoms of kapok trees.

Stars one by one take their place above us, their abundance spreading across the sky like a handful of thrown sugar, a multitude of furious, tiny, burning lights …

* * *

The Forbes Agricultural Show.

Graziers talk about lambing rates, then wander over to the sheds to study closely the beautiful symmetry of bull and ram testicles.

Farmers discuss bag sizes.

* * *

Billy and I walk past a mad old man sitting in the door of an alleyway.

'Let me shake your hand,' he says to me. I shake his hand.

Billy already has his friendly handshake out.

The old man grabs it and, looking up at Billy, says in amazement, 'You're bigger than God ... you need to go and eat some Germans!'

* * *

Parkes

Just as Mr Sharman tells a challenger to shake up the drum, a woman is out on the pitch screaming ... 'You lot are the same as Les Darcy – you are just as bad! You make your filthy money while the other boys go off and fight and do their duty giving up their lives.'

Mr Sharman reminds the crowd that all of today's takings will go to the town's war chest.

* * *

After the attack at the Nek, the bad news begins to come in …

A notice in the paper ...

Walter Gibson, Missing. Son of Arthur Gibson, Small Hills Station, Via Forbes, anxiously waiting for any news.

* * *

The woman yelling at us in Parkes, news of the battle of the Nek, has rattled all of all. Mr Sharman steers a straight course. We are best fighting here at home ... Mr Sharman's actions could almost be seen as pacifist, he does not lead people to war, the funds don't go to buying bullets or bombs directly, it goes to the sick civilians and wounded soldiers. Maybe that has been his reason. I don't really know and he will never tell me.

* * *

Bert has enlisted. He has got his teeth sorted out; he is as keen as mustard to get into the fight.

Mother has forwarded the newspaper cutting of Bert's farewell ...

Eighteen recruits were farewelled at a function at the Camden Town Hall by the Mayor and Mayoress. A heartfelt speech from the Mayor about the gravity of the times and the selflessness of those young men was reinforced to all those present. Recruit Herbert Badgery, a visiting Victorian who hopes to eventually join the Air Corps, telling the crowd he was off for a bit of a holiday. ... Recruit Blackmore, a fine straight-limbed boy, says he's ready to fight the good fight. Hearty handshakes all round as the large party followed the departing heroes all the way to the Narellan Train Station.

* * *

A letter from Aunt Adelaide:

How awfully anxious you must now be with both your brothers far away and in such danger. I bet you would want to be with them, this war a perfect opportunity to prove yourself a man. But God's revenge has seen you stop here. I trust, however, that in some small way you find a place in this great endeavour and contribute where you can.

Fond regards,

Your loving Aunt

In less than one paragraph my aunt has willed both my brothers dead, declared me God's great mistake (my leg atonement for the sins of my forefathers) and branded me a coward. Aunt Adelaide can always be relied upon to deliver a patronising, venomous letter under the pretence of caring family concern.

* * *

More and more men are leaving …

I think about the memories they must take with them. A wheat field walk one evening before harvest, the lick from a favourite sheepdog, a child's giggle.

What keepsakes do they have in their bulging pockets? A turquoise earring from a sweetheart, locks of a child's hair, bibles, photos of brothers living or lost, letters from dutiful aunts, a smooth pebble from the swimming hole.

Their memories too, the breath of their children's soft kisses, the smooth cheeks of wives and mothers.

And things to retrieve from those pockets, in the half-darkness of trenches, or on a summer day behind the lines to show their best cobbers.

Things to remind them of promises made, regrets or destinies. Items that reconfirm life's postponements.

What about the New Zealanders? The South Africans? The

Canadians? The English? What memories or keepsakes would they carry? Similar, I suppose.

Do they carry a protea leaf, a memory of mountains? The sound of crickets whirring through the long prairie grasses of Canada? Do they also carry letters, photos, bibles, earrings?

Would it be any different for the Hun or the Turk? I think it would be the same for all men.

* * *

A letter from Frank.

Well, hello there, Nipper,

Hoping things are going will with you. Things here are quite routine almost nine to five a guaranteed scrap first thing and then one in the afternoon. The Turk snipers are very annoying but the flies are ten times worse!

Writing this to you down on the beach but will need to sign off soon. When they see us all going for a dip they like to fire up this big nine inch gun we call Beachy Bill.

Thanks for the parcel; beats the jam and bully beef we get. If you could send some more pencils because despite the lead flying around here it's in bullets rather than pencils and I am down to a nib. Anyways must close. Don't worry about me I have figured this whole war thing out. Too tricky for Johnny Turk.

Yours Aff

Frank.

* * *

Cowra

A telegram from my father.

Frank missing.

No other message. I cannot sleep. I am consumed with worry, I cannot brush my teeth without gagging.

I notice Mr Sharman quietly picking up more of my administrative tasks.

* * *

CHAPTER FOUR

A call to arms

Another telegram.

Frank found alive. wounded.

* * *

The next day more information

Frank to Lemos. Leg wound. Tip-top.

* * *

Reports of militant shirkers howling down Colonel Lyster at a speech in Brisbane.

* * *

There is an open letter in the paper about football … a Sir William Irvine from Melbourne who finds the *'collective roar of young throats at games … offensive'.*

* * *

A letter on the same matter, stating that … '*there are more shirkers besides the shop hand, the farmer's boy and the mechanic … patriotism is equally lacking, and perhaps more so … among the professional classes.*'

We discuss. 'So, who's writing this letter then? Certainly, no-one heading away overseas or with a rifle in their hands; it's someone who's staying put.'

'A fire-eater,' Frank Burns reckons, 'probably an old man too fat to go who enjoys the extra drama, the sadness, the urgent glory of it all.'

'Why should he and his kind decide our fate?'

'That is the way of the world – old men telling young men how to die,' Mr Piggott said.

* * *

Debate rages in the newspapers about six o'clock closing.

> *… If the boys at the front can't drink it is the patriotic duty of those left behind at home to not drink …*
>
> *… Between 6 and 9pm there are 340,000 tired workers in New South Wales who are surely entitled to refreshment …*
>
> *… Six o'clock closing is the Patriotic Hour. Only selfish palates, greedy pockets and unpatriotic interests are asking for nine o'clock …*

We discuss the various points of view …

'Will it just increase home drinking? There is a danger that the bottle by the elbow will become handier than the bottle behind the hotel bar shelf.

Men who cannot get a glass of beer under proper licence conditions will become prey to the sly grog seller.

Mr Sharman stays neutral, other than a short instruction: 'It makes no difference for you lads, now does it?'

* * *

Pubs are all the same. Although we are not allowed to spend any time in them we walk through them almost every day as we go to and from our lodgings.

There will be a cheery barman quick with a joke and a good listener.

The permanents who hang around the door at opening with their thirsty looks.

The loudmouth who challenges anyone 'not from around here'.

The confederacy of drunks who share solidarity in endless rounds.

The five o'clock farmers just in, wetting their whistles as wives wait in the sulky.

The yarn teller.

The weather talkers.

Wheelers and dealers.

The stupid one stuck in the corner.

The bore.

The gossip.

Mr Sharman will look to stay at the best pubs, which are often also the busiest. He will always 'call in' downstairs, getting the news, finding out the local situation, dropping hints, making his presence felt.

* * *

'Is this not quite unusual?' the man is saying as I stand next to him looking at the poster advertising the troupe. 'These fit vigorous young men who relish a good fight have decided to stay and not go and do their bit. How very unusual ...'

* * *

The St Kilda Football Club change their colours from red, white and black ... Those being the same as the German ensign … to yellow, black and red … the colours of Belgium.

* * *

On a street corner in Temora ...

'Shouldn't you boys be in khaki?' says an older gentlemen who stands right in front of us crossing his arms and blocking our way.

* * *

We hear that Les has been getting hundreds of white feathers. Letters to the paper are cruel and everyone seems to think Les is the last recruit still left in the country.

* * *

Again, we hear the same comments about Les, repeated and repeated again …

'Les must join the sterner fight where the gloves are off and there is "no call to corners".'

'Put Les Darcy into Uniform and the Country will follow him.'

* * *

'Les Darcy is only one man, and can only carry one gun,' Mr Piggott is telling me. 'No-one, not even Les, can punch as hard as a bullet, or block a shell. It's a cruel game they play with Les. A cruel analogy to say one brave man from a boxing ring will win against shells and bullets. He's a boxer not a weapon; he's flesh and blood – he's not bulletproof. We don't know the half of what he's going through, I reckon, the entire country's expectations all falling onto him.'

* * *

According to Mr Sharman, Les has said that he would not lead other men to their deaths; if they wish to go that is their choice, but he wished to have no part of it.

* * *

A sign … *The war cannot be won on points – It must be a knockout.*

* * *

Slowly Mr Sharman is carefully taking out, piece by piece, the anger bottled up inside Eddie … fight by fight, day by day.

Ardlethan

A reception with the district's prominent graziers at the Turnbulls' Ben Lomond Station. Various conversations …

Suspicions of sustained and largely undiscovered cattleduffing.

Fat lamb prices.

The war …

The recent losses across the district.

How it is surely better to live well than to live long.

That the region lacks military enthusiasm and that the town's young cocks really needed to sharpen up their spurs.

* * *

The town of Harden now has a substantial fund to buy each new recruit a new wristwatch.

* * *

I pick up a two-month-old newspaper at Albury.

Albury Boys Thrilling Narrative.
How Victor Jones was wounded
How he lay in a lovely field of daises.

* * *

At Hamilton we walk smack-bang into a shire rally. The mayor asks of the crowd …

'Why won't you come forward?'

It is as if the question is being asked specifically to each of us. Billy stoops, Herbert tips his hat forward, the pace quickens, we search for an alley or a shady verandah.

* * *

Casualties from the charge at the Nek, the action at Lone Pine. My eyes rip through the list.

One of Les Darcy's best pals, Eric Newton, is dead. According to Mr Piggott, Mr Sharman had him in his Book of Men.

'A more than useful sparring partner of Les, a really nice boy.'

Mr Piggott has the saddest of looks. I sit with him alone, away from the others. He knew Eric quite well.

Then Mr Piggott tells me that he was at Wilmansrust. The fifth Victorian Mounted Rifles.

'Wilmansrust. Twelfth of June, 1901. Three hundred and fifty Australians camped out … ambushed by one hundred and fifty Boer. Twenty-two killed, forty wounded.

'The picketing wasn't right, didn't stand a chance. General Beatson called us a lot of white-livered curs, fat round-shouldered useless wasters. Well, he wasn't the cove standing in front of the machine guns … A dozen maxims mowed down our chaps like a bonny binder cutting down a crop. That's what's happened over there, all over again, that's what has happened at the Nek … no glorious charge, no stunning engagement like the papers reckon, none of that, it would have been just a slaughter, pure slaughter. It would have been horrible, the waiting, then up and over, wouldn't have stood a snowball's chance, if you didn't get killed outright, you get it in the guts and lie out there until you die.' Mr Piggott holds his head in his hands. 'Those poor boys ... poor, poor Eric.'

* * *

We are always on the lookout for the fire-eaters. The old men who stand on podiums delivering war speeches. Typically, they are …

Fat.
Balding,
pink with rage,
fat falling over belts and rolling over neckties,
quick to point out where duty lies,
they enjoy the sound of their own voices,
they are fond of repeating the old deeds from their old war.
(Wars that seem so ancient now.)

The Sudan … the relief of Ladysmith, Mafeking, Bugler Dunne, Lord Roberts …

Arms and fingers point this way and that …

Today one of the speakers says:

'The Australians would have been in Constantinople that day if the cold-footed "men": of the district had not "hung back".'

* * *

They are asking the women now to do their part …

Woman should shun the attentions of those who refuse to go.

How could any woman talk to such men, when their Belgium sisters were so hideously violated … a nurse with both breasts cut off … nuns raped, mutilation of young girls, the impaling of babies on German bayonets.

That they should assist those who remain to assert their manhood as a woman's persuasion was worth more than any men's argument.

'I can't stand by and watch all that. It's evil what they are doing, pure evil. I can't just stand by and hear about these things and do nothing, but that's what I am doing, nothing; that's what we are all doing,' Billy says.

'A lot happens in war, on both sides,' Mr Piggott says back.

We keep hearing the stories; 'where there's smoke there's fire,' Billy says.

'Don't believe everything you read in the papers, son.'

'It has to be true, or else they wouldn't write, would they?'

'It's just another way into your head, Billy. Stop reading the papers, otherwise it will do you in.'

* * *

Children gather …

Bones, bottles, iron, tin.

They dig gardens, trap rabbits, catch frogs and leeches.

They farewell brothers and fathers.

They collect wool from fence wire and bush.

They sew for cold, lonely soldiers and knit for Belgian babies.

They give away all their pocket money, they stand in costume on passing floats, they hold banners and sing in concerts.

* * *

Four-year-old Harry Richardson has collected four thousand pennies for Lady Dudley's Australian Voluntary Hospital.

* * *

There are button days or doorknocking to raise funds for the French, the Belgians, the Poles, the Serbs, the Montenegrins, the Syrians, the Russians and the Armenians.

* * *

We don't want to lose you, but really think you ought to go.

* * *

There are rumours that young single men working at local factories receive a message with their pay cheque … *'Your Country needs you, we do not.'*

* * *

The Casterton 'Win the War Day' is a success both in terms of fundraising and recruits.

Again, Mr Sharman is asked when some of his boys might be heading off.

For the first time he responds with a time frame: 'Sometime in the likely not so far distant future.'

Soon after, he says, 'In a time of their own choosing.'

Later he provides other reasons: 'When they are old enough.'

'When their brothers come back.'

He has stopped ignoring the questions, defending us, blocking accusations with his carefully crafted answers.

His donations to the Red Cross are increasing in size and frequency as does his telling of everyone about it.

* * *

A sign … *There are three types of men. Those who hear the call and obey, those who delay, and the others. To which do you belong?*

* * *

An editorial in the paper …

> *Put Les Darcy in a uniform and the men of Australia will march to hell behind him.*

* * *

It has been said that … military training is turning the country's weaklings into men.

* * *

We meet the Bendigo Mugs. These are a group of non-enlisted men, mostly those who had failed medicals. They have an entertaining concert party that tours the district raising patriotic funds. Even the most staid of the town's businessmen are giddy with laughter. Over five hundred pounds is raised.

* * *

A poster from the White Feather League:

> *To the young women of Australia. Is your best boy wearing khaki? If not, don't you think he should be?*
>
> *If he does not think that you and your country are worth fighting for do you think he is worthy of you?*
>
> *Don't pity the girl who is alone, her young man is probably a soldier, fighting for her and his country and for YOU.*
>
> *If your young man neglects his duty to his King and Country, the time may come when he will neglect you.*
>
> *Think it over then ask your young man to JOIN THE ARMY TODAY.*

* * *

'That's why I am staying back,' Frank says, 'looking after my girl and kids; my war is here, just putting enough food on the table.'

The poster is another knife in the back for Billy. Lovesick Billy who told me about an old sweetheart; what would she think of him now? What would any decent woman think of him now?

'You can't even talk to any girls just in case they are spoken for and you can't tell whether they are spoken for because they are not on a fellows arm like they used to be.'

* * *

In the local paper:

Mrs Aughtie is in receipt of the following letter, dated the 8th inst. From Mrs Carmichael Hon Secretary of the Central Sandbag Committee. We wish to thank you for your last consignment of bags and express the hope that you will continue by sending in as many as possible, as unfortunately they are as much needed as ever, and we are sending away large numbers, usually about 12,000 a week.

* * *

My brother Frank has lost his leg. I have a letter passed on to me from my parents.

Hornchurch, England

Dear Mother and Father,

In the old country now. A bit of bad news. I had to give up my left leg, so no more footy for me. The staff here are hard at work, busy making me a brand new one. A close thing, not everyone has a nine inch shell land next to them and lives to fight another day. Also a little deaf on my left side, so Mother I have the perfect excuse for ignoring your kitchen instructions. Talk that I will be heading home soon to dear old Australia soon. Cannot wait to see you all.

Yours Aff

Frank

* * *

From a local paper:

Recognising the gravity of the situation the Govt has called upon the senior public servants in the different centres to form an association, assisted by other citizens for the promotion of enlistment. Public meetings are to be held in the town of Bendigo and districts. Part of the work of the association is to make a return to the Government, classifying, on investigation, all unencumbered males, apparently fit, between 18 and 45 years into those willing to enlist and those less willing to do so and of course to do all possible to induce enlistment. It is very apparent that the Govt will resort to compulsion if moral suasion fails.

* * *

They are closing in on us. As each man enlists and leaves, the crowds thin more and more. The tide of humanity drops; then we, like the poles on a wharf, stand out and become the easy targets of any malcontents.

* * *

The local newspaper:

The public meeting heralded by the town band, was large and enthusiastic. A stirring appeal to the Empire's cause was made by Rev H. A. Peek. Recruits were then called for, and amidst loud cheers thirty-three men approached the table to have their names taken down by Sergeant Briggs.

* * *

Another poster near a Castlemaine haberdashery:

Women of Australia

When the War is over and your husband or son is asked, What did you do in the Great War? Is he to hang his head because you would not let him go?

Women of Australia, do your duty! Send your men today to join our Glorious Army.

* * *

Women are being asked to sign pledges for the active service league. I find one discarded near a drain.

At this hour of grave peril and desperate need I do hereby pledge myself most solemnly in the name of My King and Country to persuade every man I know to offer his services to the country, and I also pledge myself never to be seen in public with any man who, refused to respond to his country's call.

* * *

A cartoon of two well-dressed men causally studying a poster announcing the France's brave stand at Verdun. They are talking: *'As long as the French fight so bravely why should we?'*

'One of those looks a lot like me,' says Billy.

I tell him that he is nothing like them.

'I feel I need to prove myself, Arch, prove that I am a real man,' Billy tells me. 'Right now, I feel like a nothing, a nobody. I feel that I need to do something with my life, something big, something giant.'

* * *

News comes through about the Armenian death march, the thousands of skeletons dumped at Aleppo. The massacres under German direction.

* * *

Hero of the Dardanelles is showing at the cinema. Recruiting sergeants prowl the streets around the entrance. We steer clear. I go in front to test the waters, signalling back for them to cross to the other side the road.

* * *

They want another fifty thousand fit young men. It is hard to comprehend. If they were sheep maybe we could understand. But it is too many men.

* * *

You go fight, mate, and I'll hold your coat …

* * *

The New South Wales Universal Service League makes a case for universal service.

> *No fathers will be selected, only men over twenty will be selected, certain industries excluded.*
>
> *Numbers will go up.*
>
> *Saving of money, families spared.*
>
> *Industries safeguarded.*
>
> *Youth left to ripen.*

* * *

A new income tax to pay for the war has been approved. Mr Sharman and I are kept very busy with the new accounting procedures.

* * *

Mr Sharman:

If you work for money like a mule, don't throw it away like a donkey.

* * *

There are more and more local branches of the 'Order of the White Feather'. In Bendigo, two spinsters appear from the side of a fruit stand. Silently they hand them out as we file past. Jackie uses his feather to tickle me under the nose.

* * *

A speech I hear at Maryborough:

'What is needed is brawn and vigour, it is deplorable to see here men with muscles and brawn holding back from the task that nature intended for them.'

The bigger members of the troupe, Billy and Herbert Townsend, where they once strode, pranced, walked like bullocks, now they stoop, wish they were four inches shorter, two stone lighter and hope that the street might swallow them up and save them from their shame.

* * *

A poster:

It's Our Flag, fight for it, work for it.

* * *

A recruiting booth at Maldon's annual gymkhana has netted forty-five new volunteers.

* * *

Another poster:

The latest dispatch … send more men, age 18 to 45.

Would you stand by while a bushfire raged? Get Busy and drive the Germans back!

* * *

Yet another poster:

Will you fight? Or will you wait for this?

A picture of Germans surrounding a man and woman near a water tank and gum tree.

'Are they just over the hill? Just around the corner? Unlikely. Things would need to be a lot worse, the deadlock on the western front would need to be broken first and that was very unlikely. What then? They would need to go down right through Asia, too far; the war is half a world away, literally.

It's got nothing to do with Australia,' Mr Piggott scoffed.

* * *

Hate spreads …

All German music has been banned from orchestral concerts.

Dachshund dogs are taken to rivers and drowned in weighted down sacks.

German pianos remain unsold.

A German receives a violent blow to the nose after allegedly muttering 'Gluck fur Deutschland' in a picture theatre as a film shows the German Army marching into Brussels.

* * *

Germanton Shire Council at its last week's meeting resolved to recommend to the Government that the name 'Manton' be substituted for that of 'Germanton'.

* * *

Workers at the Sydney Glass and Bottle Works refuse to work with Germans.

* * *

At Gunning the stables and a number of sheds belonging to a Mr G Hauser are destroyed by a malicious fire.

* * *

'German Creek' on the Richmond River has already been changed to 'Empireville'.

Stones are thrown at shop windows.

Haystacks are destroyed on German farms.

Lutheran churches at Murtoa and Netherby are burned to the ground.

* * *

Accusations are made that Germans living beside harbours or overlooking towns have secret wireless sets hidden away to spy on wartime operations. From their homes the night time flashing of lights to signal ships or submarines waiting beyond the harbour can be seen. A letter to the paper …

The owner is still at large and enjoys the hospitality of this city at his beautiful home at Elizabeth Bay, whilst his countrymen are poisoning our brave men in the trenches and are sending innocent women and children to destruction on the high seas. This representative of the nation of baby-killers can obtain an excellent view of the Garden Island naval dockyard from his bedroom window ... The only safe place for Herr Plate is in the Holdsworthy Concentration Camp, or some equally secluded abode, where a bayonet or a bullet will prove effective if any mischief is attempted.

* * *

Royal Melbourne Show

Another useful looking challenger who says he's had no fights. Mr Sharman is onto this one. A liar's eyes dart down to the right as they speak. Better liars make even better fighters. It's all in the eyes.

'Done any boxing before, lad?'

'Nup.'

'What about blues on the street?'

'Nup.'

'What about on the footy field?'

'Nup.'

'So, in other words you're a liar then.'

* * *

Rumours of Fresh-faced Boys not even seventeen enlisting; boys who buy smoking pipes and somehow get in.

* * *

Big Billy Spiers reading out the headlines from the paper ... Mr Fisher has resigned because of ill health. Mr Hughes is the new Prime Minister.

'Little Billy Hughes … trouble ... never trust the little fellows like him.'

* * *

From the *Age* ...

Miss Adela Pankhurst's meeting 'Shall men enlist?' was interrupted when recruit soldiers then mobbed the stage.

While Miss Pankhurst and Miss John were singing 'I didn't raise my son to be a soldier', the men, now in possession of the piano, sung a number of popular tunes before a Major McInerney arrived and ordered the men out. According to reports there was very little heat displayed on either side, the only instance being when one irate woman pushed a soldier off the stage into the orchestra stalls.

* * *

The War Census is now underway. All males between eighteen and sixty to all those who have replied to the war census personal card receive forms in the mail. Billy has had his forwarded to him by his father. He shows me. The following questions must be answered …

Name, address, age, marital status, dependants, general health, disabilities, military training, number and descriptions of weapons in their possession and place of birth.

More questions …

Are you willing to enlist now? Reply yes or no.

If not willing to enlist now, are you willing to enlist at a later date? Reply yes or no and if willing state when.

If not willing to enlist, state the reason why, as explicitly as possible.

Also enclosed is a special personal message from the Prime Minister called 'The Call to Arms.' This puts us on the spot ...

* * *

The Call to Arms

The present state of the war imperatively demands that the exercise of the full strength of the Empire and its Allies should be put forth. In this way only can speedy victory be achieved and lasting peace secured …

The resources of the Allies are more than adequate for this task, but they must be marshalled. To wage this war with less than our full strength is to commit national suicide by slowly bleeding to death.

Our soldiers have done great things in this war. They have carved for Australia a niche in the Temple of Immortals. Those who have died fell gloriously, but had the number of our forces been doubled, many brave lives would have been spared, the Australian armies would long ago have been camping in Constantinople, and the world war would have been practically over.

We must put forth all our strength. The more men Australia sends to the front, the less danger will be to each man. Not only victory but safety belongs to the big battalion …

If you love your country, if you love freedom, then take your place alongside your fellow Australians at the front and help them achieve a speedy and glorious victory.

On behalf of the Commonwealth Government and in the name of the people of Australia, I ask you to answer 'Yes' to this appeal, and to do your part in this greatest war of all time.

Yours truly,

WM Hughes

* * *

Apart from Billy the rest of us don't have cards.

Eddie and Stanley not registered obviously.

Jackie not of age.

Frank says his card hasn't shown up.

Mr Piggott threw his out.

Herbert never got his card, all the moving around has made him a non-entity and for now he is happy to be just that.

Mr Sharman ... well, Mr Sharman always plays his cards close to his chest.

* * *

Pay off day. Everyone has complied with Mr Sharman's contract and today is the last day of the tour, payday. Paid in full. No deductions this year. We have Stan and Billy escort us to and from the bank. I divide and hand out the year's accumulated wages: one hundred and fifty hundred pounds for the prelim boys, more for the drawcards and the wrestler. The troupe goes their separate ways to bank, wire or spend.

* * *

Billy buys a new pinstripe suit which, given his size, makes him look rather garish, and I tell him so.

'Well, you know.' He smiles. 'Big man … big canvas.'

* * *

At Cole's Book Arcade I stock up. Jackie buys a pile of Deadwood Dicks and Buffalo Bills.

The little men turn out their messages …

The reign of knowledge and humanity is coming.

The happiness of mankind, the real salvation of the world, must come about by every person in existence being taught to read and induced to think.

* * *

At the Melbourne Cup …

Patrobas wins.

Large box kites are flown near the racecourse with messages painted on the sides telling young men to join up.

Scones and cakes are thrown to the crowds. As we discover, inside the food are slips of baking paper telling the eligible he ought to enlist…

* * *

The night before break-up we are walking along Swanston Street when a group of returned servicemen and drunken in-camp trainees approach us.

It starts as friendly banter, then grabbing, then pushing.

Then they try to frog march us to the recruiting centre at the town hall.

Then one returned servicemen spits on Jackie …

It gets heated.

The boys make short work of it.

* * *

Mr Sharman tells us we need to all grow a thicker skin.

* * *

My brother Frank returns early December. I go to meet the hospital ship at Circular Quay. My God. What a sight. I do not want to have to remember this. But I know I will repeat what I see back and forward in my head over and over for ever.

First, the unwell or sick who manage to walk off the ship.

The Cheer Up Our Boys Society are handing out pipes and tobacco.

Next to me one of the pretty cheer-up girls in her smart blue uniform is handing out sandwiches.

One returned soldier, excited, with a mouthful of sandwich, turns to the cheer-up girl and asks, 'Has this sandwich got Mount Pleasant Butter in it?'

'Yes,' she replied.

'I am from the South Coast. God, I have missed home! I have missed this butter! Tasting it again I can tell you what farm it's from, it's delicious!' The soldier bites again. 'I reckon I could tell you even what cow it's from!'

Next, stretcher cases, most like grey-blanket pupae, unmoving, wrapped-up packages, the sorry parcels of human suffering.

The legless, the armless, the blasted next. Winched down, one by one, in a ship's basket. Changing to crutches or wheelchairs, they wear the bravest of smiles.

There he is. The stump tucked up with safety pins … but he is beaming his beautiful smile.

He is alive! Home with us now, alive! Alive! In one piece or parts, we will have him ...

My mother grips onto him so hard he almost topples. He grabs me just as tightly.

As we leave, I look back to see the dead who didn't survive the voyage being brought gently down.

* * *

Back Again

Sick and wounded receive cordial welcome at Woolloomooloo.

Each of the 225 cases disembarking received a sprig of wattle or boronia and a packet of cigarettes.

Many of the men were in splendid physique. A fact remarked on by a first officer that it was unfortunate that such 'good material' had to be returned.

* * *

Mother has Frank on display. A parade of the town's more important women visit with a range of baked products … scones, lamingtons, chocolate cake. Nearly all are just brief acquaintances of my mother, as often they would have considered us a little below them. However, when a hero of the Dardanelles returns wounded to their hometown they come to lend support, to smooth the pillow, to cheer him up, and to find out any news to spread as whispers and gossip.

They are here today to see their local boy back from Gallipoli, ready to marvel at his bravery or doll out pity.

Frank is sick of it. His deafness frustrates him, someone sitting to his left might ask him a question, which, of course, he will not hear properly. He knows from experience that he will appear feebleminded if he attempts to answer a question he has not heard correctly. It is embarrassing to miss these questions. At times the questions, although most are well meaning, can be naive or patronising.

I sit at Frank's right. We have a system where I repeat the question into his good ear. Questions or enquiries about others over there, Frank will answer willingly. I try to redirect questions that might upset him or Mother.

One particular Sunday afternoon, a guest, Mrs Rawlins, persisted with a line of unpleasant questioning: 'Did you fear for your life? What was it really like? I hear that you were missing for several days before they found you, what exactly happened?'

Frank shifted. He had heard the question. He replied. I couldn't cut him off.

'Let me tell you, Mrs Rawlins, as you seem very keen to know exactly how bad it was, let me tell you what really happened to me.'

Mrs Rawlins shifted forward expectantly in her seat.

'The Turks counterattacked the trenches we took on the nineteenth of May.

'A Turk shell must have lopped up very close. I didn't hear it. Well, I must have heard it, but I don't remember it.

'Don't know how long I was there for. The only one alive.

'The trenches full of bodies, bits and pieces. The stink of it.

'The Turks who we had killed when we took the trench had gone black.

'They wore these green uniforms with these big belts around the waist. Because of the heat they were all bloated, the belts the last thing holding it all in … they looked like mother's roly-poly puddings.'

Mrs Rawlins pulls a queer face.

'The stink you have no idea … it smells like off cheese.'

The visiting ladies collectively recoil.

'How dreadful, how dreadful,' they mutter.

Frank is enjoying seeing the shock.

'Lost my nerve, I did. Had the wind up me. Probably could have tried to crawl off but didn't have the presence of mind to do so. The thirst … terrible. I had lost my canteen, saw another one under a dead Australian, probably old Henry – nice chap from Chatswood, minus the whole side of his head. He's right next to me, so I roll him over onto a dead Turk. There's this signing noise as I turn him over, the putrid air escaping.

'I drank the leftover water, sucked on stones after that and sat there, just sat there for a while. Quite a while.

'Listened to the groans of the dead and dying, no-one coming to get me ...

'Watched maggots from the Turk crawl along the ooze onto Henry. That's how I passed my time, Mrs Rawlins.'

Mrs Rawlins is white, shaking.

I suggested we look at Mother's roses, which seem to be doing rather well despite the weather, but Frank keeps going.

'My leg was numb, Mrs Rawlins. Bleeding from my ears and nose for three days. My ears were ringing; that hasn't stopped yet.'

'Decided then to have a good look at my leg. Open wound. Shrapnel must have gone across my thigh, long ways, opened me right up, nearly a foot long, above my knee. I look down and it's crawling, my legs full of maggots, white, wriggling bastards, eating me. Hundreds and thousands of them, like coconut shavings.' Frank points.

One of the ladies slumps in her chair. Others fan her.

Another is muttering excuses as she leaves the room.

Sounds of womanly vomiting on the verandah.

'And there all around me are the maggots' mothers and fathers. The flies. All of them trying to find a way in my shirt sleeves looking for fresh living meat.'

'Flies are the most horrible of the earth's creatures. I loathe them.'

'They seek out the worst materials – rotten food, faeces, the dead – and then proceed to dine, fornicate and raise a family in the midst of it.'

'I cannot stand them. Their sole purpose in life is to take to the wing to defile anything pure and turn it to muck.'

Frank stopped. I told him to.

'Anyways, that's what happened. Sometime later a big New Zealander, a Māori from the Pioneer Battalion, picked me up … big … as big as God he was … he carried me down. Those Māoris' will sure do me!'

'Anyway, better now. No leg, but home alive nonetheless. No leg, but that's alright; Nipper's had a bung one for years and he's getting about the country with Mr Sharman. Everything is tip-top, really. I'm fine, fine.'

The visiting ladies do not call again.

* * *

Every day Frank hops around the kitchen with a rolled-up copy of the paper, swatting flies.

'Got you … die, you bastard!'

* * *

At the Matador Café in Picton. Across the top of the menu in fancy cursive writing is the question … *Should you enlist?*

* * *

There are more and more words we read that have already become overused, worn out …

Grand Battle, died for the Empire's Cause, Sweeping Victory, Glory, Bravery, German Beasts, Turkish Beasts, Glorious Victory.

* * *

Men must work and women must weep. It had ever been so …

* * *

My brother has decided to rid Australia of all its flies. I see he has developed tables now in a notebook. The numbers of flies killed. By method …

Swatted eight,
Fly paper six,
Trapped four,
Sprayed five.

* * *

1916

CHAPTER FIVE

White feathers

The troupe for this year …

Jackie Green

Stanley Hill

Frank Burns

Mr Piggott

Billy Spiers. Yes, Billy! He's back! Mr Sharman has worked on him over the summer break – one more tour. Mr Sharman, the master convincer, master showman, salesman and gentle persuader. He could sell ice to Eskimos. I am grateful. Billy saved for another year, one more year.

'No show without punch,' he says.

I am happier than a rat with a gold tooth!

Herbert Townsend.

Taggie Young, the Chinaman, our new welterweight.

Mr Sharman.

* * *

Eddie is not with us. Eddie had, according to Mr Sharman, tangled with the Queensland Constabulary and was cooling his heels.

* * *

Mr Sharman's position on selecting any new members of the troupe: no boozers or shady characters. No ratbags – no matter how great their fistic ability might be – need apply.

* * *

There are now cigarette cards of sportsmen who have joined up.

Tibby Cotter. Cricketer.

Warrant Officer Cecil Healy. Member of the Manly Surf Lifesaving Club. Olympic swimming medallist 1906 and 1912, expert in the Australian crawl swim stroke.

McMurtie the footballer.

Arthur Cripps, Boxer.

Albert Massey, Boxer.

Sgt Major Jack Taylor, Boxer.

* * *

Mr Sharman holds a hardening session to toughen the troupe up. Once the tour starts the hits get harder and more frequent. Although the troupe have maintained some degree of fitness over the summer they, according to a new theory of Mr Sharman's, are not ready for all the knocks. Toughen them up now, condition them to the physicality early, and it will see them right through the season. He stands them opposite each other and orders them to repeatedly punch half to three-quarter blows to the arms, shoulders and torso, until skin tightens and bones harden.

* * *

This year's itinerary …

Maitland, Cessnock, Singleton, Muswellbrook, Armidale, Tamworth, Gunnedah, Narrabri, Moree, Sydney Royal Easter Show, Bathurst, Molong, Wellington, Dubbo, Narromine (rumoured to be harbouring several desperate criminals).

The Queensland Circus run still on at this stage. The Brisbane Exhibition.

The Riverina: Cowra Show, Canowindra, Grenfell, Forbes, Parkes, Ardlethan, Temora, Murrumburrah, Young, Wagga.

More north-east Murray River towns; Albury, Rutherglen, Chilton,

Beechworth (some useful types presently working at Zwar Brothers Tannery),

Wangaratta, Benalla (the Kennedy Brothers).

Then South East, Warrnambool, Terang, Camperdown (bored dairy farmers). Colac, Geelong.

The Royal Melbourne Show.

Ballarat!

Daylesford.

Bendigo, Castlemaine, Melton (stonewall crofters), Bacchus Marsh, Diggers Rest. Shepparton.

Lilydale, Healesville, Dandenong, Pakenham, Drouin, Warragul, Moe, Traralgon, Sale, Bairnsdale, (apparently there are quite a number of hefty six foot timber getters working out that way).

Call in to the mission to see if we can pick anyone up for next year.

A lot less showgrounds, more single-show towns. In fact, a lot more still-towning: stopping in little places, stopping in towns or places without shows … A lot more pulling up and pulling down the tent. The boys will not be happy; they want fights, throwing punches, not whacking in pegs.

Perhaps some of the show committees are not so keen, or asking the question why a troupe of fit young men is still at home.

Maybe Mr Sharman doesn't want to deal with this line of questioning.

Maybe it's that the new towns are too caught up with the novelty of the troupe's visit to raise war matters.

Maybe smaller towns are more polite.

Or maybe we become more of a moving target. Men without a fixed abode. The longer we dwell, the more time for questions to be asked. Mr Piggott thinks it is good to disappear for a while.

* * *

From the *Daily Sketch*, left down the side of a seat on the train.

Sixteen Army Corps of Slackers

If the 650,000 unstarred and unattested single men had enlisted and been trained and equipped, it cannot be questioned that such a force could have saved Belgium.

Triumphantly stormed the Gallipoli Peninsula and advanced on Constantinople from other points.

If such a force were now available it would make an immediate offensive possible in the West. At any time during the campaign it could have acted with decisive effect and in the critical year of 1916 it will be able, if ready, to decide the war. But the 650,000 men will be too late again unless they are fetched at once.

* * *

Billy has got even bigger in size over the summer. More muscles and more fat. To a worried Mr Sharman, a little too much of the pud. He fills in doorways, frightens people as he walks around corners, takes up more of the train seat. His Majesty's Ship … HMS *Billy Spiers* … Mr Piggott calls him …

* * *

It is a hot afternoon so we stop for beverages at the Garden of Roses Café. It is busy with chattering farmers' wives and the town's businessmen.

There is a sign advising of dress standards.

Women can remove garments consistent with charm.

Gentlemen can remove clothes consistent with decency.

The older women are trussed-up in crinoline, hot and bothered.

Bill, Stanley remove their jackets and roll up selves, but Mr Sharman's jacket stays on. He remains stoic although a little crumpled.

We arrange ourselves around a table in the middle of the restaurant. French lace tablecloths, crystal vases with violets, comfortable chairs, all very nice. Bill orders lemonade, Stan as well. Mr Sharman orders a cup of tea.

I order a round of date scones.

'Hot tea to cool down on a hot day.' One of Mr Sharman's tips.

Mr Sharman never gets time to enjoy a scone or his cup of tea as there are people lining up to talk with him.

* * *

While the others are often busy playing cards Billy and I like to play games of description. Birds are a favourite …

Crows squeeze out their regrets.

Swallows bounce past on strings.

Cockatoos screech, open and close, sharp beaks like rusty old gates.

Magpies tuck hands behind backs and inspect garden paths like headmasters.

Parrots throw themselves over hedgerows and into trees.

Cockatoos float like handkerchiefs to dab the wet boughs of gumtrees drinking in the rain.

* * *

Maitland

Taggie Young has the most unusual style. Mr Sharman wants to bottle him. Taggie can switch between orthodox and southpaw stances, confusing the opponent. Switching means the opponent never gets their defence organised. They don't have long enough to establish a platform before he switches – they never see the telling punch that suddenly springs inside out from his guard.

Mr Sharman calls Taggie's switch stance 'The Chinaman'.

* * *

The Asian fighting arts ... Taggie explains, disciplines where feet and legs are used over fists, others where most of the fighting occurs on the ground. Others that promote the use of weapons, the Japanese ninja who use a sharpened flying disk. The Chinese have a strange circular martial art known as Tai Chi – a slow spinning of the arms and legs which when sped up to full speed is reportedly deadly.

* * *

A timber wall in Cessnock. There is a peephole through the fence. Words painted and an arrow pointing to the holes. Billy, curious, wanders up and looks in. Disappointed and grim he steps back. 'Have a look,' he says, gently lifting me up.

Inside the fence is a sign: *'If you can read this you are tall enough to enlist.'*

* * *

Singleton

There is a parade of new recruits heading off. A band leads, playing 'The Boys from the Dardanelles' and 'Australia Will Be There'.

Girls throw halfpennies with their names on them, asking them to be their soldier boy and promise to write every day.

* * *

Mr Sharman tries out some new names for the boys who stand up on the boards ...

'One-punch Herbert'.

'Big Show Billy Spiers'.

'Bumper Burns'.

'Jack the Beanstalk'.

* * *

We passed a flag-raising ceremony in Muswellbrook.

Mr Piggott said it was a lot of ballyhoo about nothing more than a square piece of coloured cloth. 'The most dangerous fabric in the world, a flag,' he said.

* * *

This year's troupe is coming together … merging, joining.

'A good crop this year,' Mr Sharman has told me.

We are like a group of passengers on a sea voyage.

Like the lifting of an air balloon with us inside. We are up and away and neatly separated from others.

We are like the groups of men who, more and more, leave to fight together overseas.

We are like explorers, discovering, uncovering, renaming things, sharing things of ourselves. Learning new ways and finding new things, leaving behind our lonely pasts and becoming a collective of ourselves.

* * *

Paddy's Day. The Irish are always up for a scrap, always needing to defend ourselves throughout history. The fighting Irish. Sharman's … always were and will be good, tough fighters …

* * *

A poster: *Australia has promised Britain fifty thousand more men. Will you help us to keep that promise?*

* * *

In Armidale we see footprints painted on paths and across roads from a football ground to a recruiting depot.

* * *

Our typical arrival:

Billy fills up the foyer … Built like a bison. Broad as a door. Big Show Billy.

Mr Piggott's smile lights up the whole place.

Busy hotels fall silent as Mr Sharman speaks.

People suddenly appear from nowhere to get a glimpse of Jackie and Stanley.

Our typical departure:

Pats across the vast plateau that is Billy's wide, wide back.

Lingering handshakes.

The hotel manager and Mr Sharman in a serious ear-to-ear conversation.

Winks, nods and waves goodbye.

* * *

I listen in on a conversation between a returned soldier and a boy close to enlistment age, who asks what flying bullets sound like.

'Like the sound of small birds flying overhead,' he tells him.

* * *

Tamworth

A lecture on a temporary pulpit in the middle of town, by a Dr Hayden, on the cumulative effects of alcohol impairing the mental and moral perception of the human mind and body. Right outside the biggest pub in town.

There are angry fingers poking holes in the air …

'With the war we need our men strong sober and uncorrupted. Drunkards can march their way to an early grave, but they will not drag down our youth into the pit of despair and early death.'

'Someone shouts, 'Well, mate, the war has done that already.'

A man near me says to a friend, 'After losing my boy to the war, drinking is all I have left. Bugger me if I am going to let them make me suffer anymore.' And he throws a full bottle of beer at the pulpit.

* * *

A letter in the local newspaper …

Again, the residents of Tamworth are forced to endure drunken scenes outside a venue where we are supposed to showcase the best the area has to offer. No Christian community should allow such scenes to take place, to allow such depravity to litter this town.

Yours sincerely,

Rev Alberton

* * *

In Moree, Mr Sharman signs on two young Aboriginal brothers, Percy and Walter Collins. Seventeen and nineteen. I manage to obtain the necessary certificates of exemption from the New

South Wales Aborigines Welfare Board with little fuss. It is said the boys are trouble, and that a spell in the tent would do them good. Mr Sharman's reputation as a straight-up-and-down type of man was also made mention of. It was suggested to me that if these two worked out, then Moree could supply a long line of troublesome boys into Mr Sharman's protection.

Percy and Walter, 'The Moree Maulers', come with a reputation for hard punching and mischief. 'They are perfectly suited to my purposes; good useful, excellent,' Mr Sharman tells me.

* * *

Eight reasons why we are not going …

Jackie Green, not of age.

Stanley, not his concern.

Frank, not going to ignore his family's needs.

Mr Piggott, not required at his age.

Billy Spiers, currently contracted not to go.

Herbert Townsend, two of his other brothers have gone.

Taggie Young, not asked.

Mr Sharman, not disclosed.

* * *

Memories of the Sydney Royal Easter Show …

The smell of sticky toffee apples, soil, livestock, the tang of sap from the logs of the woodchoppers, sawdust and drying canvas.

The taste of dagwood dogs and candy floss and ice-cream,
the sounds of the toot, toot, tooting stream carousel,
the sharp ting! of the strongman's bell,
the children's hearty laughter on behalf of clowns,

the massed bands playing 'Invercargill' and 'Under the Double Eagle', their big beautiful sound that marches right through me.

Mr Sharman's constant spruiking,

the roar inside the tent, the sound of raining coins.

The sights of red, blue and green ribbons being proudly worn by mountainous cattle. The Phelan's ladder, now even higher, disappearing into a cloud.

Dr Worthing's 'Two-Headed Cow' from Bombay, eating from each of my claw hands.

* * *

Bathurst

Mr Sharman decides we are to have an outing. A trip to the pictures. Everyone is jolly.

Before the start of the feature a message is shown up across the screen …

Not for glory and not for gain have we drawn our sword to the strife.

It's a fight for our homes, a fight for our freedom, a fight for our very lives.

Your King is calling, your country's calling. Your women are calling too.

We want a hundred thousand men and the first they want is you!

There are the sounds of latecomers, shoes bumping in the darkness, hissed voices.

Now, for some reason they are moving to the front, right in front of the stage. All women with big self-important hats.

The lights are abruptly switched on.

There is a row of them. A dozen, horrible, spiteful-looking ones, others younger and probably put up by the evil old ones to undertake what is about to transpire.

Each of them reaches deep into a bag or purse grabbing a collection of white feathers. It is a Tuesday afternoon, there are two startled old ladies, two school truants and us nine. I am sitting on the outside of the row and get the first feather.

'What would the boys of Gallipoli think of you loafing about here in a picture hall?'

I am too shocked to rebuff her. I can't tell her my brother lost his leg there and I have another about to risk his life under the guns in France. I am ashamed.

The sour-faced bitches have a feather and insult for each of us …

To Jackie. 'Younger ones than you have joined.'

To Mr Piggott. 'Play your part.'

He coolly places the feather on his lap. It is the first time I have seen the look of anger on his face.

To Frank Burns. 'You have a coward's look.' They are sniffing. 'And a coward's smell.'

To Stanley Hill. A look of confusion. A hand thrust out with a feather, but no words.

To Billy. 'You look like the type to just stand by and watch the women and children of Belgium and France being raped and murdered.'

Billy takes the feather gently and holds it in his shaking hand.

To Herbert Townsend. 'Such a big man like you should be helping out your mates. You should be ashamed at your selfishness.'

Taggie. He gets a feather, but like Stanley the woman doesn't know what side he should be on.

To Mr Sharman. 'You don't look like you are brave enough to serve your country. You need to go back and hide behind your mother's skirt.'

Mr Sharman throws the feather away like a dart and returns the evil look right back where it came from.

* * *

Mr Sharman is still young enough to go – twenty-eight. Why does he choose not to go?

More use here. Finding fighting men to go. Getting them ready …

Providing skills for any possible hand-to-hand combat …

Fundraising …

A wife, and a son, young Jimmy ...

* * *

It is all eating away at Billy. One night he unpacks his thoughts for me.

He is being torn apart by a war so far away. All his mates back home are joining up, everyday questions are asked, judgements of character made just from a look, that particular kind of look.

… Self versus duty, courage versus cowardliness, honour versus justice ...

On the other side of the coin, Mr Sharman's pressure to stay.

Caught between a rock and a hard place.

I have overheard Mr Sharman's little chats with Billy, how

hard it would be to find another wrestler, how he is needed here, how his leaving might ruin the entire troupe; again with emphasis, how he is of much more use here. The decision to stay or go seems almost worse than the pain of any of the two alternate consequences. Death by a bullet or the slow death of his soul with the daily slaps of shame and guilt.

I try to tell him not to worry so much. What he does now is still important. Mr Sharman's contract is watertight. This, for now, excuses him from anything else. His duty lies here. There are still plenty of men here to wrestle, men with less significant roles to play here then Billy's. Until there are none of these men left here … he should not worry. He is stuck here, at least until November.

* * *

The guilt and the shame of the Bathurst picture hall manifests itself differently in every man.

Jackie … trains even harder.

Stanley … crawls further up inside his shell, peeking out and saying nothing.

Frank Burns … punches harder at the heavy bag, leaving a deep reminder.

Taggie … cares the least … the war is not his problem.

Mr Piggott … sleeps poorly … reminders of Wilmansrust.

Billy … all tangled up and has started to brood.

Herbert … bangs the drum even harder.

Mr Sharman writes more ferociously in his notebook.

* * *

Billy and I talk again and again, always about the same thing …

'I feel guilty all the time, guilt every time I go up on the line-up board, hold down yet another weakling, guilty even just walking down the street. I feel guilty staying here, then guilty about even thinking about leaving Mr Sharman. The shame. I wish I could just get up and shake off all the shame and guilt. There's only one way left to do it now, Arch. I reckon it would be easier to walk across no man's land than walk down a street these days.'

* * *

Frank writes and updates me on the goings-on at home …

Leg good, but feels as if it is still there, still gets pains beyond the stump. Mother is having trouble drying off all his stump socks.

Getting bored with the sit-down work at the post office.

He tells that James Franklin and Charles Harris are dead, and thirty-nine flies is his record in daily kills so far.

He is stepping out with Laura Stephenson. I know her, a pretty girl who works at the chemist in Camden.

* * *

News of the Easter Rebellion in Dublin. Twelve hundred Sinn Finners have taken the General Post Office in Dublin. They have surrounded the railway station and captured St Stephen's Green. The Irish rebel leader Padrig Pearce has read out an 'Irish Proclamation' in which he refers to 'Gallant Allies in Europe'.

'You Irish better be on the lookout for any trouble,' Mr Piggott says.

'Always looking out for trouble, always have ... always will,' replied Mr Sharman.

* * *

Daniel Mannix, Catholic Coadjutor of Melbourne, says, '*It's now or never for the Irish.*'

* * *

The rebellion is over. Ten thousand British troops saw to that … Women and children caught in the crossfire.

The 'Traitors' (as they are quickly called), Padrig Pearce and James Connelly, are captured and paraded through the streets to Kilmainham Gaol in a hail of rotten vegetables and tipped-over chamber pots.

* * *

Molong

Billy isn't happy about the wages; he says that Mr Sharman wouldn't shout even if a shark bit him on the leg.

Jackie puts him straight …

How Mr Sharman paid for all the medicine when Frank's ma got sick.

When he bought shoes for that kid we saw living out of a coal cupboard in Sydney.

Forgetting debts some had racked up and couldn't meet when they gave up the game.

Careful with his money … but kind with it too.

* * *

'It isn't really the wages,' Billy tells me later. 'Mr Sharman's a fair man, I know that, it's not him. I am feeling guilty about been here and not over there. Feeling bad that I get paid not to do my fair share, getting paid just to parade around like a peacock. Ever since Bathurst it's not been right. Archie, I should be away helping me mates out, but I am stuck here with the bond and Mr Sharman's obligations hanging over my head'.

'You are being too hard on yourself,' I say. 'You have better reasons for staying than others.'

'No, I don't think so; you need a very, very, good reason,' Billy says. 'And right now being in a boxing troupe isn't a good one any more. There would not be a single man who doesn't have a good enough reason for staying, certainly in the minds of those people that give you white feathers or stare at you. You could hide away all these years, but you would need a reason for yourself. A reason you personally could have to live with, one that wouldn't gnaw away at you day after day. For me, now, there is no reason, and the guilt … it's just all too powerful now.'

* * *

Later that day, Billy asked Mr Sharman and Mr Piggott if they thought him going off to war was better for the greater good of humanity rather than staying here for the benefit of a few.

'Is it about the greater good or helping humanity?' Mr Piggott says. 'It might be on some levels. Tell me about the greater good – tell me, Billy. What good will come from it; what exactly will we learn?'

'It's about a test of courage,' Billy says.

'Really, and what's that going to prove? Courage in spades,

they have it all, but it doesn't stop a bullet or a shell.'

'Its duty, then,' Billy says.

Mr Piggott sighs. 'Yes, duty; there it is, the misguided duty.'

'There's just as much duty right here, for me, your employer,' said Mr Sharman.

* * *

The sixteen Irish 'Martyrs' (as they are called) are executed at Kilmainham Gaol. James Connelly is so badly injured in the rebellion that he has to be shot by the firing squad sitting in a chair. Defiant Pearce asked to have the blindfold removed.

* * *

Overheard words in the main street ...

'The Irish are pale cousins of the nigger and worse behaved.'

* * *

At the Wellington Show there is a stall selling lucky charms to the newly enlisted. Fashioned in brass, penny sized, they have all the symbols of good luck on them: the horseshoe, the stirrup, a four-leaf clover, Egyptian symbols arranged around the Hindu cross. 'Membership emblem of the don't worry club' … it says … 'Good luck!'

There are almost more customers at that stall than at our tent.

* * *

We have a day off and take drays out to the Wellington Caves. We see the giant fossil of a Diprotodon, an ancient dinosaur.

Jackie is underwhelmed: 'looks just like a bloody big wombat to me.'

* * *

Narromine

We meet one of the town's minor celebrities, a woman, a Mrs Mack, who had met Franz Ferdinand in the flesh. Ten years ago, before things went very bad for him, the Archduke visited the district on a shooting expedition.

The Archduke was a crack shot, shooting anything that moved. Three kangaroos, two possums, five parrots, ten bustards, twelve ducks, two emus, three lizards, one snake, two robins, four rats and two mice.

Each time an animal was felled, all of the Archduke's staff dismounted, lined up, doffed their hats and then all go to shake his Highness's hand … every time, even for the smallest of birds.

Later Mrs Mack was invited to dine in the state car of the Archduke's personal train.

Fair hair parted in the middle, light blue eyes, tall.

A constant habit of twirling his moustache.

A menu of oysters, steak and mushrooms, turkey, ham, new potatoes and French beans, sago pudding and Charlotte russe, hock, champagne, cognac and cigars.

As they left, the Archduke took a printed photograph of himself, signed it and placed it in a silver frame with the crest of the House of Habsburg, whereupon it was presented to each of the guests including Mrs Mack.

As the Archduke slept soundly on board his train, Eduard Hodak, his Royal Highness's personal taxidermist stayed up all night stuffing every single one of the unlucky creatures the Archduke had shot down.

* * *

Brisbane (Start of the Queensland Circus Train)

A returned soldier tells us how you can actually see a flying shell as it reaches the very top of its arc.

* * *

A poster: *It's nice in the surf, but what about the men in the trenches? Go and help.*

* * *

A new circus trick.

Moitra the Human Whale.

See him drank gallon upon gallon of water.

See him swallow three live goldfish and bring them back up into a crystal bowl.

* * *

I have a letter from Bert in which he writes:

Medina Camp, Cairo, Egypt

Dear Arch,

Hi there, Nipper,

The trip over on the boat was hellishly rough and many were suffering from the 'mal de mer'. Poor fellows. They say when you are seasick you think you are going to die and when you are severely seasick you hope you are going to die!

It's a big blue ocean out there, Arch, not empty but full of life! We saw flying fish – what amazing creatures, a beautiful combination of bird and fish. I watched them for hours as they skipped along in front of the ship just like the flat stones we used to throw down at the dam. They leap twenty or thirty feet across the water. You may not believe this but one landed right in a frying pan in the galley after flying right through the open porthole! Tasted just like trout.

On dry land now, and how dry and dusty and dirty Cairo is! Saw the Sphinx and Pyramids the other day, the Sphinx reminds me of the old farm cat we had, Marmalade, you remember? He would sit just like that in front of the fireplace.

On a tour down the Nile we watched the locals catching sparrows, which they love to eat. On one side of a small stone wall they crouch with a net attached to poles throwing bread over the wall, one of them standing a distance away sees that there are birds within range. After calling out they throw the net over the wall capturing a dozen or so of the birds. Apparently, wrapped in clay cooked in the ashes of a fire and cracked open they are delicious.

Anyways just a quick note on my arrival so I need to get it away. Remember me to the others. I trust that Frank is good and Dad is managing the farm while I am away. Will write more on the goings on as they come to hand. Regards to Mr Sharman and the boys. We could do with him and his charges over here … Why will he not enlist?

Aff yours

Bert

* * *

A flyer left behind, just for us, by a woman at a café:

4 Questions to the Women of Australia

1. You have read what they would do if they ever invaded Australia?

2. Do you realise that the safety of your home and children depends on our getting of more men now?

3. Do you realise that the one word 'go' from you may send another man to fight for our King and Country?

4. When the War is over and your son is asked 'What did you do in the Great War?' Is he to hang his head because you would not let him go?

Women of Australia, do your duty! Send your men today to join our glorious Army. God save the King.

* * *

Names for men who could but do not go:

midgleys,
cold footers,
loafers,
slackers,
shirkers,
cowards,
slugs,
jibs,
milksops,
malingers,
and wowsers.
Parasites,

loons,
would-to godders,
stayputs,
dastards,
muddy-mottled wastrels,
traitors,
idlers,
murderers,
and laggards.

* * *

Sydney Stadium fans are nothing but selfish, soulless degenerates who were not fit to blacken the boots of the brave men in the trenches.

* * *

Men now wear a range of badges to avoid any embarrassing questions, accusations. To step past the evil looks and white feathers and just get on with their daily business.

The essential services badge.

Mercantile marine badges.

Sole provider badge.

Home service badge.

Transport service badge.

The badge for volunteered but medically unfit.

The silver war badge for discharged wounded, sick or unfit men.

A badge for volunteer munitions workers.

Women wear badges too, marking their sorrow … female relative badge, mothers and widows badges. A space on the ribbon to place a bar for one or two or three brothers or sons gone away or lost.

We have no badges; we think we should just make some up of our own to cover off our reasons … we could have made lots of badges:

the better money badge,
the too young badge,
the war's too far away badge,
the fundraising badge,
the cannon fodder badge,
I am black or yellow and not wanted badge,
the I've got brothers and sisters to look after badge,
Mr Sharman's got me in a contract badge,
Mr Piggott talked me out of it badge,
The I don't want to kill someone badge,
the I will go sometime badge,
the definitely thinking about it badge.
That's one especially for Billy, I am thinking.

* * *

A flyer I found left at a shop counter:

5 Questions for Patriotic Shopkeepers

1. Have you any fit men between 19 and 38 years of age serving behind your counter who at this moment ought to be serving their Country?

2. Will you call your male employees together and explain to them that in order to end the war quickly we must have more men?

3. Will you tell them what you are prepared to do for them whilst they are fighting for the Empire?

4. Have you realised that we cannot have 'business as usual' whilst the war continues? The Army wants more men today!

5. Could not women or older men fill their places till the war is over?

Your Country will appreciate the help you give.

God save the King.

* * *

People, places a fit young boy will need to avoid:

recruiting sergeants,

any men with any kind of civic standing – alderman, councillors. Mayors from the town council, the county or the shire,

any groups of young women, any wearing sashes or uniforms,

any women carrying branches of wattle or gum, colourful or well-embroidered banners or signs with large words in angry fonts,

older men, returned soldiers, any Anglican ministers, school cadets, enlisted men,

anyone wearing mourning clothes or black armbands, little children dressed in military uniform, people with certain badges displayed on their lapels.

Stay away from recruiting stations, rallies outside town or shire halls.

Avoid the tumpty tumpty tump sounds of a brass band.

Stay clear of podiums, streets and halls with any colourful bunting or flags.

Do not attend marches, demonstrations, rallies, dances, patriotic concerts or soirees.

Stay away from tearooms, mechanics halls, masonic lodges, markets, cake stalls, busy greengrocers and butchers shops. Avoid daylight and business hours.

Stay away from main streets, side streets and alleyways, stay away from popular parks and promenades. Stay away from flagpoles.

Actually, stay away from all of this, stay away from everything, stay locked well away, out of sight, to avoid them all and avoid your own embarrassment.

Hide …

***

The only proper backing for ANZACs is more ANZACs.

***

At Maryborough, fifty of the town's strongest men challenge an elephant to a tug-of-war then get asked why they haven't decided to pull together at the bigger fight by a recruiting sergeant who suddenly appears on the scene.

***

There are rumours of women, sweethearts, even wives being seen stepping out with other men.

***

From the paper:

Mr D Scott of Laurel Hill was heard to state in the Royal Hotel that it was a capitalist's war. He was charged a 100-pound fine for making statements prejudicial to recruiting. Mr Scott avoided a prison term of six months as it was reported one of his sons had served in the Dardanelles.

* * *

An open letter by Dr H M Morgan, former captain of the Wallaby Rugby Union …

Send us men, men, men and more men. It is the best game in history. There are no rules, and the only referee – posterity – has a whistle that cannot be heard. Yes, they're in our twenty-five at present, but when we heel out our ammunition more cleanly we shall move forward.

* * *

Every town is holding a Tableaux fundraiser, where people in costume stand motionless in various historical scenes… Seen one and seen them all … A plump matron type dressed as Britannia, troops of unsure young boys dressed as soldiers. Then young girls in virginal white, wearing lace and sashes deliver breathlessly loyal speeches about the Empire …

* * *

It is another long train journey; rhetorical non-war questions are raised to pass time:

The validity of other sporting pastimes, various pursuits are compared.

'What is the purest of sports?'

'Pugilism, of course.'

'Other than that.'

'None.'

'Rugby … muddied oafs … too many rules, schoolboy rules, don't run in front, don't go out, don't do this, don't do that,' Jack said.

'League starts to get exciting, then it stops,' Mr Sharman said. 'No son of mine will play that game.'

'Rules football … lots of running around like headless chooks.'

'Cricket … flannelled fools … standing in the sun for five days just for a draw.'

'Pugilism,' Mr Sharman concludes, smiling, 'is the best sport on the planet. Two men measured against a true scale, a measure of one to another. A sliding scale of courage, skill and fitness. Man to man and that alone, no excuses, only the sweet science of bruising; there is no better sport! Boxing man on man is the opening up of the soul. For every man who steps into the ring, his fight is his moment, his moment of absolute truth.'

Mr Sharman's smile is wider than the sky.

* * *

Childers

More white feathers in envelopes left for each of us at the hotel front desk. A bundle of them. Exactly eight of them. Someone has been watching, counting us. Mr Sharman dumps his and all the other envelopes into to the rubbish bin so the troupe do not need to worry themselves about it.

* * *

Bundaberg

Jackie, with his feather quill given to him that morning, practices writing *coward* over and over on an old piece of foolscap paper he has found.

* * *

Frank spends a lot of time examining his fists, big as Christmas hams. He turns them over and over, like a potter, looking for cracks or weaknesses. He sees me looking at him.

'Tools of the trade, Arch; got to keep them sharp.'

* * *

'Bully Boy!'

A man with one leg is shouting at Billy.

'Billy the fat bully boy! How about you join the real fight? If I had a spare leg, I would be up there teaching you a lesson.'

Mr Sharman says, 'Wresting doesn't need legs, come up.'

'I don't want to touch him. Cowards give me the creeps.'

* * *

Billy is missing that night. I ask around about the heckler, who he is and where he lives. I find Billy shouting at the house, telling him to come out and settle things.

* * *

Another letter from Bert:

Hello there, Nipper,

Or bonjour, I should say. After a second round of the mal de mer, including myself this time, we landed safely. Once my stomach had calmed down I set off to try some French food: frogs legs tasted like chicken and the snails were slimy and chewy but all right. Give me Mother's roast any time!

We were in camp for a boring three weeks, pretending to kill Germans in various ways.

Right now, around us are beautiful green farms. They farm the same things as us but a little differently.

They all have these wheels near their back doors about eight feet across, and we didn't have the foggiest about what they were for.

Then we see an old woman putting her dog into the wheel, she gives it a spin to set it rolling. The poor old doggy's running, running so it doesn't fly upside down; soon it gets a pace up and keeps running. The wheel connects to a drive shaft. Inside the house, the wheel is driving a butter churn! Every farm has a dog wheel.

There's a lot of hurry up and wait in the Army, but recently there's been more hurrying than waiting so I think there's something being cooked up.

Anyway, little brother, remember me to Frank and to Mother and, of course, Father. I miss you and them all terribly. Frank's scrape has made us all realise how much we all mean to one another. It sure has from my end. Best sign off now.

Love to you all.

Bert

* * *

In Rockhampton a returned Gallipoli veteran is to provide a lecture at the town hall on the 'exciting sensations of a bayonet charge'.

* * *

A poem I see in the letters column of the paper:

Wake up, boys
What of the boys of our town?
The girls are hard at work
Doing their bit to help things on.
Are their brothers going to shirk?
Why don't you go to the front, lad?
How can you stay behind
branded as a coward forever?
You've still time to change your mind.
How can you shame your mother?
They thought they were rearing men,
and now when your country calls, you're tied
To their apron strings again.
Was it for this they bore you;
Proud in each anguish throe?
For a man is born to his country
To serve her in weal or woe.
How can you face your sisters?
And other chaps' sisters too?
Do you think when our troops come back again
that the girls will look at you?
Anyway, do something –
you who are strong and fit –

If you haven't the spunk of men, boys,
get busy and learn to knit.

* * *

I see that Billy is reading his copy of the same paper. It is too late for me to stop him reading it. He is fuming as he reads each line. That evening he arranges a meeting with Mr Sharman. It's the final straw. He tells Mr Sharman he is going to enlist in Melbourne on pay-off day. No going back; there is nothing Mr Sharman, I or anyone else can say to change his mind.

* * *

'I'm not afraid of dying,' Billy said. The room is dark. I have seen people slip away before – my granny, once a man run over by a cart. Even though I don't know what happens after, I can say to you honestly, it does not scare me.'

* * *

Kitchener has disappeared in the North Atlantic. The HMS *Hampshire* sunk by a German U-boat, with all hands lost.

* * *

A hot day near Proserpine and one of the elephants pulls the emergency cord stopping the train. The elephant leans out of the carriage where the train has stopped right next to a trackside water tank and spends twenty minutes sucking out gallons of water with its long grey trunk.

* * *

Bowen

Three of the show train carriages have derailed at Euri near Bowen after an elephant grabbed onto a willow tree and pulled the carriage off the tracks.

* * *

Rumours that are the same in every town:

Who is peddling black market goods.
Who is walking out with who while their sweetheart is away.
Who is a spy for the Germans.
Who is dead and who is missing.
Who said what and what was said.

* * *

Reports of Australians in the mix …

News of the Australians' first attack on the Western Front.
Australians attack trenches at South of Armentieres.
Temporary success after enduring a tremendous bombardment until early the following morning when after eleven hours in the captured position Australians were ordered to retire.
The manner in which they carried out the operation seems to have been worthy of all the traditions of the ANZAC.

* * *

Billy and I watch as the tropical heat folds up clouds and the wind blows them past us out to the very edge of maps. As they speed by, we name each of them … Pegasus … the eagle … the ladder … the dusky maiden, the Parthenon …

* * *

More from the papers, another big push with Australians has taken place …

Pozieres Australians Win Glory

More stirring words …

Dashing successes

Valuable results

ANZACS praised

Australian gallantry

Super soldiers

ANZACs love infighting

ANZACs' daredevilry

* * *

The last house at Townsville and the infamous Mr Nugget Frater has not arrived. I wonder whether he really does exist. The troupe is disappointed and at the same time relieved he has not fronted.

* * *

There is a new show. A travelling hypnotist called Count Milivic the Mysterious is performing at Townsville before touring the Far East.

Billy, Jackie, Mr Piggott and I go along.

Billy gets to go up on stage with five other willing victims. A few swings of a gold fob watch and Billy is in this strange sleepy trance.

The Count tells them to imagine, 'when he clicks his fingers', their favourite animal.

There are two dogs barking at each other.

A cat stretching.

A goat chewing grass.

A fish of some sort.

Billy is a gorilla …

Picking away at nits, beating his chest, looking for bananas.

The Count plays a number of tricks on them.

He describes how they will be given a beautiful-tasting fresh apple, the best apple they have ever tasted.

When he clicks his fingers, they devour the big onions he has given them.

It is amazing to see how malleable a person's mind can be.

At the end of the show he goes to Billy and tells him that his belly button has been stolen and that 'when he clicks his fingers', he will wake up and go straightaway to the nearest police station and report to a constable that his belly button has been stolen.

At the end of the show Billy has half the audience in tow as he hurries off to the nearest police station. He keeps pulling up his shirt front to stare at his flat stomach and where his belly button used to be.

The police sergeant behind the counter is less than amused. Billy asked me what he has done wrong, why he is at the station. We spend the walk home filling him in on his antics. He feels well rested but remembers nothing else.

* * *

At Ingham, one of the elephants has killed a man. Feeding outside the wagon, the elephant curled its trunk around a show labourer, a warb, standing nearby. The elephant lifted the labourer off the ground and rammed his head into the wall of the carriage. Elephants are intelligent creatures. It is as if something, somewhere, something huge and overwhelmingly violent, has unsettled them.

* * *

Today's newspaper. Columns of names, photos of the dead, severely wounded, missing. The fighting near a town called Fromelles has taken a ghastly toll.

* * *

News from the Somme …

Important advantages secured near Pozieres. Large part of village won.

Enemy suffers very heavy losses in Counterattacks.

Cases of individual heroism on the part of the Anzacs are too numerous to relate.

Never has there been such enthusiasm as was displayed in the hand-to-hand fighting that took place in the narrow street of Pozieres, many men continuing the struggle after they had been several times wounded, and the officers rivalling their men in the in close fighting.

With all this fighting I am certain Bert will be amongst it and I worry constantly.

* * *

I am reading the lists in the paper.

'You love a list, don't you, Archie?' Billy says. 'You remember it all and file it away.'

I nod.

'You almost can't help it, searching books and papers. Making lists, people, places, times, dates. As soon as you see or hear it, it's filed away, isn't it? You have lists on everything.'

'Yes.'

'It must really make your head hurt sometimes.'

Billy understands.

'You remember it all, the good but also the bad?'

'Yes, it gets pretty dark.'

'Especially now, little cobber? Since the war?'

'Yes. I wish, sometimes I wish I could stop it, or just remember selectively.'

'No, you shouldn't,' Billy says. 'Think about it, imagine, one day, getting it out, putting all back together, the good with the bad, what a grand cathedral of the mind that would be! What a gift for the future! A monument for those who have lost to remember their loved ones by; so every detail, every one, becomes an everlasting memory.'

Billy has gently grabbed my shoulder, urging me: 'You need to remember, for everyone's sakes. Write it out for us, tell it again and again. Tell the good so people remember the good and tell the bad, maybe especially the bad, so we don't fall into this trap again.'

* * *

In Cairns there is another group of women standing on a street corner thrusting white feathers into the hands of any men who walk past.

'Better a hero's widow than a coward's wife … Remember the

Lusitania! What about Edith Cavell? Captain Fryatt! Consider your conscience … how can you stay?'

Billy Spiers drops his feather straightaway, Frank snaps his in half, Jackie pockets his. The rest of us with feathers drop them and return the evil eye as we walk away.

It is such a drastic contradiction. To think that these women who spit venom and throw their evil looks and sharply hook white feathers in our hands are the same mothers or wives or sisters who love and labour so tenderly those men who are away or now return sick or wounded.

* * *

Brisbane Exhibition

There seems to be a larger number of animal shows at Brisbane this year.

All the humans are going away to the big show.

There are jumping dogs, dancing ducks, counting pigs.

There are performing fleas.

With magnifying glasses, we watch 'Atlas' lift a blue and white marble and the 'Great Rodrick' walk across a wobbling tiny high wire …

There is a sign at the door … no dogs allowed …

* * *

Billy buys as much goanna salve as Mr JC Marconi will sell him. A year's supply … a cure-all … *arthritis, rheumatism, eczema, athlete's foot, lumbago, sciatica, cuts, sores and abrasions.* Billy swears by it, coats himself in the slippery smelly stuff twice a day before and after bouts. He would drink it if he could.

'Me being such a big machine,' Billy explains, 'means a lot of big moving parts that can break down from time to time and need a helping hand.'

Mr JC Marconi, the discoverer of the salve's healing properties, wears a diamond-studded iguana tie pin.

His manufacturing technique ... A six-foot goanna, hung out for half a day on hot corrugated iron, yields one and a half-pints of fresh oil ...

The secret of the salve's healing properties ... goannas seek out certain plants to eat when bitten by snakes ...

* * *

News of a large decisive action on the Western Front. Mostly British and French troops. Headlines ...

A thousand yards of trench taken.

Several key towns entered.

Capture of numerous Germans.

Heroes.

Successes.

French victories

and more words ...

Substantial gains ... Standing firm ... Desperate fight against the odds.

And more maps without any scale.

* * *

Around dinner tables, everywhere we go, gather the old men, the old fire-eaters who map out the battles. Tell war stories.

Salt and pepper shakers, knives and forks become machine gun points, lines of charging troops and German trenches.

* * *

Billy and I have our stories. We tell them, and then tell them again, crafting in new detail or deliciously ironic twists and turns. Billy has his favourites he asks me to repeat and embellish ...

A shipwreck off the coast where a group of young raven-haired Irish governesses need rescuing and it has been decided Billy is the one to swim a line out to them.

This time I strap a knife to Billy's leg so he can cut himself free of the tentacles of the Kraken, the giant squid, which threatens to molest the ship and its pretty cargo.

Sometimes I add a shark Billy can punch on the nose.

Billy laughs in delight when after scrambling aboard and deftly assembling the bosun's chair I describe how the pretty governesses remove their bonnets to reveal old cabbage heads.

I love Billy's swimming stories. The world I cannot visit. When he swam out off Magnetic Island. The underwater forest, the whispers of fish, the brightest colours of coral illuminated by shafts of light formed in the crystal prism of the glass waves that roll above him.

* * *

On the train a note left on our seat when we return from the dinner car:

> *Cowards die many times before their deaths, the valiant never taste death but once.*

CHAPTER SIX

More men to kill

We are slowly withdrawing into long silences. We turn into our own dark hallways, inside ourselves. We are weary of the war and the travelling. We never have a day off from the war. We are sick of the questions always raised, unspoken, but asked nonetheless; questions of courage, character and self. Our whole enterprise called into question, trivialised, put aside …

* * *

Six o' clock closing is now enforced in New South Wales. The Wowsers have got their way. Last drinks is a desperate fight … just like the last few spare places on a lifeboat.

* * *

Regrets …

Frank … Getting stuck in the fight game in the first place. Harder you hit someone, the more it hurts.

Mr Piggott … Going to South Africa

Billy Spiers … Not signing up immediately.

Herbert … Getting on the bottle, throwing money away.

Stanley not introducing himself to Mr Jack Johnson.

Mr Sharman … unknown … we suppose it would have to be Wagga.

* * *

Some of the 'would-to-God-that-I-could-go-brigade' are hanging around the post office. Men the wrong side of forty seem to be the most bitter and the quickest to blame or accuse. I take Billy's letters to post for him and he returns to the hotel.

* * *

Mr Sharman:

Cowardly dogs bark the loudest.

* * *

Cowra

Ten o'clock in the morning.

I saw the death knock minister leave the Telegram Office on his daily bicycle ride around the district. I see curtains in houses closing.

* * *

Canowindra

There are large, silent crowds outside the newspaper offices. Staring at the casualty lists on the walls. The men walk away wide eyed and grey, the women push their crying faces into handkerchiefs.

* * *

More news from Pozieres …

Dashing success, further results and further progress.
Australia has made a name in the world during this war – the world knows her now. It is these men – not the men who shout at stadiums and race meetings at home, but the simple, willing men who are described in this article – who are making Australia's name for her – and just at present holding on to it like grim death.

* * *

Grenfell

Every day, clergy circle the town's streets like the black crows who circle the dead lambs in spring paddocks.

* * *

There are now women walking the streets covered in the veils of mourning or wearing black armbands of remembrance.

Over there, men are doing the dying … here, women are doing the grieving.

* * *

Newspaper reports about a battle at Mouquet Farm.

A fight as hard as Australians have ever sought.

Things don't add up, all these glorious victories, and then two or three pages over, all the dead, columns and columns of them.

'A lot of newspapers and a lot of miles between us and the truth,' Mr Piggott says.

* * *

Flags are at permanent half-mast. A minute of silence begins to accrue to hours, shops are shuttered. The post office is full of people busy posting black bordered letters of condolence.

* * *

People turn to symbol or superstition to comfort themselves:

In Parkes, a mother sews a baby's caul into the left breast pocket of her son's uniform.

A man in Orange has etched the entire Lord's Prayer on a sixpence.

Tables are laid with extra places for the absent.

People are careful with umbrellas in houses, cracks on paths, handling mirrors.

People cross the road in front of the newspaper offices.

Doors are left unlocked so if he comes home …

* * *

People sit in quiet, dark houses staring at photos … look long enough and they are almost breathing, look longer and they are looking back at you …

* * *

The one hundredth and eighty-seventh casualty list ... Three hundred and eight wounded. Too many dead and too many missing.

Each day there are more and more photos.

Each day there are new headlines ...

'Pride of the Dominion'

'ANZAC Heroes'

New words ...

Killed in action ... Missing ... Died of wounds ... Dangerously wounded ...

* * *

There are more patriotic cigarette cards series ...

Victoria Cross winners.

Portraits of the top brass.

The crests of famous British warships.

* * *

Forbes

A good-sized crowd of mugs in. Mr Sharman up on the ladder.

'Today I see Rud Kee in the crowd, Mr Rud Kee down there in the middle. He's one of your locals here, a Chinese fruit salesman who now lives here right in Forbes, and a pretty handy fighter back in Sydney as I recall.'

A thick-set smiling Chinaman steps up to shake Mr Sharman's hand like an old friend.

'Surely there's another local here who'd like to spar with Rud Kee? Surely there are some good fighters in this town to match with this Sydney pug?'

A big fellow steps forward.

'Tom Feeney,' whispers a local, 'one of the best fighters in town.'

* * *

Last house of the day. Mr Sharman out jumping up and down yelling on the ladder.

'The local boy! The local boy is going to fight this house! This house … the local boy will fight!'

Feeney is all muscle. The Chinaman Kee knows he needs to make short work of him, so he goes for the doctor.

But the first punch Feeney throws lands on Rud's nose, which breaks like an egg.

Still dazed, Rud stays in close to have some time to clear his head, then he gets busy. They gave each other a right pasting. One of Rud's eyes is 'closed for repairs', but it's Feeney who turns it up first.

'A test,' Mr Sharman tells me later. He knew all about Rud Kee – heard about him at Sydney Stadium. Lost to Herb Cox, fourth round of the featherweight series. 'Had him in my book and he's as good as everyone says his is. He's good, useful, excellent.'

* * *

Parkes

Mr Sharman has his drawcard now – the only two Chinese boxers in Australia. Pity they don't like each other …

Mr Sharman has them pencilled in for the last house. He stands on the ladder with Taggie up on the board, introducing him as the Chinese boxing champion. As prearranged, Rud steps forward from the crowd and in broken English starts the pantomime: 'He not da Chinese boxing champion! I better than him!'

'A challenger, ladies and gentlemen. What is your name?'

'Cheong Lee my name and I betterer Chinese champion boxer than him.'

'Come here and I beat you like old sack,' Taggie replies ahead of Mr Sharman.

Some words exchanged in Mandarin backward and forwards.

Fingers poking the air.

Rud is up on the board, eyeing Taggie off.

Mr Sharman's instructions to Taggie and Rud.

'Don't try to kill each other.'

Both Taggie and Rud had some fought-hard nuts in Forbes. Already one of Rud's eyes is closed. Taggie has a cut lip and a cut above the eye.

A big crowd for the last house.

It's not boxing, it's a fight!

Taggie switches his stances like a cobra.

Rud throws a litany of punches.

The crowd roars.

Taggie twists punches.

Rud throws quick jabs.

Both of them are trying to prove to Mr Sharman who's the best Chinese boxer in the troupe. For all it's worth, it might as well be for the Chinese championship.

Rud has lost enough skin off his face to feed a greyhound for a week.

He's got a blood mouth like a torn pocket.

Taggie's face looks like a bag full of plums.

Mr Sharman is smiling.

'Cats got the cream,' says Mr Piggott. The crowd are beside themselves with glee.

Rud has joined the troupe on a six-week trial.

* * *

At Temora, Taggie is on the board and Rud introduces himself as 'Won Ton'. Apparently, it's some kind of fried meat wrapped in rice pastry dish. He is Won Ton, the former Mongolian Chinese boxing champion, here to fight today.

* * *

Murrumburrah

We do well in the Riverina. Mostly still towns – small towns – but Mr Sharman has the uncanny knack of coming into town right on payday.

He makes a sizeable donation to the local hospital board.

Taggie and Rud have the last house of the day and it is a real crowd-pleaser. The fighting is vicious and is a release for both of them after two days of circling each other with evil looks and whispered insults. Any technique is out the window; it's a slaughterhouse. I have never seen two people so predisposed to hate one another as Taggie and Rud.

* * *

Young

Taggie and Rud decide to have a sit-up competition. Taggie reckons he can outlast Rud. It starts at morning training and ends at afternoon teatime when Mr Sharman puts a stop to it as the show has to start in an hour.

* * *

Wagga Wagga

'Taggie's had a gutful,' Herbert is telling Billy and me.

'He's clearing out, right out.'

We see him out on the road with his suitcase. Mr Sharman standing out there holding Taggie's contract and pointing to various clauses.

We can hear them.

'Well, contract not say I have to work with very bugger bastard Rud Kee. I have enough, enough!'

'Well, I'm not paying you a cent more.' Mr Sharman is yelling as Taggie spins on his heels and is gone.

* * *

A letter to the local paper.

Sir,

For some time past some of the Germans or disloyal German sympathisers have been sending me anonymous letters through the post informing me that unless I leave Dr Haupt alone I will be shot, but are kind enough to add that if I do leave the Doctor alone, I will be left alone and inferentially, will be able to pursue the even tenor of my way without being perforated with as many holes as a colander.

Evidently this German cur thinks I can be intimidated, so I will not leave Dr Haupt alone until he either clears (or attempts to clear) himself in open Court. The fact that public opinion has compelled him to leave the district without defending himself will be my justification for following him with my voice and pen relentlessly and without mercy from one end of Australia to the other, and neither threats of prosecution or imprisonment by Senator Pearce, nor threats of Hun dogs to shoot me will turn me one inch from the path of loyalty and duty to the Empire and our noble lads defending it.

In short, to all disloyal Germans who threaten to shoot me I have only one answer and that is YOU TREACHEROUS, GERMAN BEASTS, SHOOT AND BE DAMNED.

Yours etc., T.R. Wilson.

'A sign of the times,' Mr Piggott says, 'long letters, long speeches and far too many of both of them.'

***

Names for Germans:

Hun
Fritz
boche
baby killers
beasts
thieves
ungodly rogues
murderers
torturers.

***

Rud told me how he ended up a boxer:

Left China as a boy.

Worked in a goldmine in Ravenswood, Queensland. Fought the boss and won.

Ran off to Sydney to join Snowy Baker's School of Physical Excellence.

'I love this boxing life, love it. I love to fight, fight anyone, learn from the best, come to Mr Sharman for the fitness. I do hard yards, I fight all comers, go back to stadium sometime, come to Mr Sharman and fight Taggie.'

He spits.

I asked him why he hates Taggie so much.

'Him family no good. He talk up too much; how you say it? His boots are too big on him.'

* * *

Names for Rud:

chink,

chinke,

chow,

chow-chow,

paddy pat pong,

dingbat,

canary,

dink,

John, Johnny, John Chinaman.

Things people say about Chinamen:

slant eyed,

cat haired,

blob nosed

monkey faced,

cheats,
opium fiends who eat the ears of naughty children,
the stealers of gold.

* * *

Albury

Les has signed up! That's what the papers say. Appeared at a recruiting rally at the boxing stadium where the announcement was greeted with a great cheer … 'It's not happening,' Mr Sharman says. 'His mother won't sign the papers, she is so afraid of losing him. He's going nowhere.'

In a few days Mr Sharman is, as ever, proven right.

* * *

There are two young boys dressed as soldiers, little fellas barely four; one dressed in a sailor suit the other in khaki, marching their little steps.

It is an unnerving sight.

* * *

Suddenly the lights are switched on brightly in the Albury picture house blinding us.

'There they are!' A woman shrieks, pointing at us sitting in front of her. 'Shirkers, cowards every one of them. Sergeant Bostock, I have found them, Sharman's men.'

'Right, then, let's have you up and out of here.'

'What are we being charged with? You have to charge us to move us,' Mr Piggott says.

'Creating a disturbance.'

'What! It's a comedy. We are not allowed to laugh now?'

'And for bringing niggers into this respectable establishment. I have been asked to bring you down to the station to speak with Recruiting Officer Johnson, who has been wanting to catch up with you lot. He has you all on a list.'

'What's that list then?'

'A shirkers list. Where's Billy Spiers? He has you on his list. Mr Sharman too.'

'I didn't think the police could do the Army's bidding,' Mr Piggott says.

'Who are you, Grandad? If he's needed, he's coming with me. Just because you missed the war doesn't give you the right to excuse him from his duty.'

'Well, you are wrong there,' says Mr Piggott. 'I have seen war. Have you seen it? If you have you wouldn't be so keen to do the Army's dirty work.'

'I served in South Africa.'

'Really? I don't remember you at Wilmsrust.'

'Were you at Wilmsrust?'

'Yes.'

'Well, then,' he coughed. 'Right, then. Well, the film is over anyways. I advise you to leave and return to your lodgings.'

Mr Sharman, who has said nothing, stands and motions us to leave.

* * *

Chilton

Newspapers … The War Office has requested Australia provide more reinforcements.

'How can you squeeze a lemon twice? Let alone three times?' Mr Piggott asks. 'It will be the end then, lads, the end for all of us. Conscription's not far off, then watch out.'

* * *

What is going on? The papers are saying that Les will fight his last three fights that he is contracted to fight under Snowy Baker and then there would be no more fights until such time as he had enlisted, or the war is over.

* * *

Beechworth

'I have been making calculations,' an older man tells Billy on the train.

'Calculations about the proportion of men actually killed in the war. It is not as nearly as high as you would think – no higher than lots of other ordinary occupations. You only run one chance in five hundred of being killed. Now, that's not much is it?'

* * *

There is no longer any rush for the paper before breakfast to read of any new victory; of course, the paper is full of new victories, but we do not believe them any longer.

* * *

The newspapers are still full of misplaced rhetoric …

Billy Hughes at a campaign rally at the Sydney Town Hall …

The appeal of our soldiers fighting on the battlefield falls upon

> *our ears and reaches straight to our hearts. These comrades of ours, those brave volunteers who went through the glories and agonies of Gallipoli and are now gaining fresh laurels in the gigantic battlefields on the soil of France, repose full trust in us. Shall we fail them now?*
>
> *For they go to their death unless we send support … Duty and national honour alike beckon us on … Who among us will support a base abandonment of our fellow citizens who are fighting for us to the death with deathless heroism … The nation is in peril … our duty is clear. Let us rise like men, gird up our loins and do that which duty and self-sacrifice alike dictate.*

'I'm ready to gird my loins.' Jackie laughs.

'Don't you feel like going, Arch?' Billy asks me. 'Even with the bung leg, doesn't everything you read, all the speeches, doesn't it make you feel like you should be doing something?'

'No, not in the slightest,' I lie.

* * *

Archbishop Mannix denounces the entire conflict between England and Germany over the last few years as nothing more than a sordid trade war.

This gets plenty of people hot under the collar.

* * *

Catholics are heretics and it is a well-known fact that every country the Pope has touched has withered.

* * *

As I drag myself up the street in Wangaratta I notice almost every third or fourth house has its curtains drawn dark across parlour and bedroom windows as they quietly mourn their loss.

* * *

News that Mr Piggott's nephew Edwin has died of wounds.

* * *

The approaches or tactics of the various Orders of the White Feather vary from town to town; some are opportunist, some are well planned.

At Chilton, it was a flurry of feathers thrown out of a lodging room window above us.

In Beechworth, an embroidered piece of patchwork with white feathers in looped cotton holders. And carefully stitched words: 'Cowards please take one.'

Here in Wangaratta a box of them left near the entrance of the tent with the message 'For the cowards who beat the drum and the cowards who take a glove.'

* * *

I look for a postcard to send to Bert.

On one there is a woman in portrait, Union Jack and wattle either side of her and the words '*To my dear brother serving his King and Country. We're sending our thoughts to you, dear, over the sea and foam, to say you are not forgotten, by your dear ones left at home.*' I buy it, but it is only half-suitable. There is no brother-to-brother postcard, as all men are expected to be at war.

* * *

More and more these days I see the war-wounded. They scurry at dawn or dusk along lanes and alleyways with coat lapels up and hats pulled down tight to hide their disfigurements. Portions of their faces missing, ruined, mashed, cruelly cut away.

Others I have seen appear to have had crude, quick surgery; their faces are like punched-in lumps of dough, shoved in, their skin, noses, eyes tugged in towards a hole in the middle of their face. Holes that should not be there, making once good-looking boys grotesque. Other men have the tracks of hot bullets along their throats or burrowing through jaws.

Most people will look away and forget, but my one quick glance and I remember and see, again and again, their wounds as portraits on the blank walls and in the hallways of my sleep.

* * *

Warrnambool

Percy and Walter are in Mr Sharman's bad books, as they nicked off after dinner last night. They stole a bicycle and Mr Piggott found them asleep on the beach in the midst of a pile of beer bottles.

* * *

The black market is in full swing. Certain foods are harder to come by.

At show time, men will often appear from dark corners or walk along beside you whispering. 'Tobacco, small goods, sugar, whatever you need.'

A man tries to sell me chocolate.

They beckon you to a cart, hidden down a laneway somewhere, full of half-inched goods, or get you to peer into a sack, or show you food hidden in their deep pockets sewn into an overcoat.

Some people are in desperate straits.

More cattleduffing.

More thieving generally.

More tricksters. Mr Piggott told me about a chook raffle con going around the Riverina. A cur walks into a pub at Lake Cargelligo, offering to run a chook raffle. Shifty little bloke wins it. The same shifty little bloke wins it again at West Wyalong, at Barmedman, then at Temora.

The problem is that at Cootamundra the old chook is looking more than a little worse for wear and someone recently arrived from Lake Cargelligo recognises the lucky little bloke who's just won the chook raffle and twigs the goose.

* * *

Hughes has announced that there is to be a referendum held on compulsory overseas military service.

In view of certain urgent and grave communications from the War Council of Great Britain and the present state of the war, after long and earnest deliberation the Government has arrived at the conclusion that the voluntary systems of recruiting cannot be relied upon to supply that steady stream of reinforcements necessary to maintain the Australian Expeditionary Forces at their full strength.

The Government considers there is but one course to pursue namely to ask the electors for their authority to make up the deficiency by compulsion.

Compulsory … the difference between volunteer numbers and the required is seven thousand per month. About equal with the same rate of casualties.

'Conscription! We are on the slippery slope now, lads!' says Mr Piggott.

* * *

Industrial Workers of the World … the IWW … the Wobblies as people call them, have committed up to twelve incendiary acts in Sydney in as many days.

The bombing of shops.

The smashing of bank windows.

The setting on fire of haysheds.

'What's it all supposed to prove?' Mr Sharman asks while reading. 'That we hate cows?'

* * *

Dr Hall Attorney General of NSW speaking in Sydney said that the IWW was full of Germans and read out a list of fifty Germanic names associated with the group. He went on to say that these were the men and these were the forces under the surface that were working with scrupulous cunning to achieve their vile purpose, which was to stab Britain in the back and dishonour Australia. Are you going to be their dupes or are you going to stand by Britain and the Empire? Vote yes for honour, Australia, the cause of liberty and the reinforcement of the gallant Australian Army.

* * *

Catholics and trade unionists are now considered resisters, anti-conscription and favouring the enemy by deserting the men at the front.

* * *

Sir William Irvine believes a referendum on conscription is a waste of precious time when our men are perishing every day at the front. Even the slightest delay means condemning thousands of our countrymen to their death.

* * *

Everywhere we go we hear arguments – heated conversation – about Wobblies and Unionists and Catholics. Anger follows us like sparks from a bushfire.

* * *

In England it is reported that Irishmen are taking the jobs of Englishmen.

* * *

At a speech in Sydney Billy Hughes tells us that the Australian Army will be given the immortal honour of turning the scale of victory.

Mr Sharman mutters, 'This could do me in.'

* * *

All men between twenty and forty-four are to attend for enlistment and register.

The Lottery of Death, Mr Piggott calls it.

All exemptions from the ballot will be ruthlessly dealt with.

'Stuff them,' Mr Piggott says. 'Bugger if I or you lot should even bother showing up.'

* * *

Terang

In the paper, Mannix says that conscription is a hateful thing. We talk this through; does conscription bring a better soldier? Is it the way to win a war?

More soldiers tipped in? Is it really fighting smarter? Will there be more useful men found from conscription or volunteering?

* * *

Billy says, 'Maybe conscription is needed to get the job done, to help the soldiers at the front.'

'Conscription just feeds a war being fought the wrong way. Conscription feeds the battle of attrition, which is what this war has become. Conscription is just a stocktake for the generals to calculate the numbers of allies that need to be lost against the number of Germans that need to be lost. It is such a ghastly ledger,' I say.

'To ask whether we want men to kill or be killed is not a fair question,' Mr Sharman says. 'To make a man choose between the collective good of his country and his own choices. It denies a man ownership of his own body; do you want to be a master or a slave?' This is the most I have ever heard Mr Sharman say about the war.

'For us to decide the fate of others is such a cruel question to be asked. *A man and his nation are two separate parts,'* I say.

'Yes!' Mr Piggott says, 'isn't better to live in your country than to die for it?'

Mr Sharman nods vigorously.

* * *

Is this my opportunity to convince Billy to stay home? I read from an article in the *Australian Worker* …

> *Society may say to the individual: 'You must love this; you must hate that.' But unless the individual feels love or hatred springing from his own convictions and his own feelings, society commands him in vain. He cannot love to order. He cannot hate to order. These passions MUST find their source within his soul … The man who is forced to fight is as vilely outraged as the woman who is forced to fondle. To thrust a rifle into his hand, and drive him as with whips against foe, is to degrade him to the level of a dog that is sooled on to attack another.*

We go from one side of the argument to the other. For an hour. Pushing or pulling the arguments back and forward until one by one we forget what it was about in the first place.

* * *

Camperdown

A returned soldier arrives at his old football ground wearing his old sporting uniform and speaks at halftime to his old team about duty and the need to stand with your mates.

'What's he on about?' Mr Piggott says. 'Stand with your mates here or over there?'

* * *

A man feels Billy's shoulders.

'Very useful set of shoulders we have right here.'

Apparently, he's an old retired doctor of some sort.

'And you're the wrestler, are you then? Waste of resources here really, should be overseas,' he mutters.

Standing back, he gives his diagnosis.

'Yes,' he says with some satisfaction.

'Big barrel-chested chaps like you stop playing sport, stop exercising, get fat and die of a heart attack.'

He might as well have said, off you go, lad, head off and get yourself shot, you're not long in this world anyways.

* * *

Geelong

A half-panel in the *Advertiser* …

The Other Woman's Son

Shall I vote to send another woman's son to the trenches?

What other women?

The woman who has a son as sole support? No.

The woman who spends as much as before the war on the latest monstrosity of fashion, demanding rich foods, soft living, gaiety, while other sons keep the country safe? No.

The woman who has several stalwarts on staying behind? No.

The woman whose sons are shouting themselves hoarse with applause at the stadium? No.

Ask yourselves afresh is my sentiment going to prevent me from voting to send the sons of these women to the trenches? No.

Timid women cast off your tears.

Strike for your altars and your fires.

Strike for the green graves of our sons, God, and your native land, for the sake of the mothers of soldier-sons, vote Yes.

* * *

Also, letter by 'Justice':

In Geelong there are many young fellows with the appearance of lions and the hearts of mice … the street corner loafer and the well-groomed young man who sings in the church choir are nearly all shirkers from the skin to the soul.

It is if any man who stays behind is not worth a thing. Men without any redeeming qualities. Selfish, cruel, uncaring, and these are not the men I know ...

Jackie always smiling,
Stanley so very gentle,
Percy and Walter, playful, cheeky, but good lads,
Frank who always accepts lessers as equals,
Rud … so blindly devotional,
Herbert … a good listener,
Mr Sharman always ready to lend a helping hand,
Mr Piggott always ready to gee you up,
Billy, kind, honest and humble old Billy.

* * *

Melbourne

A group of Wobblies standing on the corner of Bourke and Exhibition Streets …

'Withdraw efficiency!' they shout at us as we walk past.

'Conscription denies man ownership of his own body! Are

you master or slave? Don't be a soldier, just be a man!'

I am beginning to believe they are right. Conscription is just another cog in the great machine of war. Will conscription be the ultimate machine that destroys all men and all nations? I think it could …

* * *

Royal Melbourne Show

Mediocre crowds and challengers. Fights are predictably short or lacklustre draws, decisions awarded on points.

* * *

A letter from Bert.

Greetings to you, Nipper,

Still alive, but for the grace of God and a big dose of luck.

There's so much metal flying through the sky here day and night that I am likely to catch some of it sometime. Don't tell Mother of this. That kind of worry so far away serves no purpose.

How is the farm going?

We spend so much of our time in the dugouts that I think I am turning into a wombat.

I hear that a lot of the local girls are getting married. The local girls must be letting the standards drop marrying blokes who stayed home.

They might steal our best girls now but when we are home we will steal them right back. The best of Australian Manhood is here and certainly not in Australia.

Anyways, this is short and sweet as I need to make the post. Regards to Mr Sharman and his boys. It would certainly be nice to have some of his lads here right now. They should stop shirking and get on over to help us out.

Yours Aff

Bert

* * *

Ballarat

Why is Ballarat always so poorly attended? It continues to irk Mr Sharman.

They call Ballarat the 'showman's graveyard' – big crowds but no boxers.

In desperation, Mr Sharman throws the matching glove at the head of a likely opponent walking past. 'Come on, you're the best candidate I have seen in weeks!'

Mr Sharman gets Mr Piggott to hand over the bass drum to one of the challengers.

'Shake up the drum there, boy.'

Mr Piggott gets down off the bridge and goes out amongst the crowd ... fishing ...

We all have our theories as to Ballarat … Why there is never a full house …

Husbands under the thumb.

A meek, mild strain running through the town.

A town with better things to do.

Certain individuals dissuading any of the town's roosters to stump up.

Maybe too heavy-on with other shows, too many other in-out joints.

I think it is Meekin's Parade of Pygmies that has stolen the show patrons. 'Show time is Pygmy time,' according to Mr Meekin. They go see them first, before us. Even I have gone in for a look. It's quite bizarre, but thoroughly entertaining …

First, Mr Meekin gives a lecture on their curious lifestyle and culture …

'The tiny killers of the Congo.

'Worshippers of the crocodile and the moon.'

Then they emerge on stage to sing and play drums.

'Little men and women that never grow up.'

'There, see Princess Ubangi, their ruler, jungle associate of the chimpanzees and gorillas.'

This is followed by a demonstration of their deadly arts – arrows and spears all tipped with fatal frog poison.

'What he lacks in strength he makes up for in cunning and dexterity.'

One of them rolls his eyes back into his head and suddenly lunges toward a mug in the crowd with his poison spear.

* * *

Mr Sharman is watching what we eat. The cooler weather slows digestion. It's always a battle staying on weight … it's what undoes a lot of boxers … overeating …

Billy cleans the gravy off his plate with a slab of bread so carefully it's like he is polishing the family silver.

Mr Sharman has made his notes about weight gains … Frank … Percy … Herbert and, of course, Billy …

* * *

In Maryborough, the recruiting committee employed a Mrs Mutch, who would interview the mothers, wives or girlfriends of eligibles to try to persuade them to 'let her man go'.

* * *

The Shire of Huntly near Bendigo has sent letters to their ratepayers asking them to attend the Agricultural Hall and be privately examined to clear up once and for all his reasons for declining service. If the unfortunate man alleges any lack of physical fitness as his reason for not enlisting, he is immediately examined by the local doctor, who has donated his services for the day, and instantly declared fit enough to go.

* * *

Daylesford

Frank has caught up with an old friend until late last night and is now trying to hide his booze breath.

He goes down against a handy dairy farmer that afternoon.

'Rooster to feather duster,' Mr Sharman mutters. 'There's always a better boxer out there somewhere.'

* * *

Bendigo

The weather has turned cold, a late reminder of winter. Mr Sharman is visiting each of our rooms, checking that we have not wasted too much coal on the furnace. It's a flat rate per room, but he makes his point about saving by also turning off all necessary lights or lamps, leaving us to stumble around, bumping into furniture.

'Bloody old gorse pockets,' Frank says. 'Doesn't even have to pay for the stuff and yet he still goes on about it.'

* * *

Castlemaine

The war effort continues.

More and more committees and schemes …

The Castlemaine Tanned Sheepskin Committee.

The Fruit and Vegetable Gift Scheme for sick and wounded soldiers and their dependants.

Everywhere we go young girls stand with their hands out as their mothers roll wool over them.

Socks, socks and more socks! Eighty thousand pairs are needed and I have to say a lot of these are coming from here in Castlemaine.

The Australian Comforts Fund needs twenty thousand Tommy Cookers. No woman or child in this country will ever need to be idle.

* * *

Melton

Percy and Walter sleep in again; it is as if the colder weather slows them up. They arrive at training halfway through Mr Sharman's gee-up speech. They end up in his notebook.

* * *

A family steps onto the train. Father, mother, brother and sister … collectively, perhaps the ugliest group of people we have ever seen.

'We're all God's creatures,' Mr Sharman mutters as he notices our smirks.

* * *

Bacchus Marsh

As this tour turns into the final straight I notice how Billy has acquired an impressive medicine chest of pills, potions, medications and cure-alls …

> *Row's Embrocation. For man and beast. The best valuably specific remedy for cuts, sprains, bruises, sores, stiffness of joints, burns and scalds rheumatism, whooping coughs and chest colds.*
>
> *Bosisto's Parrot Brand Eucalyptus Oil that induces a feeling of repose and tranquillity.*
>
> *Australia Magic Mixture for gout and rheumatism.*
>
> *Dr Morse's Indian Root Pills and Dinneford's Magnesia. One for no and one for go.*
>
> *Ayer's Sarspilla blood purifier and tonic.*
>
> *De Jonge's Moller cod liver oils, Beecham's Pills and Reuter's Little Pills for the Liver.*
>
> *Clement's Tonic – a cure for nervous breakdown.*
>
> *Bonnington's Irish Moss, Doan's Backache Kidney Pills.*
>
> *Dr Sheldon's New Discovery for coughs, colds and consumption.*
>
> *Fisher's Phospherine, Zam-Buk ointment and Hudson's Eumenthol Jujubes.*

The boys have nicknamed Billy "The Doctor", and as the weeks go by, they quietly visit his "consulting rooms" seeking cures for their bumps and grazes, coughs and colds.

* * *

Diggers Rest

From the paper:

A state of Queensland Minister of Parliament, a Mr Fihelly, speaking to the Queensland Irish Association, tells them that every Irish Australian recruit means another soldier to assist the British Government to harass the people of Ireland.

England being the home of the can't, the humbug and the hypocrisy.

That a good deal has been said about Captain Fryatt and Nurse Cavell ... That Irishmen should stick to their brethren. That the shooting of Fryatt by the Germans was no worse than the shooting of Skeffington.

* * *

Shepparton

On a street corner we see people gathering, reading a just erected notice.

The Governor-General has proclaimed:

All single childless males of Australia 21 to 35 are to attend for enlistment and serve during the continuance of the present war. All eligibles are to report by 9 October.

We haven't even voted yes or no yet!

* * *

Bitterness stalks this country. Eligibles are being searched out by parties of men after failing to attest.

* * *

The Cuthberts … the conscientious objectors, as they are known, are getting a hard time, taking the war head-on. What exactly is a conscientious objector?

They argue that a man who shirks his share of national defence has no conscience.

They have their day in court and some are imprisoned. Pacifists, Quakers, Christadelphians, Jehovah's Witnesses, Seventh Day Adventists are all put through the ringer.

Warrants are sought for others evading arrest. Exemption court cases are in session everywhere.

* * *

A pamphlet:

Think!! Which way would the Kaiser like you to vote?

The Kaiser would like you to vote yes! Why?

Because yes at once pulls Australia down to the level of Germany.

Australia wants population. Conscription always has been a potent cause of emigration from Europe.

Australia has a magnificent volunteer army of 300,000 free men with more recruits coming in every day. Voluntarism has not been a failure. It has been a gigantic success. Don't besmirch Australia and Australian heroes by voting yes. Be not like dumb driven cattle, vote no.

* * *

Lilydale

Stan found himself in a tight corner last night with some drunks giving him lip. At breakfast this morning he shows where the piece of a broken tooth is still stuck in his fist.

* * *

Yes … No … Yes … No …

We don't know whether we are Arthur or Martha anymore …

* * *

The country is tearing itself apart. The yes crowd and the anti's at each other's throats.

Arguments on street corners.

Finger pointing at family dinner tables.

More fights in pubs.

At factories there are places where anti's eat lunch and where the yes people eat lunch, and there are people who just stay working to stay away from it altogether.

* * *

Healesville

A woman approaches us.

'Hey, big fellow, I have a question for you.'

I can see where this is going, but Billy, polite, affable Billy doesn't.

'Why aren't you in khaki?'

'Because he is not the type to kill,' Mr Piggott says.

'What a right feed of chutney that is; he could enlist as a stretcher-bearer. Big enough to carry back the braver soldiers.'

I see Billy's face change. It's a grand epiphany for Billy – his way out, his path forward. He doesn't have to kill and he can go and help.

'And why haven't you enlisted?' the woman says to Mr Piggott.

'Five kids, two dogs to feed and a wife that drinks, madam.'

'Don't you think it would be better to be a hero's widow than a coward's wife?'

'No, not really.'

'What are you going to tell your children when they ask you, Daddy, what did you do in the war?'

'I will tell them I managed to keep myself intact enough to ensure food on the table and coal in the hearth.'

The woman has run out of things to say, turns tail and stomps off.

* * *

Part of a letter from a soldier overseas:

We're sick, we're weary, we're wounded,

With death up above and below,

But I'd rather be here with the heroes, than back with the men who said 'No'.

What exactly is a hero? What will the boys at the front be thinking? Will they be voting yes or no?

* * *

News that Les has stowed away on a ship to America.

Sunday Times headlines:

Cold-footed Les Darcy bolts from Australia to escape home defence, government should seize his property

This paper regards with indignation the conduct of any man who bolts from his country at the hour of its need. It regards with unspeakable contempt any and every person who connives in any way to such levanting. For a fellow who bolts when he begins to deem it possible that his duty may be thrust upon him, there can be nothing but disgust and scorn.

Mr Piggott says, 'Don't the rock choppers sure cop it from the Proddies about Les not joining up? The Anglican Bishop says that unenlisted eligibles of a certain religious background are all pro German.'

'Disappointing ... a foolish move, led astray by others ... will be forever branded a coward; this is not who Les is,' says Mr Sharman.

'No choice,' says Mr Piggott. 'He was right to chase the good coin on offer – a family to support, no decent fights arranged here out of spite by Baker and McIntosh, couldn't get a passport to leave, mother wouldn't sign him off to enlist ... Caught between a rock and a hard place.'

* * *

The titles Les won at Sydney Stadium at Rushcutters Bay stripped from him ...

> *Owing to Les Darcy's unpatriotic action in clearing out from his country, at a time when he should be doing his bit with his Australian comrades, it has been decided to strip him of his middleweight and heavyweight championship titles.*

Mr Piggott notes that those stadium operators haven't put their hands up for the war just yet.

'Nor has Mr Sharman,' says Jackie.

'Sure, but you won't see him commenting in newspapers on the character of others,' says Mr Piggott. 'He who casts the first stone.'

* * *

Pakenham

More letters in the paper about Les:

What has Les Darcy done for Australia? He has turned tail and made a bolt for it the moment when it seemed that he could no longer dodge his plain duty to the country that has fed and pampered him. The Commonwealth might reasonably request that United States will refuse permission to Darcy to land. He can be barred quite easily as an undesirable immigrant. If you conceive an immigrant more undesirable than a disloyal pugilist with a yellow streak, your imagination is fine.

* * *

We are glad to be shot of the main centres. It is easier to hide out here in Gippsland, moving from town to town, telling people we reported ages ago: 'Yes, yes, back in Flemington, at Dandenong, three weeks ago in Ballarat.'

* * *

Drouin

A pamphlet from the anti's:

I didn't raise my son to be soldier,
I brought him up to be my pride and joy.
Who dares to put a musket to his shoulder,
To kill some other mother's darling boy?

* * *

Sounds of Billy crying.

Darkness. Complete darkness in the room we share.

'Billy, are you alright, mate?'

'Yes, little mate, right as rain.'

'No, Billy, what's wrong? It's the war isn't?'

Silence.

'Yes. Yes, it is. I can't keep touring, I need to enlist. But if I go I let down Mr Sharman; on the other hand, I feel I can help more as a stretcher-bearer. What should I do?'

'Do what's right by you,' I say.

'Yes, I suppose. I will miss you, my little mate.

'And I will miss you terribly, big mate.'

'Leaves Mr Sharman without a wrestler.'

'Mr Sharman is cunning enough to work through all that. I mean, he's being ducking and weaving though the war since it started.'

'Right, then, I will go. Can you talk to Mr Sharman for me?'

'Yes, of course.'

Thanks, little mate.

I start thinking about whether I should have argued more, convinced him to stay, stay here with me, safe.

'Are you crying too now, Archie?'

'Yes, I am.'

'Oh dear,' Billy says, 'we better watch we don't go and dehydrate ourselves.'

* * *

Warragul

It is time to vote in the referendum I remember the premise on the voting form, word for word …

Are you in favour of the Government having in this grave emergency, the same compulsory powers over citizens, in regard to requiring their military service, for the term of this war outside the Commonwealth, as it now has in regard to military service within the Commonwealth?

***

Does it mean those on home defence duties could be forced to serve overseas? None of us know what it really means.

Some towns want the remaining men to stay; others want the men to go to protect those already there …

***

Have we done the right thing? Hold men back and let down those over there? Send men to their deaths? Have we done the right thing? Will this help us win the war or lose it? Will it help us save our country or destroy it?

***

I vote no. Mr Piggott's a no as well. Billy votes yes, as it provides him with a back-up excuse. The others don't vote. I am not brave enough to ask Mr Sharman which way he went, but I think it would be a firm no from all Irish Australian and Catholic gentlemen like himself.

***

Morwell

The butter factory put up a young burly freezer packer who doesn't seem quite right in the head. A strapping village idiot to do someone else's damage.

Mr Sharman's fighting instructions.

'Don't fight a fool ... fiddle a fool ...'

* * *

Sale, East Gippsland

A close-run thing.

Yes: 1,087,557

No: 1,160,033

The Governor-General blames …

The Irish Catholics.

The women's vote.

The general agricultural population objecting to labour shortages.

* * *

An angry letter from a sore loser …

The loss of the referendum is a sorry state of affairs which has brought a smear of dishonour on the Australian Flag.

Enough about flags and smears and honour, I just want this horrible war to be over. I hope this referendum is the last terrible decision we will have to make.

* * *

In the paper, it seems, that war enthusiasm is waning …

The Bairnsdale Women's Patriotic Guild will suspend its operations for December and January to meet the domestic demands generated by Christmas.

* * *

Pay-off day and Mr Sharman holds Kangaroo Court at the Golden Fleece Hotel in the restaurant he has arranged to be empty.

I read out the year's entitlements for each of the troupe. Then Mr Sharman, with some feinted reluctance, ceremonially reads out the deductions for misbehaviour. He reads from his notebook each of the offences, its location, the incident and the section in the contract they have contravened, the level of financial punishment per offence and then the total deduction. I will then hand over the pre-prepared pay packets like there aren't any no's, ifs or buts about it.

'Percy and Walter at Warrnambool, contravening section five, consuming intoxicating liquors and misappropriation of a bicycle. Ten pounds each.'

They smile sheepishly and look down at their feet.

'Percy and Walter, Ballarat, Melbourne and Melton, three counts of contravening section eight, sleeping in, two pound per offence.'

They look surprised and appear not to recall the incidents.

Frank, section five, consuming intoxicating liquors, found out after drinking at Daylesford. Five pounds.

Billy. As I expected he cops it from Mr Sharman for his repeated sleeping in or lazy training. 'Various locations, fourteen counts of contravening section eight, sleeping in, poor or uncompleted training …

Billy takes it on the chin; he doesn't care, he's out of here in a few days.

'Jackie, two counts of contravening section eight in Brisbane. Unexplained absences. Attending an associate's party without permission and spending time with the same associate in a

Fortitude Valley billiards hall.'

Jackie is open mouthed. Mr Sharman must have followed him.

In Mr Sharman's considered opinion: the biggest downfall of many potential champions are pals and parties.

Mr Sharman's ruling is final.

* * *

Melbourne Cup

According to Mr Piggott there are a lot more dips here at the cup this year. Groups of pickpockets down from New South Wales to work the racegoers. Mr Piggott recognises two of them: the Mouse and Codmouth Hughes. The races are a perfect place for the dips to work. They spend the morning sizing up the best marks. The ones with all the cash, the ones easy with the cash, the drunk ones, the big talkers, the stupid and the carefree. Once they know their mark they move in as a pack. One chats to the mark, asking for directions or making a flattering remark about a hat; the second one bumps into the mark, apologising and loosening straps or opening pockets; the third dips in, grabbing the purse or wallet, deftly handing it to the fourth who strolls away.

Mr Piggott nods at Codmouth and Codmouth nods back. No dip is brave or foolish enough to try it on any of Sharman's men.

* * *

Sasanof wins the Cup. Billy takes some heavy losses. He doesn't care. Just happy to spend the day with his best mates, he tells me.

Mr Piggott wins several long bets on the later races.

'Well, haven't I been kicked up the ass by a rainbow!'

I come up even in terms of pounds and fond memories. There are certainly fewer young men here having a punt than the last few years.

* * *

Back at Cole's Book Arcade.

Frank buys a copy of *Cole's Funny Picture Book.* There is a drawing of a thrashing machine for naughty boys and a scolding machine for naughty girls. Jackie is very keen to have a look at the real device …

Cole's little men and their signs make their suggestions …

A future religion will not be one of ceremony and mystery but one of reason, simplicity and love.

Always do that which you believe is right.

* * *

We walk Billy to the station. He shakes everyone's hand, winking at Percy and Walter, joking with Jackie, nodding back to Stanley, looking Frank and Herbert, straight in the eye, staying tough.

Billy shakes Mr Sharman's hand.

'Goodbye, Mr Sharman.'

'Call me Jimmy,' Mr Sharman says as he leans forward to place his other hand over Billy's. There is a stammer, a whisper, in his usually booming voice.

'Go well, Billy, and come back safe to us.'

I feel as if I am about to break in half.

Billy, out of focus through my tears, leaps forward and bear hugs me.

'See ya, little mate.'

I hold him.

'Please,' I say, I can't help it. 'Please don't let this be the last time I see you.'

I feel Mr Sharman's hand firmly on my shoulder. Billy has unwrapped from me. I look up and my friend Billy Spiers the wrestler is gone.

1917

CHAPTER SEVEN

Fighting at home

This year's troupe …

Jackie

Stanley Hill

Gilbert, a black fighter in his late fifties

Frank

Arthur Norgrove

Bill Robinson, the 'unconfirmed' New Zealand middleweight champion

Mr Piggott

Nick the Russian, the new wrestler, also currently 'unconfirmed' in terms of skill or temperament by myself or Mr Sharman

George Cook, the troupe's new heavyweight

Rud Kee, Chinese boxing champion

Mr Sharman.

'I have some changes for Arthur's contract, Archie.' Mr

Sharman hands me a series of notes. 'A couple of extra clauses to add in there; he needs to be on a tight leash.'

'What do you mean by that?'

Mr Piggott tells me. 'Most of the pugs we have signing on are on the way up. Arthur, he's potentially on the slide down.'

'He's an overeater and a slack trainer,' Mr Sharman says. 'The protector for Aborigines has put me in charge of him. If he makes any mistakes he's leaving us.'

* * *

Although there are some new 'ins' there are more notable 'outs'.

Percy and Walter Collins have found more trouble and have ended up under a police curfew back in Moree.

Herbert is gone too. He is training with Snowy Flynn.

'From the fat and right into the fire,' Mr Sharman says.

And, of course, Billy. All the rooms and tables and spaces on trains are all left empty and quiet.

* * *

The first altogether training session for the troupe. Mr Sharman like a fisherman, checking his new season nets.

'Leave your reputations at the door. You will start again. I will reconstruct you piece by piece.'

He takes them back to the bare-bone basics: training regimes, boxer's wind, stretching techniques, leading, counters, parries, combinations, bread and butters, ins and outs, tent tricks, rules and regulations, expectations and contractual obligations.

After all this, Arthur looks a little bored. He punches the hard bag for a while, leaving a huge dent in it. Then he shadow boxes, makes excuses and sneaks away.

* * *

Lunch at the Coronation tearooms.

Arthur has second helpings, thirds, fourths and is now well into his fifths.

* * *

This year's itinerary:

We are on the run …

Some of the usual New England sites to start with … Maitland, Cessnock, Armidale, Tamworth, then out further. Tenterfield … Staying out quite wide, staying out west much longer … working around the Goondiwindi Irrigators, Moree, then Narrabri and Wee Waa. We are running away from the war, out west … but then back for the Sydney Royal Easter Show.

The circus train through Queensland is not to run this year, so we will go inland, chasing the rumours of good fighting men …

Beaudesert, Toowoomba, then search for a gang of railway ballast men currently located at Dalby. Miles, Roma, up to Rockhampton, Yeppoon (big dark-looking Kanakas), into Blackwater (miners).

Emerald, Barcaldine, up to Townsville, quickly into Charters Towers (calling in on the Beveridge clan), the Cairns Show.

Then back down south. The Brisbane Exhibition.

Parts of the Riverina … Ardlethan, Temora, Young, Gunning, Murrumburrah, Cootamundra.

Bypassing the usual North East Victoria trip, instead heading through the Mallee by paddle steamer … Echuca, Barham,

Swan Hill, Nyah, Robinvale, Mildura and Wentworth. A raid into Snowy Flynn's territory … Renmark, South Australia. He has stopped touring because of the war … Mr Sharman merely filling the gap … offering a temporary substitute … not breaking his word.

The usual Victorian run … Port Fairy, Hamilton, Bendigo.

A lot of still-towning: stopping in little places, stopping in towns or places without shows … Winslow, Mortlake, Romsey.

Hide and seek …

Finally, Mr Sharman has seen sense to drop Ballarat from the schedule.

Bacchus Marsh, Lilydale, Warragul. The Melbourne Show. Melbourne. Short trips out from there … Cranbourne, Berwick, Gisborne, Warburton, Lara. Gippsland … Traralgon, Sale, Bairnsdale.

South Gippsland … Korumburra (coal miners from the state railway coal mine), Loch, Leongatha.

A slight price rise this year. Less people around but there is still enough money about … Sixpence for adults, threepence for children.

* * *

Maitland

Mr Sharman starts a new patter with the fighters just as they shape up and the bell goes, firing out the words, quick, dramatic; like it's not just two baggy-assed local roosters having a slugging match, it's like a world title fight ...

'I want a good clean fight. I want a good three rounds. I want nothing below the belt. I want nothing around the back of the head. If he goes down you wait for him and he'll do the same for you. You go down three times and you lose. Win and you get the money, draw you get nothing, lose and you get the experience. Now, shake hands. Now, box!'

* * *

I watch Arthur in his first fight inside the tent. He is a weirdly constructed man. A massive reach. He is fat from chest down to waist but he moves surprising quickly considering his weight and his thin and short chicken legs.

* * *

Nick the Russian.

He looks Russian enough – a square-looking face, a strong nose.

He isn't really Russian, he's a Dalmatian. He's not really that either – born in Australia. Does a good accent, though. All part of the show.

Bill Robinson – a class act on the run. A conscription dodger … Conscription brought into New Zealand last year. Bill getting out before they got him. New Zealand's Les Darcy. Fights under an alias; and Bill's not even his real name – it's Clarence, Clarence Wright. Here in Australia to make his fortune and just stay alive.

* * *

Tamworth

I hear the singing first. I know this time that they are coming for us.

'Onward, Christian soldiers, marching as to war … '

Mr Sharman tells us to all wait inside the tent. He stands outside the tent flap entrance, eyeballing them.

After a stare-off they assume the tent is closed today and they turn away to find another target they will all approve of disapproving of.

They march off towards the leg show, with 'Vanessa the Undresser' firmly in their sights.

* * *

Tenterfield

There are more and more returned servicemen out begging on the streets. At the railway station they sit on the ground, missing arms or legs.

Bill Robinson gives one of them who is missing an arm as well as a leg a shilling and asks how he is keeping.

'I'm not broken, I am just falling apart,' the man replied.

* * *

Moree

Mr Sharman gets Walter and Percy out for the day. Back for a day's fighting in the tent. They are as cheeky as ever. They want to tour again but the local protector will have none of it.

* * *

Now we leave the comfort of trains. The road and wagon section of the tour to the towns outback. 'Can never understand why Mr Sharman wants to come all the way out whoop-whoop,' Frank says.

On the road we stop to water horses and meet a Dutchman

with all his processions on top of a bicycle. He tells us he has come from White Cliffs and is on his way to the Opal Mines at Ducks Creek. He unwraps a tin and from inside that he unwraps another cloth and inside that opals from Cooper Pedy. And another tin and cloths, yellow sapphires from Anakie: 'They are beautiful if you permit me to say so,' the man says.

Jackie asked why he had not sold some of his treasures to buy a car, as surely with such a haul of loot he could afford one. The man replied, 'I cannot sell these, they are my pets! They are my babies!' Then as quick as he appears he is on his way.

* * *

Despite the emptiness, the great distances, out here there are always people showing up.

Shearers. Bagmen.

Drovers making back, telling us where good rain had fallen.

Drovers making out, pushing their loud mobs of dirty orange sheep past us like Saturday football crowds.

Fossickers despondent in their misfortune, but gleefully hopeful about their next big find.

Bushmen, horse breakers,
Afghan hawkers clanging pots and pans,
spielers, buskers.
Wandering fencers, rabbitos,
sewing machine agents,
piano tuners,
book canvassers,
saddlers and general tinkers.
Water diviners.

Teamsters, the long bullock trains … what an impressive sight! Twenty or thirty bullocks all pulling. They are like great wooden ships. Cutty sarks of the dusty inland. Cargo, living and sleeping quarters all self-contained within the giant wagon. The top deck where the teamster and family sleep on top of cargo, then underneath the tucker box and water, cooking utensils, the wire chicken coop that provides a regular supply of fresh eggs.

We see the teams heading out, heavy with roofing iron, provisions furniture, a giant ornate cedar wardrobe, even a grand piano.

Sometimes a plump and grumpy governess riding on top of all of it. Then, alternate days, we see others on the turn-about, coming in from far-off stations, stacked high with the wool clip.

* * *

We discuss the art of water divining. How much can we really trust some cur holding on to a piece of wobbly willow stick?

'All a load of claptrap, bumpkin … ' Frank states his case. 'Local knowledge is all it is, the use of old records, old stories passed on.'

A reading of the land's upturned palms.

Divinity ... Magic.

No. Just a close look for the tell tale signs …

Where hills drop away, where certain bushes grow, the colour of leaves, grass. Where you find extra rabbits or kangaroos.

A cruel confidence trick, wobbly wire, words of hope, creative finger pointing, praying on the desperate.

On the other hand, I argue, it gives hope for the hopeless.

'It gives them what they want but not what they need,' Mr Sharman tells us.

A water diviner … a genius? A prophet? A saviour? … No … we decide … a gentle trickster, a part-time illywhacker, a minor spieler and nothing more than that.

* * *

A letter Frank has received:

Dear Sir,

Unless you have some genuine reason for not enlisting, I advise you to off and join the Army before you are made to. Compulsion is not far off. I am only waiting the order to call up every eligible and as you can see I have you on my list. You will be mightily sorry in the end if you wait until you are fetched. Those who are fetched will not be asked where they would like to go.

Sergeant Johnson

Frank's concern isn't the threats. It's being singled out that worries him – that they are focussed and closing in on him especially. And that he found him out here. The tour has always been a good place to hide. He isn't worried about running into Sergeant Johnson, a town bully that's all. 'We'll see who'll be mightily sorry,' he bristles.

* * *

Mr Sharman:

Beware the man who tries to fit you out in his idea of a hat.

* * *

Some more reasons for not going:
The Irish situation.
Waiting for the right time to go.
Brothers and sisters to support.
Mum won't sign the papers.
Bad teeth.

* * *

Reasons why men join up:
I couldn't help myself.
To see if the froggies really eat frogs.
Good money.
Didn't want to be called chicken.
To prove I can cut it.
'You just have to be in it. Don't you?'
Duty.
To stop Billy Hughes sending my sister.
Avenging a brother's death.
More money for me and my dear old lonely widowed mum.

* * *

Narrabri

A returned man, drunk and mumbling, wandering around town.

'Gone to God. All of them. Gone, gone to the bright beyond the lucky bastards.'

* * *

'What's your favourite music?' Jackie asks George.

'Chin music,' he replies.

* * *

Wee Waa

New towns we have not visited discover us with such delight. There is nothing people will not do for you. A farmer who has travelled five hundred miles to see us fight. Offers to join local families for dinner. People who have counted the days until we arrive. Invitations to visit gardens, stores, to ride in motor vehicles.

Words used to describe us … Fists like sledgehammers … handsome as film stars … fit as Mallee trout.

Out here. Way out here, out back, we can forget about the war for a day.

* * *

Mr Sharman has some new spiels to drag in the mugs …

'Take your pick, take your pick. Any fighters out there today?'

'Roll up, roll up and test your fists and test your guts.'

'Come here! Come here! Where they wrestle, where they fight. Come here! Come here!'

'Bill Robinson here with us today. Bill Robinson here with us today, ladies and gentlemen. He will please all except his opponents.'

* * *

A letter from Bert:

Hello there, Nipper,

Well, I think I am the first Blackmore to see snow. The novelty has certainly worn off – it's just frozen rain.

Away from the front we are billeted at old farms, sleeping in the hayshed, burrow down deep into it, which will do me just fine!

Thank Aunt Adelaide for the socks and mitts. I tell you they are sorely needed here, you could wear another twelve layers of them and still be colder than an Eskimo.

Anyways, my favourite little brother, I hope this will be the last winter I have here; hopefully I don't get knocked and can get home to enjoy the proper sunshine.

We have heard that conscription has been turned down. The cowards have won out! What a waste of oxygen all those anti's are.

I have seen a few lads from home, Roy Shennan and John Morrow send their regards. They are fine fellows and think very highly of you, as of course we all do. Signing off then.

Your loving brother

Bert

* * *

Almost every woman you meet now wears an enamel brooch with the colours of a battalion in which someone they love is serving.

* * *

A brochure; given, found or abandoned …

Free tour of Great Britain and Europe … the chance of a lifetime … do your duty …

* * *

In America no-one wants to fight Les.

He is mixed up with some trickster called Sully, who apparently used to hang around Randwick racecourse. A real dead loss.

Les is banned from fighting by various state governors. Stuck doing Freeman Bernstein's burlesque and vaudeville tour. Les is reported to be quite down. Mr Sharman hears that Les's mother is receiving fat postal sacks of anonymous letters, cruel letters, many with East Maitland postmarks …

* * *

The war has now reached a point where most families have sent all their sons but one, left at home as 'insurance'.

* * *

Some of the Linseed Ladies are still around with their cheeky looks. Based on Mr Sharman's advice, the members of the troupe who may have once liaised with such types will no longer do so. Too many complications.

She might be about to cheat a sweetheart in France …

No more real fights to win, no chance to demonstrate their prowess, before claiming their prize.

Not the done thing to approach any such a lady unless you are certain of their circumstances.

'You can't even talk to any girls just in case they are spoken for and you can't tell whether they are spoken for because they are not on a fellow's arm like they used to be. You can't step out with a girl because you don't know who they step out with because all the fellows they step out with have gone,' says Nick.

A whole generation of young womanhood now promised to ghosts.

* * *

Mr Sharman tells Mr Piggott and myself that he will need to donate, depending on the sentiment of the tent, the mood of the town, the entire proceeds of some houses to war causes in order to justify the operation …

Sometimes the decision is not hard to make especially when …

One of the important townspeople takes Mr Sharman aside for a quiet word of warning on show eve. Beware;

If there has been a recent loss of a particularly popular boy. (They are all popular boys.)

If out front he sees people standing back muttering or shaking their heads.

Or if the mugs stand in the tents, arms folded, unsmiling, silent, waiting because their local boy is there to teach the one of the shirkers a lesson …

* * *

On the train back to Sydney, Mr Piggott points out a couple of card sharpers, magsmen, after two of them board at Stroud.

'They like working the North Coast Train back to Sydney – plenty of stops, lots of time. They set up various card games and they cheat money out of people; people lose their life savings,' Mr Piggott says.

Mr Sharman and Mr Piggott move to briefly sit with them. 'Beautiful scenery on this train, isn't it?' says Mr Piggott.

'Yes,' they reply.

'Well, today's not the day to be playing your special kind of card game, is it, lads?' says Mr Sharman.

They alight at the next station.

I am glad there are men like Mr Sharman and Mr Piggott here to stop this mad world from becoming even more poisonous.

* * *

Royal Sydney Easter Show

The worse numbers of challengers we have ever seen … almost no men …

We can't put women and children in the ring, so we cut the number of fights in half.

The visiting station owners grumble about the lack of men and boys to help with farm work.

* * *

Tom Uren visits to referee some of the bouts. This brings in a few more mugs.

Mr Uren is a tough man, Mr Piggott tells me. During his career he kept fighting on with burst eardrums as a result of repeated double vision punches to the head.

A man absolutely without fear. As a boy he worked as a power-monkey on the Hurlstone Park Glebe Island Railway and for bets chewed down on explosive detonators.

* * *

As well as refereeing, Mr Uren substitutes for the missing fighters by performing a series of wonderful tricks with a skipping rope, pleasing what is left of the half-empty house.

* * *

How to tell the difference between a good fighter and a great fighter.

'Forget about looking at cuts on faces and bent or broken noses,' Mr Sharman tells us. 'That just means they have bumped into a few fellows who know how to fight. Look at their hands. Look to see if his knuckles are fused together, that tells the real story.'

* * *

At Dave Meekin's tent I meet some of this year's new freaks.

As always, the names and characters he has found are interesting …

'King Chong and Princess Wong'

'Jo-Jo the dog-faced boy'

A new tattooed lady who has four hundred and sixty-four individual designs (she shows me Raphael's Madonna and Child)

Other freaks …

'The Skeleton Man'

'The Human Fairy'

'Zimme the Human Fish'

'Chang the pinhead Chinaman', his head no bigger than an orange.

* * *

Before we leave Sydney, it is time for the purchase of new suits and clothing.

Nearly everyone in the troupe has brought the Murdoch 'Everrite' blue serge suit.

'The front ranker suit', which advertisements tell us Les Darcy, the middleweight champion of the boxing world, wears.

Advertisements that tell us confidently that Les is a 'Murdoch man'.

'Those who know him,' Mr Sharman says, 'know he is much, much more than just that.'

* * *

The *Sunday Times*:

Les Darcy sells birthright for mess of pottage

Les has applied for American citizenship and intends to enlist in US Army to fight in France.

* * *

The Canadians have taken the coveted Vimy Ridge. The Australians are in a fierce fight at Bullecourt. I brace myself for bad news.

* * *

Beaudesert

Mr Sharman sends the whole troupe out for a long run. To get them used to the Queensland sun. They returned later exhausted. Arthur is missing. He returns half an hour later covered in sweat.

One of the lads told me later he stopped at a café just a half-mile down the ways, where he enjoyed a leisurely breakfast of eggs and bacon, then splashed himself with water in an artistic way, so it looks like he has sweated and toiled in the heat. He was puffing when he got back. Mr Sharman and Mr Piggott are none the wiser.

* * *

Great feats at Bullecourt

The Australians are right in the heart of the Hindenburg Line at the village of Bullecourt. The village conquered with imperishable glory by these man hunters.

It is hardly possible to yet realise what the unflinching valour of these Australians must have meant, what sublimity of endurance was theirs, what added lustre they have bestowed on their countrymen, what their feat of arms now, and what it will mean in history.

A series of counterattacks and bombardments at Bullecourt …

Never in the war have our countrymen shown more clearly the qualities of brilliant attack and stubborn resistance.

* * *

Toowoomba

The reverends are out on their bicycles. Casualty lists grow longer. We have all had enough of tragedy.

* * *

Dalby

A telegram from my father.

Albert seriously injured. No more details.

* * *

CHAPTER EIGHT

All that might have been

Miles

Another telegram …

Is this it? The worst kind of news?

Albert recovering from gas.

At least he is alive, for now.

* * *

Alf Parsons, a neighbour's neighbour, who loved to collect flowers, pressing them into books, is missing after Bullecourt in France. He was in the same battalion as Bert.

* * *

Roma

The big oil rig on Hospital Hill cranks up and down.

We visit the graveside of Peter 'The Black Prince' Jackson. At fourteen he quelled a mutiny with only his fists. Beat Old Chocolate Godfrey for the Australian heavyweight title. Died here of the consumption, his headstone inscribed *'This was a man.'*

* * *

Rockhampton

Rud gets called a yellow devil by a challenger out on the pitch.

Rud winds up like a clock.

'Don't worry 'bout big man, white man, don't worry 'bout brack man, you try to beat yellow man … you try! Up here, you try!'

The man is far bigger than Rud and useful looking. Rud is itching to get stuck into him.

Mr Sharman likes Rud's gameness. His anxiety to mix matters with all comers, no matter how big or fierce they might be, is admirable. He pulls in large crowds.

'Rud Kee,' Mr Sharman says, an arm around his shoulder and pointing at the full house, 'I think this the start of a beautiful friendship.'

* * *

From the paper clipping sent to me by my mother:

Gassed

Mr JH Blackmore, Camden, has been notified that his son, Corporal Albert Blackmore, was gassed in France. All sincerely trust that the trouble is only in a mild form.

* * *

My brother's misfortune allows the others to mention their kith and kin who have gone and had their own troubles.

Jackie's brother has copped the gas as well.

Nick knows lost neighbours, friends.

George knows a few.

Rud knows no-one at all.

Mr Sharman listens to our discussion, and when it is his turn, he says nothing and opens up his Book of Men and marks it with his pencil. Like scoring a cricket match he records each dismissal reluctantly.

* * *

Yeppoon

Frank writes to tell me that he has asked Laura to marry him and unbelievably she has said yes and the wedding is this spring, November, when I am off the tour and I can be his best man.

* * *

Blackwater

Bill Robinson has earned himself the nickname Dog-guts, his farts, silent but violent, regularly drive us from rooms or train components. His tenure in the lavatory makes it off limits for a good hour. How could something so evil come out of a man so polite and quiet as Bill? We all eat the same food – how could he produce such poisonous smells?

* * *

Emerald

Too hot too early, a full publican's booth, angry types drunk spitting and swearing.

Mr Sharman has sensed that there could be a bit of a boilover, an all-in brawl.

'Ladies and gentlemen, there are two types I don't want in this tent: drunks and idiots. We don't want them, do we, ladies and gentlemen? These chaps down the front here have been waiting a long time. Give them a go,' he says, bringing a sense of calm back into proceedings.

* * *

Barcaldine

In the main street we pass the tree of knowledge. Rud knows all about it.

'Shearers bloody sick of working all guts out. Come here, this place, strike, first strike in Australia, start of the workers parties.'

* * *

At night screaming sounds from a returned man's house that sits close to my hotel window.

* * *

Only very occasionally now, a useful local comes forward and fights very well, even upstaging one of the troupe. Mr Sharman is straight onto these snags, as we call them, chatting with them after bouts, getting their details for his address book and future reference.

* * *

Turning back towards the coast and then heading north, talk turns to Frater. From what Mr Piggott has told me, Nugget Frater sounds terrifying.

A husky five foot eight and fourteen stone, a bristling moustache, broad as a piano and as strong as ten men.

Away from the ring, he is as nice a fellow as you would ever want to meet, apparently. A very quiet, very polite man. But in the tent, he goes wild, as if he has never heard of the Queensberry Rules and looks to slaughter anyone he meets.

He is a very well to do dairy farmer. On show day, he will first inspect the animals he is exhibiting then he comes to the tent, asking Mr Sharman who he has lined up for him today.

Mr Sharman will ask him what he wants and Frater will always say, 'Anything on two legs' and 'The bigger the better'. By this stage, all the cattlemen have left the cattle pavilion and crowd the tent.

Frater has never been knocked out and you do well to stay the three rounds without damage.

There is a point where a normal man will see that his opponent has had enough, when he knows he is beaten and will make his mind up to go easy. That point in a fight when the victor looks into the eyes of the vanquished and decides, based on their own upbringing or moral compass, that the victim is done in and enough is enough. Frater gives nothing up; he is an ancient gladiator and the tent is his bloody colosseum.

'If there were any more Fraters on tour there wouldn't be half as many as you tent boxers,' Mr Sharman says.

* * *

Rockhampton

We stay in Rockhampton overnight, waiting for a morning train. Arthur eats thirds then mops up the plates of the others before asking Mr Sharman for more. 'You'll ruin me, Arthur Norgrove,' Mr Sharman says. He seems to worry more about the outlays so much more on days that we don't fight.

***

Early morning.

Trees noisy, heavy, coloured, full of singing birds …

I overhear the cellarman and the barman talking in the hotel courtyard.

'Did yer hear? Les Darcy is dead. Died in Memphis from a fever.'

'Oh, good riddance to bad rubbish,' the other said.

'You reckon? Poor Les, he was alright.'

I hurry to the sitting room where fresh newspapers await, tears blurring the hallway as I rush.

Death of Les Darcy

The death is announced at Memphis, Tennessee, of Les Darcy, the Australian champion boxer. Darcy's death was sudden and unexpected. He had rallied, and he told a fight promoter that he was 'feeling fine,' but he died quietly a few minutes later. Darcy's last statement was for his parents. His greatest wish was to have five fights before joining the United States Aviation Corps, and so be able to send money home. He had arranged a match at Milwaukee, but this was cancelled owing to an infected tooth. The infection spread to the tonsils, which were removed, and then spread to the heart, causing dilation. Rheumatism and pneumonia supervened.

Another one taken from us. All the boys are terribly upset.

Mr Sharman stays in his room.

***

Les died of a broken heart. Man without a country.

* * *

Rud pulls out his old travelling box, reaches inside, grabbing something carefully wrapped up in newspaper and string.

An old cracked pair of gloves.

'I spar with Les.' Rud holds up the gloves, tears running down his big sad brown face. 'After this sparring, I put away forever.'

* * *

Later Mr Sharman shows me a recent letter from Les.

I have two ambitions. I want to be middleweight champion of the world, and I want to be a good tradesman, a first rate blacksmith …

I will be home soon …

* * *

Reports from Memphis …

The last Mass for the ring favourite Les Darcy was celebrated at the little church of St Brigid's by Father Mogan, who had known the champion well. The funeral cortège to the New Orleans train escorted by the Catholic Boy Scouts, Chickasaw Baseball Team, and a large company of friends, many wept. A military band from the local Defence Depot played 'Nearer My God to Thee'.

* * *

Mackay

News of the Russian Revolution.

Petrograd … the people want peace, land and bread not war.
The Italian Army are striking.
A series of mutinies throughout the French Army.
The whole thing is tipping over …

* * *

A newspaper report from CW Bean of more fighting in Europe:

The Australians fighting side by side with the New Zealanders in their first great common battle since Gallipoli swung around to make the flank of a great attack on Messines, and penetrated into the strong German position behind the Messines Ridge. The Anzacs attacked under a hurricane bombardment, after the explosion on the right and left of seven great mines. The whole attack kept more precisely and mathematically to the programme than any ever made by either Germans or British so far as I know. Australian troops came through the gas drenched woods without the cover of its shell-fire. It was not long before the figures of the New Zealanders were seen moving on the ridge top close to the ruins of Messines.

* * *

Proserpine

A series of posters appearing at each bay of the train station:

Golfers take your caddy with you. Enlist in the Sportsmen's One Thousand.

Tennis players stand the racquet. Join the Sportsmen's One Thousand.

Oarsmen pull together for victory by enlisting in the Sportsmen's One Thousand.

Footballers be in the last quarter with the Sportsmen's One Thousand.

* * *

A poster with a picture of the Victoria Cross on one side and a pile of sports equipment on the other:

Which? You are wanted in the Sportsmen's One Thousand.

Lay aside your playthings and play the greater game.

The Sportsman's One Thousand.

Camp together, train together, embark together, fight together.

Play up, play up and play the game.

* * *

Bowen

Sportsman's recruiting day. We donate all the takings. Mr Sharman gets Nick to demonstrate wrestling techniques. The rest of the troupe keep a low profile. Speeches are made about the qualities learned through sporting endeavours such as bravery, teamwork and fair play; about preparing Australia's fine young athletes for the greater game. That the prowess displayed on the sporting field would see victory overseas.

'While it's a close in and under here in the tent, it's a courageous up and over and at them over in France.'

Mr Sharman makes a short speech, wishing people luck.

We all can't help think that if there wasn't all this hullabaloo about sport and the war Les Darcy may well not have died so far away. The tent is only half-full of old men; only two boys, probably too young to enlist, come forward.

* * *

'The sportsman's one thousand!!!'

'There's a thousand of them at least in Mr Sharman's Book of Men, and you won't see him handing that over to anyone.'

* * *

Ayr

From the *Bulletin* …

Sportsmen of Australia
Blokes and coves and coots
Shift yer blanky carcasses
Move yer blanky boots
Gird yer blanky loins up
Get yer blanky gun
Get yer blanky enemy
And watch the blighter run.

'What a load of rubbish,' Mr Piggott spits. 'Just because it rhymes don't mean it's right.'

* * *

Les's body has arrived back in Sydney. The cortege passed through the crowded streets to Wood, Coffill and Co Undertakers. A viewing organised by the Catholic Guild.

* * *

It was estimated that over twelve thousand people filed past the body in the first few hours. Sobs, groans and subdued weeping made the atmosphere one of curiously personal mourning.

* * *

More and more file past Les. The numbers growing so much that the weight of people pushed in windows. All of Wood and Coffill's windows were smashed. Three hundred thousand file past.

* * *

Mr Sharman has decided that we should all attend Les's funeral. Train to Townsville, then we travel by steamer to Brisbane and straight on to Newcastle. We join the lines of motorcar taxis to Maitland.

* * *

We are invited to see Les at his family home in Emerald Street, East Maitland.

Winnie, his sweetheart, and his poor mum and dad there looking ruined. People lining the hallway.

Dave Smith there. And Mick Hawkins there too … a faithful friend to the very end.

And there he is … poor, poor Les.

Dressed in a neat dark suit, new shoes, a stiff Persil white collar and shirt. A black crepe band around one arm. He looks at peace. A small smile, the glimpse of a gold tooth.

* * *

The service at St Joseph's.

The cortege, two miles. Estimates that over one hundred thousand mourners attend. There are plenty of soldiers in the crowd. Fritz Holland there after leaving the vaudeville troupe he was travelling with somewhere outback.

Wreaths from miners in Kalgoorlie, patients of the Heidelberg Repatriation Hospital, hundreds and hundreds of others.

At the graveside, Father O'Gorman spoke up for Les …

'We are proud of Darcy, and never have we been prouder of him than today, for we are able to give his calumniators the lie by virtue of this great demonstration. Before the grave closes over him, in his name we can forgive his enemies.'

Mr Sharman sheds a tear.

* * *

In the paper the next day, with poor Les barely in the ground:

The exhibition at East Maitland was an insult to our boys at the Front.

Rev Killworth

* * *

The *Sunday Times …*

Why don't they canonise him!

* * *

Sunday Times! Sunday Slimes more likely. What else would you expect from a paper owned by Hugh McIntosh? He hounded Les alive, and he hounds him dead.

Signed Father Joe Coady

* * *

Townsville

Straight after Les's funeral we restart the tour back in Townsville on the last show day.

Frater is here.

He has been waiting for us.

Not even as big a man as Mr Piggott said he was … but certainly a very scary-looking one.

Rud volunteers to take him on. Arthur is also as keen as mustard, but Mr Sharman decides, perhaps for tactical reasons rather than sentiment, just to let Rud have a go.

Rud covers up well for the first three rounds as Frater fights unleashed. In the third round Frater shouts, 'Cop this one!' and punches Rud across the ring. His collarbone is smashed into pieces. Mr Sharman and the others carry him off to the quiet corner of the tent; he is in a world of pain. Frater collects and is straight off not looking back.

* * *

It turns out that a non-fighting Rud is actually a very handy man to have:

As a lookout.

Setting up speedballs, training bags.

Applying salves.

Making soup for swollen, battered mouths.

Giving rubdowns.

Geeing the boys up.

Collecting tickets.

Fetching things.

Light sparring.

Friendly advice.

He calls Mr Sharman 'Mr Boss'.

* * *

Charters Towers

While Rud is taking a break from fighting Mr Sharman gets him to check tickets at the front tent flap. He undertakes this task ruthlessly, checking every ticket.

'Look at him; he could teach the Sphinx to keep a straight face,' Mr Piggott said laughing.

* * *

It is Jackie's eighteenth birthday. A lot of mothers will not sign their sons off early and Jackie's mother is no exception.

* * *

Mr Sharman's training is as intense as ever. The open sparring sessions seem more brutal. As if he is readying them for something.

Maybe Mr Sharman wants to show the challengers the true brutality of conflict, sow the seeds of doubt, give any young fellows thinking about joining up a crisis of confidence, something to turn them off all forms of fighting.

* * *

Ingham

A lot of Aboriginals here today to watch Stanley and Arthur fight.

Mr Sharman works the crowd all day. He finds the town's best prospect and boosts him up as the town's best.

Arthur is in the ring, ready for the final house of the night. A cur in the crowd shouts out …

'Look at the honker on that one! Huge! That's one real big coon nose, that is.'

'Imagine it full of gold dust!' Arthur replies, smiling back.

The crowd is laughing.

Arthur stamps his feet like he's doing a Māori war dance. He pokes his tongue out and then says, 'Come to me now, you little boy.' His opponent, mad with rage, rushes in.

Then in one brutal punch he rearranges the town's hierarchy.

The Aboriginals in the tent are cheering, and gather around Arthur and Stan.

* * *

Tully

Women are encouraged to wear a badge with the words …

Qui s'excuse s'accuse.

He who excuses himself, accuses himself.

It is hoped that women will wear the badge to arouse the curiosity of men. When a man is persuaded by them to enlist, they are able to send away for another badge.

Some women, most often the town's prettiest, have large collections of the badges crowding on sideboards and mantelpieces like swarms of brightly coloured beetles.

* * *

Ministers now wear their own coloured badges or peculiarly shaped hats when delivering the bad news, so they will be welcome and approachable at other times. Not that there are many of these other times left these days.

* * *

Cairns Show

Mr Sharman and Rud have developed a silent understanding out on the pitch. A series of simple gazes shared between himself and Mr Sharman across the flat grass. Rud has different kinds of faces: one for when things are slow; others when sales are brisk, feverish; one when he thinks the tent is full, when Mr Sharman can ease off; another when he needs to shout louder or spin in some tension.

Although Rud's face never changes dramatically, I know there are messages going back and forth. It is as if he and Mr Sharman are passing notes. It is barely discernible to most, but I can see it.

I suppose that this skill is from their shared backgrounds. Every good boxer studies the face of his opponent … the eyes are the windows to the soul as Mr Sharman will say. He has spent a lifetime on the study of faces. An opponent's eyes wide and staring show a boxer who has given up hope; one with eyes hooded and close is ready to surprise; another who looks right at you, watching you, he may be the one who has your measure …

* * *

Rud has eyes like a hawk. No longer fighting, he has assumed the role of cook and twenty-four-hour guard. From putting up the tent to bringing it back down, he has his eyes wide open.

'Me always looking, looking, looking,' Rud says pointing at his eyes.

As soon as the gates open he is standing on a high point watching for trouble. An eye on the money bag, an eye on the tent flap, an eye for spielers, an eye on the bridge, an eye on the pitch, an eye on the gate. Dawn to dusk, Rud is watching. Nothing ever goes missing; no-one as much as even touches the tent or equipment without that look from a nearby hovering Rud.

The entrance to the tent is even more tightly guarded.

Rud's rule …

Look at the ticket not at the face.

'Look at him.' Mr Piggott marvels as we watch him catch a kid sneaking in under the tent flap. Rud, in one movement, grabs the collar, sticks his foot fair centre on the back of the boy's trousers and swings him out of the tent.

'He wouldn't even let a draught of wind past that front door!'

* * *

More pressure is being applied …

We hear that in some towns down south young men are given twenty-eight days to submit themselves for medical examination in preparation for enlistment or produce a certificate of exemption or leave of enlistment from their employment.

* * *

The Queensland White Feather League suggests the names of shirkers be listed in all the local papers.

* * *

More than halfway through this year's tour. Little insights, quirks, habits continue to reveal themselves …

How Jackie will wave one hand with food in front of seagulls, swinging his arm back and forth like a famous conductor.

I notice how Gilbert, when sitting, gently places one hand upon the other to rest, heavy and tired on his lap.

Frank is the one who always holds doors open for others the longest …

Bill Robinson's politeness, his 'I beg your pardons', his 'excuse me pleases', and his 'I am terribly sorry'. His apologies for the slightest of inconveniences caused.

How Mr Piggott always seems to be the first to enter any room and how everyone smiles back at his twinkling eyes.

How Nick grinds his teeth when deciding on something.

George's cracking of his knuckles on any mention of a fight.

Mr Sharman's reading of a newspaper on a table. How he carefully folds it into exact quarters, confirming the straightest creases flat with the sharp side of his hand.

How Arthur stops in every bakery we come across and buys at least one sticky bun.

Rud Kee and his growing devotion to the troupe and Mr Sharman.

* * *

More nicknames … The Choirboy, the Grinder, the Mollydooker …

* * *

Local fortune tellers consulted weekly as mothers and wives, anxious to know more about where their sons might be and how they were bearing up, throw away good money to them.

We are all waiting. Waiting for each of them to come back.

* * *

There are more welcome home events.

A dance held in their honour …

A returned man badly maimed and up there on the stage.

(Those who go to war must take risks and expect to lose something.)

Everyone staring at him, waiting for his exciting accounts of dashing troops that never come.

The call for new volunteers.

Singing by children.

The usual speeches.

A lovely spread.

A gold watch or medal presented.

A flow of people wanting to shake the hero's hand.

And him just wanting to go home to find some soothing quietness in dark and lonely places.

A dance floor crowded with the trippers of the light fantastic, seats around the dance floor where the broken men sit.

* * *

Brisbane Exhibition

Memories:

The clanking dim of apparatus up on Machinery Hill.

I visit sideshow alley ...

The Fabulous Flealinnes.

The extraordinary entomological exhibition featuring trained fleas executing acts of skill and daring ...

Mighty Fred, who lifts a strongman's equivalent of twenty-two tonnes.

The fantastic Freda, who shot from a cannon high into the air protected only by its natural exoskeleton, lands, with pinpoint accuracy, on its own tiny little satin cushion.

The large colourful banner that proclaims, *"The Fabulous Flealinnes who face daily peril unafraid.'*

* * *

Arthur has no time for strategy; he is an instinctive boxer. He has a punch like a hind leg of a horse. One punch, that's all he needs.

Every time Mr Sharman tries to talk tactics with him all he will say is, 'I know the right time to hit them, Mr Sharman, and so that's what I'll do, if that's alright with you, Mr Boss.'

* * *

The usual snakebite remedy men are here. Those who call themselves Professor this or Doctor that.

A large stall piled with *Doctor Mueller's Snakebite Antidote Pocket Cases … a hypodermic injection of strychnine and Cody's Crystals.*

* * *

In a Brisbane department store, women travel in from the suburbs on day trips especially to abuse the male shop assistants for not enlisting.

* * *

More words that are overused …

England in dire distress

England above all

Your country needs you

The war to end all wars
Saving the world fit for heroes to live in.
Will they ever come?

* * *

The house of King George V, the house of the Battenburgs, is now to be known as the house of the Mountbattens.

* * *

My Aunt Adelaide writes. She tells me that men are marrying for convenience. It was these women she was truly sorry for, one who had married since the war, in this way, because the children of those marriages would come into the world as cowards and be raised by cowards. Hasn't there been enough dissolution of our brave manhood already?

* * *

Pictures in newspapers of German-owned properties in Sydney, Melbourne, Brisbane and Perth.

* * *

Rumours that the Germans are distilling glycerine from the dead at a corpse exploitation establishment.

* * *

A poster: *You are wanted today in the trenches far more than you were ever needed on the football or cricket field.*

* * *

The Riverina

More high jinks; this time it is Arthur who leads several astray.

A night-time raid of a nearby orchard is uncovered when several of the troupe complain of stomach aches the next morning.

* * *

I think you can tell a lot about a person by how they kill an insect.

Jackie is quickly in with the newspaper.

Bill Robinson doesn't go anywhere near any insects – all of them much scarier than anything back in New Zealand.

Mr Piggott winces.

Nick smiles and takes his time.

Rud is a Buddhist so won't kill anything.

I have seen George kill a spider. Whispered something under his breath before killing.

I remember the saddest of looks on Billy Spier's face after killing a mosquito.

Mr Sharman. Mr Sharman sights the insect, then if it is considered to be vermin, there is swift revenge for his dead infant brothers and sister.

* * *

Temora

No-one is showing up to the recruitment parades. I drag myself past what was supposed to be one in the main street in front of the shire offices. The mayor and councillors uncomfortably check their fob watches. The Lone Pine recruiting band have put down their instruments and stand around with their hands in their pockets.

The fire brigade is not marching down the street as they were supposed to.

A small group of school children hold disappointed limp flags. There are no fit men anywhere.

* * *

Frank has visited his family and Mr Sharman has excused him from tent duties for the day.

Recruiting Sergeant Johnson, all puffed up and self-important, comes calling for Frank, and a few terse words between him and Mr Sharman are exchanged before he is on his way.

* * *

Very few show up at the tent. With the war, aside from the absence of men, it is as if the population has lost its appetite for sport, joy or any form of happiness whatsoever. This is what Mr Piggott believes.

* * *

Young

Rud has caught a skinny kid sneaking in. Crawled in under the tent flap. Said he had lost his ticket. The sawdust across his chest and stomach of his shirt gives it away.

A skinny kid about fourteen …

'Boss … second time this one, very bloody cheeky bastard sneaking in … make him fight!' Rud said. 'Punish bad for sneaking it.'

The kid is up for it.

'That'll do me! Get me someone me own size.'

Young Billy Grimes reckons he's a fighter, here to join up.

* * *

He can fight, kind of. He's a strange one … flat footed.

He drops his opponent in Young.

He follows us to Gunning, to Murrumburrah and Cootamundra.

He has the strangest style … something like a wind-up toy crossed with a praying mantis and a drunken sailor.

Mr Sharman decides to sign him up.

* * *

More of Mr Sharman's hints for young fighters on boxing success …

Turn a deaf ear to the street corner and the billiard room and the so-called boxing expert.

Keep clear of Mr Booze.

Train properly, eat wholesomely, take plenty of rest, cut out the parties and fair weather friends. One sincere pal is worth a million of the latter breed.

Learn to crawl before you can walk, learn the tricks, don't think you are a world beater after a few fights.

Don't let your head swell because wherever there a good man there's always another one who is better.

* * *

Echuca-Moama

We are walking past the town cemetery; some wag has tacked a stolen recruitment poster onto the cemetery fence:

Wake up, your country needs you!

* * *

Swan Hill

Mr Sharman has started, with the absence of young roosters about the town, to try to lure out some of the town's older men to fight ancient old Gilbert.

* * *

Gilbert is tired, barely able to push out one or two of his punches.
'Come on, Liquorice!' a voice in the crowd shouts.

* * *

Mr Sharman is considering letting old Gilbert go. He can only manage one fight a day and even that was pushing it. He's past his best …
'You can't keep reheating old soup,' Mr Sharman says.

* * *

Nyah

We are a country of women, old men and children. Fights for the troupe are too easy, as the quality of men left behind is telling. There are almost no men left.

Mr Sharman arranges a fight between two old pugs he knows who live in the town. According to Mr Piggott the much touted fight might as well have been two old men leaning on each other as they argue over the use of a park bench.

* * *

Mr Sharman has decided to keep old Gilbert on … personal and family circumstances ... As he would often say,

Deeds speak louder than words.

* * *

The Mallee is overrun with mice. A letter in the paper …

Sir,

I write to complain about the Mallee mice plaque. At night mice run up and down our beds and also our babies' bed, tearing at the mattresses and pulling out the kapok. I know of one man who said they began to start on his ears. They are an industrious lot. They have cleared out our store, chewed corks level to the tops of bottles, they chew boots, shoes and tablecloths. We poison with poisoned wheat but if we kill one, a hundred come to its funeral. We pick up from 1000 to 2000 every day. We got tired of counting them so we measure them by the bucket. The overflowing and poorly constructed wheat stacks are the problem, a bumper crop, but with the war no fit men to hump it away. I wish the Railways Commissioners would hurry up and truck the wheat away; then perhaps the mice would be starved out. I wish some of the 'swells' lived up here to see what we have to put up with; then perhaps we would get a little attention.

Yours etc.,

Beth

Cocamba

* * *

Senator Pearce, Minister for Defence has announced that horse-racing, football and boxing is to be curtailed.

Major contests of twenty rounds are only to be allowed in each state once a fortnight.

It has not been considered necessary at present to restrict the number of mixed boxing and vaudeville contests, so we are off the hook for now.

Mr Sharman pens a number of letters to Senator Pearce outlining the benefits of the boxing tent in terms of the fundraising for the war effort as well as the formidable fitness and readiness it provides young men.

Mr Sharman, the gentle persuader ...

* * *

Robinvale

A woman from one of the town's most wealthy families has brought in a bag of false teeth that her husband, who was serving overseas, will not be needing anymore.

* * *

Word in the newspapers that Sydney tramway men strike over time cards. This tips the balance: a general strike of railwaymen, miners, wharf labourers and other unionists is now underway.

* * *

Mildura

Another poster:

Why not join in the greatest sport of all ... Hun-hunting.

* * *

In Renmark there are twelve thousand names listed on notices placed on the most important and most frequented institutions around the town.

These were the original Anzacs they had spent a thousand days without any home leave. Pleas are made to replace local names with new volunteers.

* * *

Port Fairy

Saturday. I am resting. A heavy cold keeps me in my bed away from the tent. I listen. There are no voices of men. It is as if they have all gone. There is no bellowing from the nearby football ground. No laughter from hotel bars. No calling for others to help as heavy carts are unloaded. No shouting out to cobbers across the street. Older or weaker men who replace the younger ones are not in the habit of shouting. There is nothing worth shouting about.

* * *

Hamilton

One of the show committee has decided to have a few stern words with Mr Sharman about the 'lack of excitement in the tent in comparison to previous years'.

Mr Sharman replied straightaway: 'You can't put a cow cover over a horse and expect to get milk in the morning.'

* * *

Massive crowds strike in Melbourne: ten thousand protest against general living standards. A group of strikers attack two loyalist truck drivers and one is killed. The IWW is declared illegal.

* * *

Mr Sharman has decided to reconstruct Billy Grimes.

Despite his success, winning all his fights, his whole stance is wrong in every aspect.

'Stands like a drunk giraffe,' Mr Sharman says.

Cack-handed, wrong footed, clumsy and dangerously exposed.

Mr Sharman goes right back to basics …

Present the least amount of vulnerable space.

Stand balanced for attack or defence.

Legs bent with some weight on the back leg.

The forward arm up to match the nipple height of the opponent.

Despite all this Billy reverts back to his spidery style, breaking every rule and winning every fight. Mr Sharman is exasperated.

* * *

The newspapers again:

Great success east of Ypres. Positions of importance won, heavy casualties inflicted on the enemy more than two thousand prisoners taken.

A tremendous attack launched by Australian troops pushing into German positions to over a mile depth and captured Veldhoek and parts of Polygon Wood.

Never before has a battle carried to such a success in face of formidable difficulties.

We know what will be coming soon to the front doors of houses.

* * *

Jackie has been crying in his room. The white tracks which mark his face and his red eyes signal the hard flow of tears. His brother is dead.

* * *

At the post office the lines are long as people post black-bordered envelopes with letters of mourning to friends or relatives. People cry into black-bordered handkerchiefs.

* * *

CHAPTER NINE

More men

News of a battle at a place called Broodseinde …

On the crest were moving men, bunches of men at intervals everywhere, walking with their rifles generally slung, with the splendid nonchalance which marks our men …

Anzacs disappointed at the lack of opportunity to use the bayonet …

* * *

Local reverends reassure their congregations that *despite the suffering God is squarely on the Empire's side. God was using the war to call the country back to the path of righteousness.*

They speak of the cleansing effect of sacrifice … through the dour struggle there will be the discovery of a new land … a fire purged civilisation in which the King of Kings and Lord of Lords will rule …

* * *

The pen portraits and photos of the dead we first saw in newspapers are now posters on walls at railway stations, outside churches and public halls.

* * *

There is an hour for mourning and an hour for tears, but also an hour for bucking up and belting despondency to leg.

* * *

'Why can't we go back to 1914, Archie?' Mr Piggott asks me. 'They were the marmalade days, weren't they? Happy days. Before this stupid war, before we started losing everyone. How carefree the days they were, fun filled and bright, no big axe hanging over our heads, no sadness, no guilt.'

* * *

At Bendigo a police inspector steps forward to stop a fight that has barely started. Mr Piggott slows the inspector by grabbing his elbow. 'The fight's off when it's clear the fighter has no chance of winning; it's too early right now, Marquess of Queensberry Rules.'

The Inspector pushes Mr Piggott politely aside. 'Well, I am the Marquess of Queensberry around here, mate, and I say this fight is over.'

* * *

General Birdwood has called for more reinforcements with the losses at Passchendaele; the collapse of Russia and the reverse in Italy has … *imperilled our national safety* …

'You cannot always squeeze a lemon twice,' says Mr Piggott.

* * *

A reverend tells a grieving family who lost a second son that …

We are members of one glorious body marching forward, the Captain of which is Christ. The rooms of his mansion are being filled, that is all.'

* * *

A woman describes how at church before her son left how she saw a glow around his head and knew at that point that he would be safe.

* * *

A postcard from Billy …

Dear Archie, Mr Sharman and the boys,

Was in the old country for a while and had some leave in London. I saw The Pearl Fishers *at the Royal Albert Hall. My favourite opera. Today had a good feed at the ANZAC house to start the day off right. Then, running around to see the tower, parliament, the palace, the abbey, the waxworks and the museum, so much to see. Then another good feed and then straight off to bed. A lovely nice, warm, soft, clean bed.*

After lots more training and lots more people shouting at us we're off somewhere.

Anyways must sign off, will write again soon.

Your friend

Billy

* * *

'I worry about Billy,' I overhear Mr Piggott and Mr Sharman saying. 'A brave, good boy, but too much surface area, it's the wrong place for a big man like that.'

'You can't block flying metal.'

'He's going to cop something sooner or later; we'll need to especially look after Archie if any bad news comes.'

* * *

Sulkies and drays and carts and horses wait patiently outside the houses where people have come to pay their respects to those now marking their loss.

* * *

There are new recruiting sergeants who harangue passers-by from hotel balconies as they step out on Saturday nights.

* * *

In Warragul the local Girl Trench Workers Association hold a Freaks Ball. They provide a dinner and dance but refuse to admit any of the 'poor creatures alleged to be males'.

* * *

With the lack of useful opposition, Mr Sharman decides Billy Grimes can fight two at a time, three in the ring! Billy does very well.

Billy's usual is the un-usual for most others.

* * *

A number of young boys, close to military age, come to the tent to avenge lost brothers, to punch out all their grief, but end up sobbing weakly in their family's arms.

* * *

Melbourne Show

The leather-lung calls of spruikers.

'Turn the ducks around, Walter!'

'Penny to hoopla, penny to hoopla, hold a duck, hold a duck.'

'Prizes for all comers.'

'Pie for a zac! Pie for a zac!'

The worse numbers Mr Sharman has ever seen … no men … you can't put children and old men and women in the ring. Again, Mr Sharman cuts the number of fights by half.

* * *

The Pacifists Vida Goldstein and Adela Parkhurst hold a lecture at Bacchus Marsh … 'The War and Industrial Democracy'. It is enthusiastically well attended.

* * *

Mr Sharman's advice to me …

This is the about the right time to start to cultivate a little more shrewdness.

* * *

Rud has been reading the *Australian Worker* again, I don't know where he gets his hands on such a publication, but I ask to read it after he has finished … He gives the paper over to me with a flourish and a vigorous shaking of the head.

I read …

… If every person ought to defend the state in time of war, the state ought to defend every person in a time of peace. But does it? Does it defend the wage earner? Does it protect him

> *against the sweater and the exploiter? Does it make it its business to see that every man and woman are given equal opportunities? Does it protect its citizens against the useur, the landlord and the profiteer?*
>
> *Does it give the poor man's son the same opportunities as the rich man's son? No.*

Rud is watching me read. He asks as I look up.

'Bloody bad, the government? Yes, done the workerman very bloody bad …'

He springs over, grabbing at the paper,

'You read this, read, you must say no, yes?'

'Yes.'

'You mean no?'

'Yes, Rud I mean no.'

'Blimey heck! What you mean? says Rud.

'Let me read it then!'

'Ok, ok!'

* * *

Traralgon

Billy Grimes is Mr Sharman's problem-solver.

If Mr Sharman can't fathom someone out he gives them straight to Billy Grimes. After a round with Billy they don't know whether they are Arthur or Martha.

* * *

I wander past a schoolyard and watch the children's lunchtime games …

British bulldog.

Playground wars … Gallipoli, Britishers versus Turks and Germans,

Conscripts versus Non-Conscripts.

* * *

Mr Sharman admires how Rud watches his spending and his savings. 'He's very careful with his potatoes,' Mr Sharman whispers to me.

* * *

The owner of the Korumburra photographic studio shows me a picture of a returned man who arrived for a portrait, paid the fee, removed his shirt, turned side on, lifting up his arm.

Several photos taken of the large hole in his torso that, in his client's words, 'will show any future generations exactly what a war did to men'.

His face as bitter and as vicious as his jagged wound.

War brings out the best in a man, but it also brings out the worst.

* * *

Reports of a gallant cavalry charge at a place called Beersheba in the Middle East. I brace again for the totals that will add themselves one by one to my memory.

* * *

There is a letter from the New South Wales Commander of Recruitment, a Mr A Dawson.

Dear Mr Sharman,

In recent discussion with the Australian Boxing Federation Chairman and a prominent boxing promoter the New South Wales recruitment board has determined that at this urgent and grave time of war your resources are better redeployed to training and enlistment of yourself and your boxing troupe. The Australian Boxing Federation now requires you to stop touring immediately and attend the Holdsworthy Barracks to teach close quarter fighting to recruits and further, the remainder of your troupe enlist.

From this instance the Australian Boxing Federation declares your boxing troupe operation as non-compliant.

Please advise of your expected attendance date at Holdsworthy Barracks.

Yours,

Commander A Dawson, New South Wales Commander of Recruitment

'It's *ultra vires*, Mr Sharman.'

'What exactly does that mean, Archie?'

'Where one acts beyond one's legal power or authority.'

'Yes, useful.'

'There is no conscription law in place that allows the Army to require enlistment or service without consent. There is also nothing in the constitution of the Australian Boxing Federation that defines non-compliance or allows the federation to declare it upon third parties.'

'How do you know about all that?'

'I read the constitution.'

'Of course you did, Archie boy! Well done! Your blood's worth bottling. Write back to all the signatories and use those words, *ultra vires* and anything else you can throw right back at them. I will never stop touring.'

* * *

Leongatha

Newspaper reports that there are eight hundred Maltese waiting, anchored, in a ship off Brisbane ready to land.

Mr Sharman … 'There's bound to be some blokes keen for a fight after six months stuck in a leaky old tub.'

'And what's more, there's plenty of blokes on land who would want to have a crack at them,' says Mr Piggott.

'Something to keep in mind for next year,' says Mr Sharman writing in his notebook.

* * *

The Golden Fleece Hotel, Melbourne

On the street outside the hotel, I see one of Mr Sharman's business regimes. The same one he applied to me when I joined in 1914. On the footpath opposite the hotel are some of the hopefuls waiting to talk to Mr Sharman about touring next year. If you are uncontracted and have no appointment to see him you must wait outside on the street, below his window, until he sees you and waves you up.

Outside the Golden Fleece Hotel there are always young, keen ones waiting, looking up at the windows.

* * *

This year's Kangaroo Court. Mr Sharman has his list of fines to be deducted from end-of-year totals.

George, three pounds for a stint of lazy training from Ardlethan through to Cootamundra.

Bill Robinson, two pounds for flatulence shared with the travelling public in numerous train carriages around the continent. Laughs and graceful acceptance.

Various consumption of liquor infringements for Frank and Nick.

None of Arthur's misdemeanours rate a mention – the poor training, the hijinks and the overeating. He is so well regarded, men would crawl over yards of broken bottles or a dozen naked women to see him fight. Mr Sharman will do anything to hold onto him.

* * *

Rud has arranged for us to have a kind of Chinese lunch to be held at Ting Sing's Cafe, one of the restaurants frequented by the immigrants in Chinatown. A banquet known as yum cha. Inside, we can barely see whatever Rud has brought us here to eat. Cooks clutter and bang pots and plates. Rud speaking in his tongue to the waiters who wheel little noisy trolleys with little plates of food. It is as if Rud is herding them all around and around the restaurant like wild cats, all of them yelling at those sitting at tables, throwing down plates or rushing off to the next table.

It is wonderful and strange, it is also exciting and terrible. Everything is either shell, fungi, tentacle, testicles, fish, skin, foot, claw or paw of some kind.

Bill and George dare each other to eat things.

'Pity the poor bastard sharing a room with Robinson tonight!'

Bill gets George to eat something that looks a lot like a cockroach.

George makes Bill eat a spiky sea urchin, cracked open green and oozing like a raw egg.

Both are shades of green.

***

On the way back, Mr Piggott lets out a rather extravagant fart. 'Better an empty house than a bad tenant, as dear old Billy would say.'

The others laugh at his comment, but all it does is remind me of my dear old mate now gone. Billy Spiers the wrestler, Billy Spiers the singer, Billy Spiers, my friend.

***

Westcourt wins the Melbourne Cup.

Rud berates any of the troupe who lose even a penny on a bad horse.

'Bloody hell, you flame idiot, what you do! You flame idiot and very silly bugger.' He shakes his head in disbelief.

Mr Sharman, who isn't one to have a flutter, does the same, but silently, with a serious frown.

***

Back at Cole's book emporium. More signs on the wall around the store.

Religion. The three grandest truths of universal religion are the fatherhood of God, the brotherhood of man and progressive immortality.

***

Mr Hughes has decided no is not good enough and has called for a second referendum. From the paper …

'In the last referendum the soldiers voted Yes by a majority of 13,505 [cheers]. At the last election they voted for the Win-the-war party by an overwhelming majority of 51.520 [cheers]. These figures speak for themselves. They are an appeal for reinforcements more powerful than my lips can frame. Those of you who have relatives in the trenches cannot heed their cry unmoved. If they hungered, would you not send them food? If they were sick, would you not succour them? Their need is for reinforcements. They need rest, they need help.'

'Now is the hour when men of weaker fibre would quail, appalled by the danger that menaces them, now draw yourselves erect, and turn to the world an indomitable face. Courage, like cowardice, is contagious, let us set an example that will hearten our soldiers, encourage our allies and show to the enemy that he cannot break our spirit [cheers].'

'Fellow electors, the Government proposal is before you. I tell you plainly that the Government must have this power.'

Mr Hughes, on resuming his seat, was enthusiastically cheered. Mild hooting came from the few anti-conscriptionists at the back of the hall.

* * *

Well, the huff-and-puff merchants are back out again. Swells who love the sound of their own voices.

* * *

Archbishop Mannix has drawn a crowd of fifty thousand to Richmond Racecourse to rally against conscription.

'It's not right to kill and certainly it's not right for one section of the community to compel another to take life.'

Camden

The capture of Passchendaele crowns the hard work of the British Armies in Flanders of the past two months.

* * *

A letter from Billy:

Arch,

Had our first quarrel with the Hun and I did alright. You go through something like that and you find something extra in yourself. I have figured it out: you are fighting for your mates here, certainly not for the generals or King or even Country.

In fact, the other day Mr Windsor, the King himself, came past in a big motorcar and we couldn't much be bothered cheering or saluting. Some French officers came past later and we cheered and cheered and saluted until our arms nearly fell right off. They were very happy with themselves and smiled and saluted back.

It's funny over here, Archie; when they want something done tough it's always the Australians or the New Zealanders that they send in to sort Fritz out. Then we read the British did this or did that.

Arch, things get pretty hot here and I wouldn't be surprised if I could meet my end sometime soon. They say if Fritz has a bullet with your name on it doesn't matter if you're here or out sweeping the streets of Paris he will still get you. Nothing you can do, so you can't worry about it, just hope its quick. If I do go, Archie, just remember me to the others and remember the good life and special friendship we had. Just think if that dodgy bookkeeper hadn't cheated Mr Sharman we would have never met.

Anyways the other day we were on a route march, another one, out to nowhere and back again. The Army loves a bit of hurry up and wait … We passed a couple of eucalyptus trees, God knows how they got there. One of the boys broke off and starts pulling off the leaves, all of us gathering around. He gets a bunch of leaves and crushes them in his hands. 'Smell that, boys!' he said, 'Smell it … that's Australia! Australia our home!' I smelt it, and I remembered home and all my good friends and family so far away and all of us have been awfully homesick ever since.

It reminded me especially my tripping around the countryside with you and Mr Sharman and the others, so remember me fondly to all of them.

Yours truly,

Billy

* * *

An advertisement for armour vests:

Are you going to protect your soldier boy? Send away for an armour vest, top grade protection from bullets, shells and bayonet thrusts.

* * *

The *Australian Worker* has several articles about the Hughes Bendigo Speech:

Are we ready to be the dupes of the gang of capitalistic spielers who control the game? Militarisation of labour to break the independent spirit of Australian Workers.

If Australia accepts the scheme of military compulsion formulated by the Prime Minister at Bendigo it will abandon every pretension to be a democratic nation and reduce its citizens to the level of cannibals drawing lots for an obscene feast.

Conscription is to take the form of a lottery; lives are to be drawn for on Tattersall principles; souls to be made the subjects of a hideous sweep.

Thousands of men will be despatched to the shambles of the old world. May who remain be robbed of their industrial liberty and be forced to become mere conscripts of toil. Are we unworthy of a better fate?

Answer, people of Australia, with a thunderous NO!

* * *

Politicians deliver more long-winded speeches, touching on all subjects without actually illuminating on any of them.

* * *

From the paper … Billy Hughes cops an egg on the scone:

An extraordinary and disgraceful riot occurred at Warwick this afternoon when the Prime Minister alighted from the southward bound train to address an open air meeting on the platform. The moment he stepped from his carriage he was surrounded by a howling mob: 50 men, most of them of military age, were waiting on the platform. The moment they saw the Prime Minister they commenced hooting and groaning and hurling vile epithets at him. He had not gone more than a yard or two before a struggling, jostling crowd was wedged around him. An egg thrown from the crowd just missed him and broke upon the platform railing. A second one, better aimed, broke upon the Prime Minister's hat and knocked it off.

The thrower of the egg did not enjoy his triumph long. A returned soldier on the platform hurled himself upon him, and in a second a free fight was in progress.

Fists were flying everywhere, and the Prime Minister was in the thick of it, striving to get at the man who had assaulted him, and who was one of the biggest in the crowd.

It was only under the most insistent demands of the Prime Minister that the police could at last be induced to escort the man off the platform, and then, apparently, they released him as soon as they got out of Mr Hughes's sight, for he appeared on the scene again almost immediately.

Although Mr Hughes demanded in capacity as Attorney General of the Commonwealth that they should take action against the assailant, Senior-Sergeant Kenny declined to do so, declaring that he recognised the laws of Queensland only, and would act under no other.

* * *

A pamphlet:

Mothers of Australia. Now is your trial and opportunity. Will you be the proud mothers of a nation of heroes or stand dishonoured as the mothers of a race of degenerates?

* * *

Australians, why not celebrate our conscription victory with a deportation day as early as possible?

* * *

A card found on the footpath:

Women vote 'no' and guard against cheap black labour now landing.

* * *

Frank's wedding.

A happy day.

A beautiful bride.

Rings in my pocket; no prouder a best man.

Mr Sharman there as my special guest, smiling.

A toast to the absent.

* * *

News that Tibby Cotter, the cricketer featured on the cigarette cards, who joined the twelfth light horse, has been killed at the light horse charge of Beersheba. Such a well-loved man.

* * *

A poster: *Vote* No, M*um; they'll take Dad next. Vote No.*

* * *

The *Australian Worker* suggests conscription means the enslavement of women and children. This is what is happening in England – apparently women are working long hours in wretched conditions on low pay; over three hundred children working in factories for 7s.6d a week.

Conscription is not only an instrument for national defence but a bludgeon to break the stand of industrial classes.

Industrial magnates and big business have grown fat on the blood of slaughter.

* * *

The country said no the first time; why are we going through these burning hoops of debate again? I cannot stand it.

* * *

A notice I read from the paper:

The anti's creed

I believe the men at the front should be sacrificed.

I believe we should turn dog on them.

I believe that our women should betray the men who are fighting for them.

I believe in the sanctity of my own life.

I believe in taking all the benefit and none of the risks.

I believe it was right to sink the Lusitania.

I believe in murder on the high seas.

I believe in the IWW.
I believe in Sinn Fein.
I believe that Britain should be crushed and humiliated.
I believe in the massacre of Belgian priests.
I believe in the murder of women, and baby killing.
I believe that Nurse Cavell got her desserts.
I believe that treachery is a virtue.
I believe that disloyalty is true citizenship.
I believe that desertion is ennobling.
I believe in Considine, Fihelly, Ryan, Blackburn, Brookfield, Mannix, and all their works.
I believe in egg power rather than man power.
I believe in holding up transports and hospital ships.
I believe in general strikes.
I believe in burning Australian haystacks.
I believe in mine-laying in Australian waters.
I believe in handing Australia over to Germany.
I believe I'm worm enough to vote No.
Those who don't believe in the above creed will vote yes.

* * *

Also, more and more poems … Long rhyming parameters speak of loss, courage, duty.

* * *

A report in the papers. Archbishop Mannix speaks to over twenty thousand people at the Exhibition Building, Melbourne …

'I say that this cheap talk about equal sacrifice is galling, absurd, and ridiculous. [Applause] The wealthy classes would

be very glad to send the last man, but they have no notion of giving the last shilling, nor even the first. (Loud applause). I warn you not to be under the delusion that the capitalists will, in the end, pay for the war. You know that these people have a remarkable facility for passing these obligations on. [Laughter] In reality, the burden in the end will be borne by the toiling masses of Australia. [Applause].

'Recruiting will suffer while sectarian bigots are allowed on the platforms. These bigots have antagonised a large section of the community by their abuse and their insults. In abusing me they have hurt the Catholic people more than they have hurt me.

'The sectarians should be shunted off the platform. When they are gone, and the platforms were purified and disinfected, those engaged in recruiting might expect to get a more calm and patient hearing from a large section of the Australian people.

'My last word is to advise you to keep the little power you have, and to vote NO on December 20. [Loud applause] You will be acting in your own interests, and in the true interests of the Empire, by keeping Australia free, and not giving a blank cheque to Mr Hughes or anybody else. [Applause] If you surrender your freedom by accepting conscription, what assurances have you that the rights you give away will be used to the best advantage of Australia?'

At the close of the great speech, the audience of 20,000 rose and sang 'God Save Ireland'.

His Grace left the Exhibition Building amidst a perfect storm of cheers, which continued for some time.

* * *

The anti's hand bill …

The blood vote

Why is your face so white, Mother?
Why do you choke for breath?
O I have dreamt in the night my son,
That I doomed a man to death.

* * *

The rhetoric goes on and on …

* * *

A conscription question … Are you letting men die?

* * *

A conscription meeting at the Melbourne Cricket Ground …

The scene at the hundred thousand meeting held in advocacy of the Reinforcements Referendum proposal in the Melbourne Cricket Ground last night was remarkable, and the proceedings should become historic. Though a disgraceful attempt to mar it was made by anti-conscriptionists, the meeting was intensely enthusiastic, and a striking demonstration in favour of a 'Yes' vote.

Amongst the throng were a few thousand men, nearly all of military age, who had broken pieces of glass which were hurled viciously at the speakers, and the Prime Minister (Mr Hughes) and the Lord Mayor (Councillor Stapley) escaped serious injury by the narrowest margin. Special and ordinary constables charged the mob with batons and handcuffs, and many bruised and cut heads were the result.

> *Despite the dastardly tactics of the opponents, nearly the whole programme was carried out. Five bands, distributed in the stands, and at half past seven commenced to play patriotic airs. The crowds joined in as one huge chorus, and the loyal fervour was given to vent to deafening cheers for the 'Yes' campaign, cheers for Mr Hughes and hoots for Germany.*
>
> *The patriotic spirit was intensified when several returned soldiers entered the enclosure within the arena. A young woman carrying an Australian flag took up a position in front of the returned men, and they were induced to march around the oval. As they passed, the crowds in the stands rose and cheered them.*

* * *

The day before voting day, everyone is either wearing a 'yes' or a 'no' badge.

* * *

So here we are again voting in the second referendum … what part of no does Billy Hughes not understand?

> *Are you in favour of the proposal of the Commonwealth Government for reinforcing the Australian Imperial force overseas?*

* * *

The second conscription has been defeated!

This time there is an even greater NO: 1,181,747 to 1,015,159 YES.

Hughes is furious.

I hope this time this is the end of it.

1918

CHAPTER TEN

Better off dead

Frank shows me an article in the *Referee* about Mr Sharman.

'The shine is starting to dull for your man Mr Jimmy Sharman,' Frank said. 'People starting to ask a few questions, Archie boy.'

I read the article Frank has hobbled all the way over to give me …

Jimmy Sharman at Temora

'Jimmy Sharman,' writes the Referee's Orange correspondent, 'takes up the cudgels for the sports, and hands out a dirty left to those who delight in stating that the boxing men of the state are not responding to their country's call … Jimmy claims two records for the local stadium, viz., that there have been more boxing contests staged by him there than in any other country town throughout the Commonwealth, and secondly that more of his boys have joined the colours than from any other

individual section of the community. During his half–a-dozen years sojourn … he says he has managed 74 contests, in which 70 different lads were engaged, and out of that number 45 joined up, 15 of the remainder being married men, while one was exempt; one was interned, and one died, which leaves seven, who were single at the time of their matches, who have not volunteered. Jimmy has certainly put a good one over his calumniators, and his figures speak well for the body pugilistic.'

* * *

Mr Sharman has gone to the Holdsworthy Barracks to teach self-defence and boxing to new recruits. We will start much later, missing the New England leg and starting at the Sydney Royal Easter Show.

* * *

Bert returned in early March.

The legless winched down first.

The armless give away their sad half-hugs.

The gassed have swollen faces.

The cheer-up girls hand out tobacco and pipes.

We see Bert walking off. Crumpled, folded and thin.

I grab him first, pulling him into me, pulling him to safety, wrapping him up.

We hug him tightly. We hold him so tight like he is made of gold. But his arms, his shoulders, are just sticks and knobs.

I see a dozen men being helped by orderlies down the gangplank.

Some stare furtively off into the distance. The thousand-yard stare …

Several sputter tears and hesitate as they try to step off. They stand one step away from their beloved homeland and yet in their minds it is a cliff, a terrible vast abyss.

They shake.

A number hold their hands over their ears.

They cower, duck. Others mutter.

One slips each step as he walks, a queer loping gait, his legs wobbling as if battling against the wind.

Another flaps his arms like a chicken. A young boy near the gangplank laughs at him and points before his father pulls him away.

Lastly there is one man who has a look of horror across his face, as if he has seen the most horrible apparition. His face remains unchanged, fixed in some terrible moment that happened months ago on the other side of the world. He scurries off the ship and along the wharf onto a truck without windows.

* * *

Night after night Bert visits me.

Pulling up a chair, sitting at the end of my bed, in the darkness.

The sound of his rasping breath. Swigs from a bottle of something he's brought from somewhere.

'Don't tell Mother, Father … don't tell anyone', is how he always begins.

The same stories every night. I can smell him sweating. A strange toxic sweat.

'Armentieres, straightforward enough, bit of a picnic really.

'Pozieres … a different kettle of fish there … Oh, the stuff I've seen, Archie … The shells, Archie, the shells, ripping men to pieces, like mincemeat. Sometimes you can't even stand, the ground shaking so much. I got buried three times, me mates dug me out. Stinking mud, all piss shit and bits of other men, going down me throat, couldn't tell whether I was up or down. Seen it all, blokes with no arms, or without a leg but still running. Brains … bits of people everywhere, all over the place. All over you.'

'Saw a poor bugger with his stomach blown wide open, still walking, tripping over his own guts. Like sausages, his intestines, like a line of sausages and he's dragging them along.'

'It's not clean, war; it's not like one clean shot that ends it – it's the rumble of artillery coming closer and closer and you under it all … shitting in your pants … waiting … waiting … hoping that if it comes it finishes you off good and proper. It's not a real fight, it's just maths, the trajectory of shells. It's a giant machine … a huge horrible piece of machinery that men … millions of men are fed into.'

'Things I have seen, Archie … dead men buried, then thrown up, by shelling, blown clear out of their graves and torn apart again, Archie, again and again. The dead dying and dying two three times … no rest for them, killed again and then killed again.'

'You listening, Arch?'

'Yes.'

'I killed a man, a boy really. Stuck the bayonet in his guts; the look on his face, his eyes popped out like prawns.'

'Funny, though … it's the animals I remember the most. That's what stays with me: the horses, poor things, they didn't know what was going on – the sounds, explosions, terrified them. Got stuck with one in a shell hole at Pozieres; tried to calm it, it was so frightened, like a child. It never had the choice to be there. Remember it sighing as it died. Remember that for the rest of my life. See it every time I close my eyes.'

'Anyways, Nipper, got even worse at Bullecourt – the mud, the tanks didn't work, men stuck in the shell holes, asking to be shot rather than swallow any of that stink. Rats, big fat things everywhere, eating the bodies. In winter, the snow, all the bodies all frozen so then the rats turn on us. You got to be ready, Archie … Archie, keep your gas mask on, cobber, stops them nibbling your face.'

'Got lucky, didn't I? Just a bit of the gas, just got a bit of a wiff, yes? Could have been worse, Nipps, yeah? Should cheer up, yeah? Not blown to bits … Should count my chickens, thank my lucky stars, eh?'

* * *

Every night that I am home he visits and recounts his story, over and over.

Every morning, the sounds of him unpacking his coughs.

* * *

An advertisement:

Hopkins Radium Salt. Shell shock, trench nerves, rheumatism, neuritis, muscular disorders. This well-known treatment has done wonders for officers and men.

I know it won't help and Bert probably won't even touch the stuff but I buy a packet of it anyway.

* * *

Bert has been diagnosed with pneumonia and emphysema; there is nothing else his poor lungs cannot get. Wet old bags of wind.

Every day, every breath drawn painfully out of him. The cough tears at his throat, rips away at his sodden and burning lungs.

* * *

Mother tries every kind of treatment …

mustard foot baths,

eucalyptus massage,

garlic soups,

asthma powder that makes us all sneeze.

* * *

Bert has to attend a clinic each fortnight for an aspiration procedure. A long thick needle is inserted through the chest wall and the fluid and pus is pumped out.

* * *

This year's troupe …

Mr Sharman back from his twelve weeks at the Holdsworthy Barracks. Pushed into a corner, he negotiated a cunning compromise: he has, for now, done his bit. Of course, he tells me nothing.

Stan still with us.

Artie McShane, a promising youngster. 'Bags of art, this one, bags of it,' Mr Sharman says enthusiastically. 'Useful, good, excellent.'

Mr Piggott

Nick the Russian

George Cook, heavyweight

Rud Kee

Mr Sharman has picked up a mission kid. A new kid called Lester. This kid who showed up at the Brisbane Exhibition last year with a pack of six wild dogs in tow.

Mr Piggott says that the wild kids like him are good finds ...

They have all the natural abilities needed for fighting in tents: courage, a quick eye, strength, perseverance, speed, toughness, fighting brains, a seventh sense.

The mugs either hate them or love them; they are feared or despised. Some of the mugs say they wouldn't lower themselves to fight a mission kid. Mr Sharman usually convinces them and the belting they get makes them seriously rethink all things.

The mission kid grows up tough and knows his business, he knows what he is there to do … and the best thing is they won't be going off to war …

It is not much of a troupe this year. We don't even start out with a full complement of fighters to cover half of the weight divisions.

Arthur Norgrove gone.

Jackie and Billy Grimes have both gone to the stadiums.

Gilbert's not been heard of.

Frank has bowed to the pressure of Sergeant Johnson's recruiting.

Bill Robinson has gone back to New Zealand and is training recruits in self-defence at the Trentham Army Camp.

'It's like a big revolving door. Champs going in and champs going out,' Mr Piggott said.

'Mostly going out at this stage,' I say.

Stan is now the last original fighter left from my start in 1914. Apart from him, I decide, there is not much class as previous years; maybe the McShane boy, and George, he has promise.

We regroup at Circular Quay, and we are off to a bad start when Mr Sharman realises some of the troupe have been sampling the refreshments available at the First and Last Hotel directly opposite.

Mr Sharman is quite flat. He seems less keen than previous years; certainly subdued for the first day of a tour.

* * *

'Right, we need to box clever this tour. Not just in the tent, but in your minds,' Mr Sharman tells us.

'We have a war to fight here at home. From my point of view the war is hopeless and I don't want to see any more men wasted. Regardless, you are all contracted to me. I am here to protect you, my assets. The enemies for us are the recruiting sergeants, newspapers and prime ministers, and pretty much everyone else. So, if you are troubled by what these types say to you, direct them straightaway to me.'

As we have less fighters and less challengers, Mr Sharman changes the fight card, dropping bouts, making some of the troupe fight more, but instructing them to get into their opponents quicker. He holds shorter bouts and looks much harder for the opportunity to arrange more local town fights. We increase the amount of boxing and wrestling tuition so more younger children can become involved.

* * *

Mr Sharman has arranged the trip. Broadly the same route as other years, but we set up twice as much and go out even further. Out all the way to Bourke, the furthest west Mr Sharman has ever been, as if to check whether the war has crept out that far. There are new sites between the shows. Any excuse or date in the calendar – town jubilees, workers' half-days, end of harvest, mining town sprees. And a lot more still-towning: more villages and small towns where nothing ever happens. Little towns with barely one hundred yards of street and maybe a single horse trough …

I am instructed to write ahead and place advertisements in local papers before we arrive so we can ensure anyone from the district who is keen for a fight knows about it and will not miss us. The troupe are not happy with all the bumping in and out, travelling on night trains, one or two night houses only, but they know that to find any men to fight we have to search.

* * *

Mr Sharman says, 'No fish in the smooth water, so let's try the rough.'

* * *

We start at the Royal Easter Show.

The Sydney vaudeville circuit, in various half-empty picture halls.

Then the central west … Bathurst, Blayney, Orange, Molong, Parkes, Forbes, Peak Hill, Narromine, Nyngan, all the way out to Bourke, Warren, Dubbo, Gilgandra, back via Lithgow and Katoomba.

Queensland … Nerang, Beaudesert, Jimboomba, Ipswich, Toowoomba, Dalby, Chinchilla, Miles, Roma, Maryborough, Bundaberg, Gladstone, Rockhampton, Blackwater, Emerald, Barcaldine, Longreach, Mackay, Townsville, Charters Towers, a benefit show at Innisfail to help with rebuilding after the cyclone. Cairns. The Brisbane Exhibition.

Goulburn.

The Riverina … Yass, Murrumburrah, Young, Cootamundra, Wagga Wagga, Temora, Ardlethan, Griffith, Hillston, Leeton and Hay.

Country Victoria … Wodonga, Benalla, Shepparton, Seymour, Broadford, Wallan.

Ballarat (to test the waters).

Maryborough, Donald, Ararat, Stawell, Horsham.

Western Victoria … Hamilton, Portland, Port Fairy, Warrnambool, Camperdown, Colac, Geelong.

Royal Melbourne Show.

Central Victoria … the goldfields … Castlemaine, Bendigo, Kyneton, Gisborne.

Gippsland … Warragul, Morwell (hopefully dragging a few good pugs out of the butter factory).

Traralgon, Sale, Bairnsdale and Orbost.

* * *

Mr Sharman decides to apply a permanent patriotic surcharge to all ticket prices and has it printed on all tickets.

* * *

Mr Sharman trains the new ones extra hard. An hour of full sparring.

'Walk up, walk up,' he shouts. 'Keep walking up, keep walking up. You're a fighter, a fighter, walk it up to them, walk up.'

* * *

More advice from Mr Sharman at dinner:

Learn something from every fight.

Overcome the brawler before he overcomes you.

Remember, some fellas you meet out there would have waited and trained all year for this one chance to knock your block off.

* * *

There have many peace rallies over the summer.

The Loyalists … Equality of Sacrifice …

The Australian Peace Alliance held a mass rally at the Brisbane Exhibition Hall with various speakers, Joseph Collings,

Senator Myles Ferricks,

Jim Quinton from the IWW,

the Quaker Margaret Thorp,

from the women's peace army, Vida Goldstein.

They are stepping out of the shadows now. Others list their names as they curse them in hateful open letters to the press.

* * *

A poster:

Why should I be asked to enlist?

Is my country in peril?

Yes!

Then why am I hanging back?

Am I a coward?

* * *

Reasons as to why any of this year's troupe will not be going:

Defiance. The Irish situation.

Thinking about the right time to go.

Brothers and sisters to support.

Mum won't sign the papers.

Helping with fundraising back here.

No address.

Bad teeth.

* * *

Another letter from Billy:

Hello there, Archie,

I have been struggling with a cold I couldn't seem to shake and had some trouble with my feet as well. With so much surface area I suppose, Archie, the germs are always finding somewhere to get in. I had a bit of convalescence in Blighty with a diagnosis of mild trench fever and trench foot. Standing in mud made my feet swell up and go every colour of the rainbow. Still, it was very nice to get the lovely nurses' full attention and enjoy the nice soft warm beds they tucked me into. I even got a kiss on the cheek from one or two of them. Mr Sharman would be happy though – I've lost me a lot of my pud and maybe even too thin now. Moving back to the big argument next week. I wish it could be the big agreement instead and I can get back to my people as quick as possible. Regards to Mr Sharman and

Mr P and good old Stan. I miss them and the tour. I even miss the training. How is Nick working out? Any good wrestlers still left out there? How was Ballarat this year? A dead loss? I can tell you why – it's because all of the Ballarat boys are over here. I have two brothers from Sebastopol serving in my section, the best chaps you would ever meet. I hope your brothers are on the mend. From what I heard Bert went to hell and back where he was, the Huns chucking tons of steel over for a week. Hopefully the big heads get together soon and sort this whole thing out with a nice cup of tea and a gentleman's handshake. I hope you are good, Arch. It must be tough on any young fellow still at home. It's a lot simpler over here; the grief only comes over from the east, not every which direction like it did at home. Anyways, keep that mind of yours busy but don't try and think too much.

I will sign off now. Your staunchest friend,

Billy

* * *

Time for Mr Sharman's annual lecture …

C_2 H_5 OH in any of its forms is the worst poison known to young men.

Train as if your life depends on it because it does.

Flash friends can quickly turn into the biggest foes.

Let your fists do the talking.

* * *

For the first time Stan and I room together.

We talk his favourite boxers … Jack Johnson, the Boston Tar Baby … Sam Langford, Sam McVey, Joe Jeanette.

* * *

There are reports of a mass movement of German troops across Europe. With the collapse of the Russian front there are now fourteen German divisions … half a million men … likely to push west. Paris under threat, then England.

'Looks like we are in quite a fix now,' Mr Piggott says.

'The last four years could all be for nothing,' I say.

'Always has been for nothing, Archie, always has been.'

* * *

More reports from newspapers that the Germans are advancing rapidly. Even the papers are glum. This must be bad! In two days, anything gained in the Somme has gone. Long range guns are shelling Paris. Villers-Bretonneux, Arras and other parts of the allied line are overrun. I worry about where Billy might be. Every one of us has the urge to help those men. We all know people facing the Germans right now. We should be standing by them, but we can't. We feel useless.

* * *

Royal Easter Show

Sideshow alley as big and as bizarre as ever …

There are some new variety shows: *'Dancers of the seven veils', 'The fire-eating fanatics from the Philippines' … illusionists, conjurers, 'Leonardo the Levitator', Indian Fakirs and their rope tricks, escapologists … 'the hand-cuff King' … sword-swallowers …*

'Isom' who climbs a ladder of swords and walks twenty yards over a corridor of broken beer bottles ... 'Mrs General Mite the Midget.'

> *A man has brought over from Perth a galah that shits whole shilling coins, one after the other.*
>
> *There are lots more Aunty Sally knockdowns and shooting galleries than past years. There is an 'in and out show' with a man who we are told has descended into a deep trance for the last three weeks and can be seen lying in a coffin for the run of the entire Easter show without taking food, water or cigarettes.*
>
> *'Valescar the Ice Girl' is enclosed in one ton of ice.*
>
> *Another joint has 'Wee Jimmy', the world's smallest horse ... with gold hooves ...*

There is a brand new fat lady from New Zealand ... Fat Fanny from Bluff ... unloaded by ship's crane.

She beckons to the young men with a low, sweet voice: 'Here, my boy, come here, you beautiful boy. Come here and feel my leg. Touch me, touch me here.'

* * *

We also hear that there is a larger than usual collection of miscreants working in and around the edges of the showgrounds and the city.

Willy 'Donkey' Wright, a con artist who works the trains – a card sharper – boards with banknotes falling out his pockets, eating a raw onion and raving on about seagulls. He finds his gullible mark and takes all his planned show day spending money.

'Sharky' Simpson, who tricks local shopkeepers and even some of the showies. He might buy a packet of matches, offer a large note, then change his mind and offer coins, then change his mind again, until the confused shopkeeper hands back the original note and change.

'That's why you put the note to be changed on top of the bag, then dig down for change,' Rud says.

Mr Sharman is suitably impressed. 'Excellent Rud, useful, yes, useful, good.'

They are all here, at the Easter show, the pickpockets, conmen, petty thieves, madams of the night, spivs and tricksters.

It is as if all the good people have gone and all we are left with is the bad.

Then again, what are we these days? Real fighters? With our stews and canny matching, our spieler. Maybe we are just a step up from the tricksters? Maybe we are just the same as them. Pretending the fights are close and mean anything much at all.

* * *

Business mottos ...

Mr Sharman ... *Business may bring money, but friendship hardly ever does.*

Mr Piggott ... *Every crowd has a silver lining.*

Mr Sharman ... *A fool and his money are soon parted.*

Mr Sharman ... *Take care of the pence and the pounds will take care of themselves.*

* * *

For future reference and trip planning Mr Sharman asks me to confirm the towns with the biggest operating goldmines ... If you want to make money go to where the money is.

* * *

News that Australian troops have recaptured Villers-Bretonneux …

Australians, together with some British battalions, moved upon Villers-Bretonneux at ten o'clock on Wednesday night. They fought all through the dark hours, and it was not until seven o'clock the next morning that the news came back of the recovery of the place.

One has never admired our men and officers more than at the present moment. However the Australian divisions may be supported by Australia, they are fighting with such magnificent spirit that they are a tower of strength in this crisis of strength of that democracy which made them. It is right that democracy should know this, and also know that its force may diminish through a shortage of reinforcements.

* * *

News that the retreating French civilians saw the Australians marching up the road and began to unstack their belongings off carts and back into their houses.

Vous les tiendrez, Vive Australie!

A number of Germans were found in a fully stocked cellar full of wine and cheese. A lot of the prisoners taken were too drunk or full of food to put up a fight …

The others, though … the others fought like devils. Australian bayonets were kept very busy …

Soon, I know, for sure, my grim war tally will grow.

* * *

Sydney Vaudeville

More than the usual collection of spivs at the rail stations, well dressed and friendly, try to sell you anything not tied down and also things that were tied down but then ripped off.

A man in an overcoat offers me a range of smallgoods stitched carefully on the inside.

***

Fights are harder to find, especially midweek; we are part of a mixed card at the Civic in a boxing exhibition and vaudeville show …

Jake Freidman the Happy Hollander performs his Tyrolean and Swiss yodelling.

George Cook and Artie … biggest versus the smallest in a half-hearted slap and tickle.

Bird call imitators.

Dancing dogs.

Little Edith the child wonder shot.

The laughter songster.

Whistling Rufus.

Nick the Russian wrestling half-drunk old men.

The minstrel troupe.

***

Some of the returned men still have the faces of children, but the eyes, the eyes are much older.

***

Our theatre season is mercifully drawing to a close … Our one-trick horse and pony show. We are as bad as the recruiting films that they show over and over: *Advance of the tanks, Hero of the Dardanelles, Will they ever come? Australia at war, Sons of the Empire, Australia's peril.*

All variations of the same thing – guilt and misplaced glory. I have no favourite one that I hate more than others. It is all lies.

* * *

The Green Parrot Restaurant on George Street. A thin returned man opens the door to the restaurant and approaches the waiter, asking for spare food or kitchen scraps. The waiter softly shakes his head and the man leaves. I wonder whether the waiter and his fat clientele know anything of what this man has seen. Mr Sharman sends me out with a ten pound note to hand on to him.

* * *

Bathurst

A platoon of young girls with pretend rifles marching up and down the red brick main street with flags and a banner reading … *If you won't go, we will.*

* * *

Debate among the troupe about which year has been the best so far. The new ones fishing for compliments, checking themselves against Sharman's scale.

'All different,' I say diplomatically. Mr Sharman is more accurate.

'Nineteen fourteen. Good across the board, something on offer across the weighs and Billy wrestling. Good trainers and Jackie going particularly well. Good gates and challengers back then,' he said wistfully. 'Bit lean since then.'

The boys look disappointed. Mr Sharman reassures them ...

'Above average standard this year with the odd exception ... it's up to all of you lot to prove me wrong.'

* * *

Blayney

Artie steps up to his opponent who is an older and bigger but much weaker minded boy. Artie releases a sudden flurry of violence up and down his opponent's body.

The boy is up on his bike and running away. 'Oi come here!' Artie yelling at him: 'What do you think this is? A goat race?'

* * *

Mr Sharman likes the determination shown by the young fellow: 'The fight bee is well and truly buzzing around in his bonnet.'

* * *

Mr Sharman's advice for young up-and-coming boxers:

Avoid blatherskites, larrikins, slack trainers and know-it-alls.

* * *

Stories from recaptured Villers-Bretonneux ...

A French mother forced to hold a spotlight into the face of her son as the German firing squad shoots him.

The Germans give a young French girl a box of chocolates, which, upon opening, exploded.

* * *

We meet a world traveller, a Mr Tremain, spending all his inheritance after selling several mills in England. He decided that all he would need was a suitcase, a good coat and sturdy shoes – that was ten years ago. The things he has seen …

Temples that grow up through clouds in Mexico.

The burning of bodies on the funeral ghats of Varanasi.

How the Māori people of New Zealand cook their food inside volcanoes.

The Indians, whole families, generations of them, who all live on rafts made of reeds on Lake Titicaca.

Perhaps after the war when we are touring with Billy's singing we can go see such wonders with our own eyes ...

* * *

Orange

We have brought a big bag of apples. Apples from Orange … Lester thinks this paradox is hilarious and we are into them.

Stan's cheeks bulging.

Artie bites down like a large bronze whaler.

Mr Piggott rolls a piece of it around and around inside his mouth as he tells his new jokes.

Nick is full of juicy salivation.

George Cook has finished four already.

Rud shines it up like a new cricket ball before finally biting into it.

Mr Sharman savours slowly, making it last. He eats methodically.

Lester chews noisily, laughing with his mouth open.

I nibble away like a tidy little rabbit, holding it in my bent claw of a hand.

* * *

Molong

Artie has a real bag of tricks, Mr Sharman likes what he sees: a quick hand and eye, outstanding footwork, a great bread and butter. Useful, excellent, good.

* * *

JJ Leahy the pastoralist is on the train. According to Mr Piggott, JJ Leahy owns half of Australia; at least everything between Forbes, Condoblin and West Wyalong … huge stations we have heard of through the comings and goings of men, stock. And we've seen the stamps on wool bales … Manna Park, Wongajong, Ina, Namina, Eulo, Myamley, Moonbi-Fairholme, Hopes Manna, Stezelle and Block A. Then there's his other properties. We make a game of it naming them all … *Baden Park* at Ivanhoe, *Benah* at Nyngan, *Oxley*, Hylea, *Ardsley*, *Bundilla*, *Kelloshiel*, *Killongbutta*, *Freemantle*, *Willow Glen*, *Porter's Retreat* at Oberon, *Fullerton* and the *Burra*. And to top it off he has even more properties in Queensland: *Bon Accord* at Dalby, *Mt Sturgeon* and *Oban* south of Mount Isa.

Mr Sharman spends two hours in earnest discussion with him.

* * *

My parents write telling me that Bert cannot find any work. Businesses prefer not to hire any 'sub-efficients'; there is concern about their headaches, their coughs. Concerns about production rates of even the mildly affected returned men. Worry about whether some of their joints might slip out. It seems as if everyone is looking for light work.

* * *

'Are you Mr Sharman?' a boy asks.

'Yes, I am.'

The boy, only seven or eight, comes closer and spits right into Mr Sharman's face.

* * *

Mr Sharman on the art of counterpunching and life:

> *Sometimes before you throw a big punch you have to take a big punch.*

* * *

Parkes

Every single one of the towns we visit is littered with pieces of soldiers, incomplete, missing an arm or missing a leg or losing their minds.

A returned man outside a draper's and haberdashery store asks me, 'Can you spare a deener for a digger down on his luck?'

Mr Sharman gives him a five pound note.

* * *

We have gone far enough to have a new round of nicknames for this year's tour:

Artie is called 'The Wasp'.

Nick the Russian is known as 'Tricky Nicky'; also likes to be referred to as 'The Barnacle' because he is so hard to pull off an opponent.

Stan and Mr Piggott stay with 'Snake' and 'Mr P'.

Lester sometimes calls Stan 'Brother Darkness'.

George Cook is called 'Bumper'.

Mr Sharman stays as 'Boss' or 'Mister'.

Rud is still Rud or sometimes 'Tickets'.

Lester is called 'The Fang', 'Pester', 'Lurch' or 'Bushy'.

I keep 'Pencils'.

* * *

Forbes

A pilot offers Mr Sharman a free biplane ride. Mr Sharman refuses politely and tells us later that if man was born to fly we would have feathers and a better head for heights.

* * *

Peak Hill

Artie is to fight a much taller opponent …

Some advice from Mr Sharman:

You can always lower their height with a quick round of jabs into the belly.

* * *

With the young ones, Mr Sharman is always present to demonstrate the right way of doing things …

How to tie a tie.
How to greet people of a high social standing.
How to respond to a compliment.
How to shine your shoes efficiently.

* * *

People with more money than sense:

A man Nick once met who owned five terrace houses in Carlton but lived in a roughly converted stable with a thousand rats sharing his bed and dinner plate.

Another at Mount Morgan who rolled up five pound notes and smoked them.

* * *

Narromine

Mr Sharman takes Artie aside and gives him his special 'boxing clever' talk. Is he fond of the boy or fond of his boxing abilities? I think it's both.

* * *

Nyngan

This troupe has turned competitive. Artie and Lester starting it, not saying anything, just watching each other train and fight. The fights are quicker and punches harder. Their rivalry oozing into training, the speedball drumming faster, faster, the skipping rope whirrs, weights lifted, then lifted again. Arm wrestles on trains and at dinner tables. Mr Sharman is waiting for the right moment to put them all together in the ring.

* * *

We go further afield. We travel as far west as we dare to find new men to fight. But the war has reached most places.

* * *

We stop in small dried-out towns.

'Any rain lately?'

'Not much, but the beer's still flowing and that's the main thing.'

* * *

Bourke

On the outskirts of Bourke, we see the Afghan cameleers.

What a sight! They have set up their camp at the railhead. From here they go deep into the interior. It is hard to think that anyone could live past this point.

There are great trains of camels, arriving or departing, the head camel colourful with its tassels, hanging from its nose and lead. Thirty other camels follow carrying wool bales or crates of provisions for farms that I cannot imagine could be any lonelier.

The crates are loaded on the flanks of the camel, with a rope drawn taut between the tops of the boxes lifting the weight off the camel's sides so as not to crush the animal's ribs.

What animals they are! Long eyelashes as thick as paintbrushes. Soft feet that cup over sand, cushioning each stride. Giant ladder legs. They bellow in contempt at their handlers, their teeth and lips mumbling ancient insults as they are loaded down. The Afghans manage them so efficiently.

* * *

Warren

Mr Sharman, Mr Piggott and now Rud Kee are discussing the benefits of purchasing trucks to tour with next year. Saving on hotel room bills. The troupe sleeping and eating in a tent joined to the ring tent. It means tiring drives between sites. It means visiting some of the harder-to-reach places, places where pugs are supposed to be – Omeo, Corryong, Batlow, Bega. Savings to be made on train fares, cartage. Not being at the mercy of rail strikers or timetables. The outlay for the trucks and benzine costs are quite steep.

'Save one match and build a house,' Mr Sharman said.

* * *

The Commercial Hotel Dubbo

In preparation for Saturday night's long awaited and heavily advertised prize fight it turns out that both George Cook and Phil Walls need a doctor's certificate. They return to the hotel after visiting Doctor Burkitt's surgery. They shift around the parlour and Mr Sharman like naughty school boys and their headmaster.

Mr Sharman snaps, 'Right, tell me what the hell is going on then, George?'

'Well, that doctor, Doctor Burkitt, he's a strange old fish that one. Sure is.'

'Yes, go on.'

'Well, first … he didn't even lay a hand on us … then he said, straight out, he wouldn't issue either of us a certificate for the fight.'

'What?' Mr Sharman said. 'That's what I discussed directly with him myself just yesterday and he was very keen to help.'

'Yes, well, then Doctor Burkitt said he would provide us with certificates conditionally …'

'Conditionally?' Mr Sharman said.

'Yes … um … yes, on the condition that he would be allowed to enter the ring before the fight and give his reasons for his refusal.'

'But you have the certificates with you? There … you are holding them!'

Mr Sharman is pointing at their big sweaty nervous hands.

George and Phil are both holding on to pieces of paper.

'Yes … um … actually he meant to talk about his reasons for his conditional approval. Yes, that's what he said. That's right, Phil?' George said.

'Yes, yes, that's about right, his conditional approval,' Phil said.

'This is some kind of a trap!' Mr Sharman said. 'Are there any other doctors we can see?'

'Not now,' I said, 'it's after five.'

Dubbo Mechanic's Hall

Doctor Birkett is only a little fellow; a lot like Mr Sharman – little and fierce. And he has a set of lungs on him …

'You all know that I am a sport and a lover of sport. You have come here tonight to see two fine specimens of young Australians enter into a contest. I venture to say here that young Cook is one of the finest specimens of manhood that I have ever had under examination. I hear that his parents will not give their consent to his going to the front because he is only nineteen years of age. Still they allow him to enter this ring and engage in a prize fight. Cook is as good as any

three Germans and I would like to lead a thousand such as he into battle.

'Friends, twelve months ago, at Messines Ridge, I saw your own Australian brothers coming out of the trenches after twenty-one days of continuous and strenuous fighting and if you had seen those tired Australians there is not a man in this audience but would have said, "By God I will take their place." Yet, here in Australia, men of the physique of Cook and Walls fight for amusement while our brave Australian boys are dying for want of assistance on the fields of France.

'I would not have given these two men a certificate but for the fact that I know Jimmy Sharman is a right good sport and I would not put him in a corner through this fight not coming off. I make this offer to George Cook: if he enlists and goes to the front, I will insure him for two hundred pounds and if Phil Walls will go I will get a friend to insure him for a like sum.'

Then Doctor Birkett is gone.

Then there is polite applause.

Then cheering. 'Go get him, George!'

'Go, Phil!'

Mr Sharman starts the fight immediately.

And George punching harder than he's ever punched before.

* * *

Dubbo

News that Billy Spiers has been seriously wounded at Villers-Bretonneux …

CHAPTER ELEVEN

Grief, the price we pay for love

Billy has died of wounds

Billy … the namer of clouds … Billy the singer … Billy the wrestler … Billy, my best friend … Died in terrible pain and alone, away from his beloved country, so far away from those he loved and who loved him.

***

Gilgandra

I am destroyed. I lie in bed awake all night. I linger at breakfast, search out quiet and lonely places. I am in a spin.

Rud places a hand on my shoulder whenever we pass or sit near one another, saying nothing.

Mr Piggott goes a whole day without a joke.

Stan is restless. He paces and sighs.

The rest didn't know him but keep their distance.

Mr Sharman says nothing; he stays in his room. He goes about his business.

* * *

Later Mr Piggott tells me he and Mr Sharman are just holding on from completely falling apart. 'For the sake of the troupe we need to keep a brave face and carry on.'

* * *

Another train journey discussion. They defer to me, one of the old hands: 'What's the prettiest town in Australia?'

Orange? Grafton in Spring? Daylesford, down on the lake?

Bright?

I think about this. I shut my eyes.

Orange, its bright gardens and beautiful trees.

Grafton and its jacarandas in November.

The Lake at Daylesford. Me and Billy, playing ducks and drakes in the rowboat, Billy smiling.

'Daylesford,' I reply before excusing myself as tears start to lick my face.

* * *

I receive a newspaper cutting from my mother:

The Supreme Sacrifice

Private William Spiers

Sad intelligence was received that Pte William Spiers of Campbellfield has died of wounds. The late Pte Spiers was twenty-six years of age. He was one of the finest types of Australians and citizens, of a most genial and estimable disposition and the most sterling character. Smallness or meanness knew no place in his nature, which only had room for openness, manliness, straightforwardness and kindliness. Mr J. Sharman, for whom the fallen soldier worked as a member of his well-known boxing troupe, speaks in unstinting terms of praise and admiration of his industry, trustworthiness and sociableness and regarded him as a member of the family. William was also well known as a talented singer. He was hoping to attend the Sydney Conservatory of Music after the war. In the world of sport the deceased man was the very soul of honour. He was an enthusiastic wrestler and while striving his hardest for victory ever acted in a clean manner. Truly, Australia is much the poorer for the loss of Billy Spiers and we join with the whole district in extending the deepest sympathy to his family and their sad bereavement.

I had no idea Mr Sharman had made correspondence with the newspaper. I feel bad that I thought ill of him. He too carries the loss of Billy, but shoulders it more gracefully than I do.

* * *

Lithgow

A man sitting at the railway station with the plaque around his neck which reads:

Help a blinded digger.

Mr Sharman folds pound notes into his hand.

* * *

The toughest town in Australia? The new ones ask me again.

Newcastle, the foundry men?

Roma?

Blackwater?

'Townsville,' I say, 'if Frater has made the trip in.'

* * *

Katoomba

We pay a visit to Mr Medlicott's pharmacy. It's not potions or lotions we are after. We are there to see the girl who works behind the counter. The prettiest girl in all New South Wales, Miss Eureka Jones … her beautiful face, her beautiful eyes and her mystery.

* * *

Nerang

Lester comes over to me and puts a hand on my shoulder telling me, 'We all got to stay strong … all of us … got to stay strong.'

Rud tells me, 'If you keep thinking about someone they never die.'

But with this heavy grief …

I see things in a different light now, as one does when he shakes hands with the shadows.

* * *

Beaudesert

Lester is put against a police constable from Toowoomba. The tent cheers the policeman to win. The policeman says something to Lester. I have a feeling that they are old acquaintances. Shouts of 'Boong', 'Coon' and 'Nigger' are spat out of the mouths of an angry crowd.

The policeman is big but knows little about boxing; all he wants to do is teach Lester a lesson. Lester gets out of his way for the first round. As he tires, Lester starts picking him off, cutting under the eye, blooding the nose and loosening a tooth. Right near the end of the last round Lester smashes the policeman's chin.

As the policeman lies groggy across the sawdust Lester walks up to him, leans over and says, 'Got you back for what you did, yeah?'

* * *

Jimboomba

My father writes to tell me Bert is wandering at night out on the streets like other returned men.

Men whose minds the dead have ravished …

* * *

Mr Sharman:

Everyone needs to run their own race.

* * *

Ipswich

Mr Sharman changes tack and tells the troupe that they need to take more punches; they need to let a few more in to give the local boys that are left a bit more heart.

* * *

My Tuesdays are meatless.
My Wednesdays are wheatless.
I'm getting more eatless each day.
My home it is heatless.
My bed it is sheetless.
They're all been sent to the YMCA.

* * *

Chinchilla

Coal is half-inched from railway sidings collected in baby perambulators.

* * *

Roma

A letter from my father.

He has found Bert wandering across the home paddock in his pyjamas three nights last week.

* * *

Maryborough

Mrs Mutch has been engaged by the recruiting committees of several surrounding towns to interview mothers and wives of eligibles to persuade each women to let her man go. She is both methodical and well-travelled.

* * *

What town has the prettiest girls?

Ballarat.

St Kilda Beach on a Sunday.

Warwick, Hobart, Wollongong.

The Randwick Races.

Brisbane.

'Katoomba has just one … Miss Eureka Jones,' I say, 'whose beauty beats all of the prettiest girls in Brisbane put together.'

The others rue that they did not pay a visit, instead choosing instead to go to Echo Point and standing there leering through the fog and seeing nothing.

* * *

Bundaberg

Mr Sharman has some new patter to drag the mugs in …

'We'll fight anything; we don't care if you are big or little, black or white, brown yellow or brindle.'

'The bigger they are the harder they fall.'

'Test your wits and test your mitts.'

* * *

'What is the ugliest place in Australia?

Innisfail after the cyclone.

Maitland.

Cessnock.

'Lithgow – it's the true ass-end of the Blue Mountains,' says Nick.

Debate rages for the next hour about here or there being worst, until they give up and Lithgow wins out.

* * *

Gladstone

We set up right next to the meatworks at Parsons Point. A good house at knock-off time. Slaughterman throwing their meaty-smelling fists at each other.

A man said to be recently struck by lightning removes his shirt. Red rivers of burned skin twist down his body where the rain had run down him and then a bolt from God above had passed through him to the ground. Think about it: he was once where heaven and earth collide.

* * *

To pass the time we make up moments. Meeting famous people or attending historical events …

Meeting Napoleon.

Walking with the dinosaurs.

Cleopatra, grapes, wine, handmaidens, the hot desert and the cool Nile.

A soirée with Nellie Melba.

I tell them about dinner with King George,
the huge table like a glacier shining with crystal glasses,
small talk about English weather,
duck a l'orange,
Four kinds of pudding.
I save them from the smaller details …
the footman's shoes across the crackle gravel outside,
the pause in the waiter's breathing,
the King's whiskers speckled with the tiniest drops of soup.

* * *

Rockhampton

More often now Mr Sharman arranges preliminary bouts between young lads – boys aged between eight and ten who fight with oversized gloves to fill in time for absent men.

More wrestling hold demonstrations, more skipping and speedball displays also fill in the gaps.

* * *

George dismantles a highly fancied canecutter in Mackay.

'He looks like a good match against a certain agricultural gentleman in the Townsville area,' says Mr Sharman with a glint in his eye.

* * *

Townsville

Frater is out front yelling and pointing. 'I want to drop that big bastard there,' he says, pointing holes in the air and pointing specifically at George.

He wants to fight George and George wants to fight him.

Mr Sharman spends the whole afternoon dragging a huge crowd of mugs into the tent. So many mugs want to see it that we lift up the tent flaps and charge half-price for all the mugs who watch from outside.

'Bill Frater will fight! Bill Frater will fight in this tent!'

Frater … the man we love to hate, the locals' favourite, the angriest man in Australia.

George manages to get a few away early. Frater is shocked and not impressed.

Then Frater goes berserk.

'Come here, you fucker, I'll kill ya!'

George stays clear of the storm until it blows itself out.

Next round and both fighters are keen to mix it up.

George doesn't let Frater throw a full arm-length punch, staying in close.

Tight short punches are punched, back and forth, back and forth.

Last round and George stays inside. Frater is ropeable: 'Fight like a man!' he yells.

The bell rings and Mr Sharman declares a draw. Frater storms away.

George has a face so puffy it looks like it has been stung by a swarm of bees.

* * *

Brisbane Exhibition

More new sideshow acts:

The man magnet and his diet of steel.

The incredible Volton.

The fireproof sisters from Saturn.

Spidora, the half-spider–half-woman. See her within the tangled web she weaves all by herself.

Professor Doyle the Mnemonist.

He remembers each card from a sequence of a freshly shuffled pack, just from a quick glance, but then so can I ...

The pill and potion men are here in force.

Absolute quackery.

According to Mr Sharman, no qualifications are needed. All that is required:

a face of stone,

a tongue of treacle,

contempt for the truth,

and a complete indifference for the soon-to-be-ruined health of your latest victim.

We are to stay well away.

* * *

We hear about a man with severe jaundice who has recently cured himself by eating three peeled beetroot a day.

* * *

Mr Sharman's word is his bond, whether he is dealing with the show secretary and president or the lowest tent hand.

* * *

An advertisement in the paper.

Digger J Thompson

Who was blinded in the war.

Is now open to receive your razors and scissors.

Razors ground and set 1/6 scissors 6d. Country orders promptly attended to. Orders may be left at Messrs Bell & Bradshaw, William Street or 24 Balmoral Street Westend.

In the morning Mr Sharman gathers all our razors and visits Mr Thompson personally.

* * *

It is four years since this war started. Four years of the country having the guts ripped out of it.

Tributes and anniversary memorials in local papers use the

same words again and again …

A popular favourite …

A true Australian type …

A cheerful, happy youth, whose nice manner and winning smile made him a general favourite …

A young fellow of the highest character …

A keen sportsman of grit and determination …

A good and loyal servant … lost to us now for the past three years …

* * *

Daddy

Every day I think of you as you once thought of me.

* * *

Look at us. Mr Sharman, Mr Piggott, Stan, me, Rud and all the other members of Jimmy Sharman's Boxing Troupe. This little crew, navigating our little ship through the rocks and storms of war and conscription. It is remarkable we have got this far. You couldn't have hidden away for the last four years and not gone away without a good reason or a lot of cunning. How could you stay without a reason? A strong enough reason, a reason that you could live with, one than wouldn't nag away at you day after day. The guilt would be just too powerful in the end.

* * *

Mr Sharman is doing his usual research. This time he's reading the stockyard sale reports. Good one-year lambs or heavy lamb prices from six months back should see the crowds larger and spending more.

* * *

Goulburn

No young roosters are left. Mr Sharman matches two fifty-year-olds for later in the day. The 'fight', according to Mr Piggott, ends up to be nothing much more than a glorified tickle match.

* * *

Yass

George gets handed another white feather.

'Christ, more bloody white feathers! Poor farm chooks! All of them poor buggers must now all be plucked bald and freezing cold.'

It would be strange for him not to get a white feather within an hour of arriving in any new town.

* * *

An unfortunate man on the train relates his sad story of how he was once a successful smallgoods trader but sold the lot for a racehorse that died three days later. Mr Sharman is almost physically sick with the grief and the worry about this man's sad story.

* * *

Murrumburrah

Mr Sharman's standard list of nicknames for every size and type of challenger …

If they are short: Titch … Half-pint … Nipper …

If they are tall: Lofty … Stretch … Spider …

If they are heavy set: Ox ... Nugget ...

If they are thin: Beanpole … Lanky … Stick Insect … the Splinter … Muscles …

He even decides nicknames by hair type … red becomes Bluey, bald becomes Curly.

The cataloguing never really ends with Mr Sharman …

* * *

Young

At the post office a man unwraps a parcel from his son that contains a torn bloody tunic sleeve and a small jar with twisted shrapnel that has carved away its pound of meat. Proof of a close shave.

* * *

A discussion about how the weights of boxers and their divisions always seem to match a certain type of person, certain behaviours …

Heavyweights. Friendly, gentle, trusting, terrifying if pushed too far.

Middleweights. Always struggling with their weight, the halfway men.

Lightweights. Moody, dark, aspiring for a bigger share of the glory.

Featherweights. The cheeky ones, talkative, tricky.

Bantamweights. The angry ants. Always needing to prove themselves.

* * *

More news about Bert not going too well.

Bad dreams, screaming and fighting, keeping everyone awake all night.

'In life and in war each man measures up differently,' Mr Piggott tells me.

* * *

Cootamundra

News of a battle featuring Australians at Hamel …

By the end of the first day of the great attack the Australian infantry had advanced 10 miles into country which yesterday morning was German, on a front of about nine miles. Our losses in all this were ridiculously small. One battalion which we found at the farthest point of the advance had only three casualties. The troops now are looking out over country where they can see quietly clearly the familiar old line of trees topping the Peronne road. They are in tremendous spirits.

* * *

Wagga Wagga

Another substantial donation to the Wagga Wagga District Hospital Trust.

You can almost set a sundial by Mr Sharman's promise and handshake.

* * *

Temora

A curious situation no-one, not even Mr Sharman or Mr Piggott, have ever seen or heard of. A double knockout. Both locals punching hard at exactly the same moment, both connecting with each other's jaws and down they both go like two sacks of spuds. Mr Sharman awards the purse equally to each of them.

'That's not every day you will see that, ladies and gentlemen. But if you are going to see it anywhere it will be right here, in Sharman's famous boxing tent.'

* * *

Talk suggests that there is a great drive of British and Dominion troops heading east across Picardy … Are we finally winning this war?

* * *

Ardlethan

A local boy dies of a snake bite. A spring snake, more powerful venom, stored up over the winter. The death brings up a number of stories about snakes …

They swallow their young when in danger.

They can outrun a man, especially uphill.

They hypnotise their prey.

Play music or leave out a saucer of milk and this will entice them from their hiding holes.

They drink milk by biting into cows' udders.

Snakes will always avenge a mate's death.

* * *

Griffith

Rumours that the Germans are close to finished, that the war will be over by Christmas. But we remember hearing that before.

It doesn't stop us dreaming, laying out our future plans:

Stan to keep boxing in the tent. Maybe save up to go to America and go spar with Jack Johnson.

Rud to stay with Mr Sharman.

Artie wants to go all the way, the stadium and the titles (and he might just do it).

Nick wants to buy land near Adelaide and start planting grape vines.

George wants to travel the world, fight in Europe and America then go back home, get married, have a dozen kids and sit on a porch.

Mr Sharman wants to discover a dozen new champions so he can keep on keeping on.

Lester doesn't have a clue.

They ask me. It is the first time I have reconsidered it; as if until the war is over, I am unable to think of anything about the future. A visit to where Billy rests.

A writer, I say, travelling new far-off lands then returning to Camden sometime to maybe open a bookshop. They all laugh. 'Planning on selling the books or just reading them all?'

* * *

Hillston

Mr Sharman decides to put Lester and Artie in the stew. He builds them up as Artie the New South Wales schoolboy champion and Lester the wild farmhand run away from his cruel employer somewhere up north. Lester gives Artie dagger looks and Artie gives him dagger looks right back.

Mr Sharman has me up on the bridge as we are short. It's all tops of hats and faces staring up at you from here. Everything speeds, rushes … people become so much smaller. I am almost floating above them. I grip the drumstick, I bang the drum! I feel the power in my hand. The strength. I am here in the moment. Banging the drum. Archie Blackmore is up here banging the drum.

* * *

News that Cecil Healy, the swimmer on the cigarette cards, has been killed at the siege of Peronne. Poor Cecil. Cecil who insisted his great friend Duke Kahanamoku – who was nearly disqualified for being late – be allowed to complete in the swimming final at the Stockholm Olympics, is dead.

* * *

Leeton

Mr Sharman starts some banter with Lester, who is going to be the gee today.

'You've had a fight or two have you, son?'

'Done a bit,' says Lester scuffing at the dust with his boots.

'Well, then, you better get up on this board if you have done a bit. How about taking on the fellow down the end? Have a go at him. I'll give you two pounds for two rounds.'

'Not enough for my kind of fighting. Three pounds, Mr Sharman.'

'Three! If you want three pounds, it's three rounds. You know … up go the pounds, up go the rounds … You know what you get if you fight him and he beats you?'

'I don't … I suppose nothing, Mr Sharman.'

'Don't worry about that; you'll get nothing but a lot of good boxing experience, my lad.'

* * *

Hay

Down by the river we meet some Murrumbidgee whalers, the swagmen, the sundowners who walk and live up and down the river.

One we meet takes a leisurely circular trip of four hundred miles – from Wagga Wagga to Gundagai along the left bank to Hay then back to Wagga up along the left bank. A round trip of twelve months.

The sundowner has two tuckerbags: one full of food and another pitifully half-empty.

He arrives near dusk, promising to put in a hard day's work tomorrow after a good feed, then at the crack of dawn he is gone.

Another kind of swagman is the kind known as a silvertail, a disgraced English lord, a family's black sheep on the run – there seems to be a lot of them in these parts.

* * *

Benalla

Hardly any men step up to fight. The last fight in the tent proves only one thing ... big fish ... small pond ...

* * *

There are more reports of soldiers dying of influenza. They call it the Spanish flu or Spanish grippe.

* * *

Shepparton

'How are your hands?' Mr Sharman asks each of his boxers, checking each of them, carefully rolling them over, like their wrists are the fetlocks of racehorses. Wear and tear on the hands halfway through the tour needs careful management.

'The harder you hurt someone the harder it hurts you,' Mr Sharman says. Knowing Mr Sharman better now I can see how much regret he has squeezed into those words.

* * *

Seymour

Mr Sharman has a collection of new spruiking terms …

'Boxer or brawler? Let's find out what you're all about!'

'Come on! Come on! Give it a go! Give it a go!

'Survive three rounds and get three pounds. A round or two for a pound or two! Whoa!'

* * *

The boys have set up a competition among themselves to see who is the toughest. Various painful tests are set ...

A barefoot walk across a paddock full of bindies.

A bare-chested run down a hill infested with gorse.

Hanging off a tree for as long as it takes to be the last man hanging.

Juggling hot coals.

* * *

Mr Sharman, all of a sudden, has asked for more speed and flair in each of them; a few more tricks, more fire, more go-getting.

There is a lack of excitement sneaking into the tent.

* * *

Broadford

'What do we have here!' A man right in front of the ladder shouts at Mr Sharman.

'Cowards, bullies … picking on little boys and old men!'

'I can assure you, sir, there are only fair fights here,' says Mr Sharman.

'Isn't it strange ... odd ... this lot we have here?'

The man waves his hand across us up on the bridge, painting us all in guilt.

'The fighters who don't want to fight!'

'Boxing is a craft ... killing is different!' Mr Piggott shouts.

The man is not rattled ... Mr Sharman is …

'Killing is different, yes. Killing is necessary. Killing is needed to finish this thing off, to avenge, to pay back. I see you all up there! And I see my sons, one lost to us now, and I know for certain where you lot should be. I know what kind of fighting you should be doing.'

Mr Sharman jumps off the back of the bridge, disappearing through rows of tents.

Mr Piggott starts up beating the drum again. The boys file off into the very back of the tent.

Rud and I open up the tent flap and no-one from the crowd follows us in.

* * *

News that Bert has had a general breakdown and is in the Graythwaite Anzac Hostel to rest and recover. He is nervy and in a right state. Father is worried that he might try to harm himself.

* * *

Wallan

Aunt Adelaide writes warning me of the white plague. Tuberculosis! Tubercular soldiers are returning home from the cesspit trenches of Europe full of disease.

These Soldier Spreaders, as she calls them, are carelessly infecting their own families and others. I had best take care with all the dirty showground types I choose to keep company with. The government should detain all these men until all are proven healthy.

I don't remember Aunt Adelaide ever receiving any medical training.

* * *

I have noticed how many of the returned men with tuberculosis have built sleepouts on verandahs enclosed with dark canvas curtains. It is thought that the cool air helps treat the condition.

I also heard of a tubercular who, over the summer, cured himself by sunbathing naked beside a waterhole for the hottest two hours of every day.

* * *

Ballarat

Lester and Artie unleashed in another stew.

I see them out on the ground, pushing each other on the chest. Toe to toe, it's getting heated; perhaps the pretend bootmaker and the pretend farmhand are about to have a major disagreement. Then, it is on for young and old: the pushing turning to shouting, cursing and punching, followed by series of wrestles and headlocks.

The mugs crowd in. Dust kicks up.

Young boys in straw boater hats scream excitedly, 'Fight! fight!'

Mr Sharman calmly steps in, telling them the best way to sort this out is to sort it out in the tent.

The crowd roars with agreement.

Mr Sharman works the mugs all day. Telling them about the big fistic tournament on offer. A rumble. In all his touring experience Mr Sharman has never seen two young men so angry.

'Come watch the angry ants. Six o'clock!'

* * *

A good mob hangs around for the last house.

'Get your seat, get your seat. The program's full, the program's full!'

'Come over, come over. Where they wrestle, where they fight!'

Lester wins on points. According to Mr Piggott it has all the fighting ingredients we need: a fair fight, furious and fast.

That day we drag a reasonable crowd – the best we have had for Ballarat, which might rate as a fair gate at any other site.

* * *

Maryborough

The town's shopkeepers are always a mixed bunch, but wherever we are, each shop has a certain type serving behind the counter …

Bank tellers briskly re-lick their fingers after every tenth pound note they count.

Postmasters are efficient.

Bakers are plump, tired and grumpy.

Pharmacists count and pour their pills and potions coldly.

Butchers, big men with knives, are always the friendliest.

* * *

Aunt Adelaide writes about a returned soldier who was shot through the neck.

It is amusing to see him cheerfully whistling through the two holes. He can even blow out a match! He cannot speak that well but otherwise he looks quite fine.

* * *

Donald

A mother whose son was shot in the jaw handfed him liquid food for a year before he died earlier this week.

* * *

Ararat

An unhappy place. Wardens (half-mad themselves) from J ward, the mental hospital for the criminally insane, feel they have something they need to prove and they fight like demons.

* * *

Stawell

Unusual types or sad cases you often meet boarding in hotels …

The landlocked sea captain in Moree who never wants to see a drop of that evil blue stuff ever again.

The disgraced English lord who was rumoured to occupy a floor of the Golden Fleece Hotel and demanded every Friday a full silver service luncheon laid out in his private dining hall for twelve very important guests who never came.

Various wealthy old ladies who live with their three cats … always three … Cats who drink off the best china plates.

And here in Stawell, a returned serviceman. Returned from 1914. A VD case …

'Syphilis … from Egypt,' the nosey landlord tells me. 'Didn't even make it on to Gallipoli. Likes to keep his own company. Keep it quiet; I twigged the goose when I saw letters from the hospital at Langwarrin. Not a normal kind of hospital as I found out later. A local boy too; well, from one town over … Horsham. Can't go home, can he? The shame of it. That close to home and he just can't do it; no-one will ever go near him again.'

* * *

Horsham

We often talk about our own liaisons with the fairer sex. Today, Mr Piggott, Rud and Mr Sharman sit away from us so we can provide each other with filthy details, real, imagined and hard to verify …

Artie tells us how a girl invited him for a walk along the river at Brisbane. How she stopped by a tree suddenly lifting up her skirt.

Nick tells about a well-to-do housewife who appeared at her window in French lingerie, beckoning him to leave his bicycle on her front porch and call in for a special noontime luncheon.

I imagine away my virginity and tell them about summer swimming, an isolated cove only visited by boat, her salty swimsuit, the sounds of her and the cicadas travelling in the trees.

Hamilton

Lester knocks out three of a farmer's front teeth.

'That cur has a bad case of summer teeth,' Mr Piggott says.

'What?'

'Some a teeth here,' Mr Piggott points, 'and some a teeth over there,' he points again.

* * *

Portland

Mr Sharman is a prolific folder of things. He folds and refolds. Table napkins, newspapers, pound notes, show programs. All folded sharply, tightly, precisely. Out on the board he rolls up his shirt sleeves before starting his spiel. Folding perfectly over the width of his cuff, over and over exactly up and up his arms.

* * *

Port Fairy

To mark George's twentieth birthday, they sneak in some hard liquor and we all drink far too much of it. Mr Sharman, Mr Piggott and Rud Kee are dining with the show committee chair so we shouldn't be caught.

We are drunk! Swearing like forty bastards, singing, falling, stumbling around all over the place. Hungry, we raid the hotel's pantry, dropping things, breaking things. We are drunk! We are messier than a mad woman's breakfast.

* * *

Warrnambool

'Old Blueass' is what some of the mugs call Rud. 'There's no chance of sneaking in when the old blueass fly is buzzing around.'

* * *

Camperdown

Father writes a long letter about Bert. Doctor Horsley believes he needs extensive treatment for his worsening condition. Mother is at her wit's end. He is to be admitted to Broughton Hall.

I write back immediately. I am at pains to ensure that he does not end up with the lunatics; he is not one of those. Mr Sharman tells me that Broughton Hall has new repatriation wards for returned men separate from the civilian insane. I write a series of letters to the repatriation and hospital boards to ensure Bert is kept far enough away from the ordinarily insane.

* * *

Colac

What is it with redheads? The carrot tops, blueys, beetroots, brick tops, rustys, coppertops? They are always more fiery than other fellows. A gingernut and Lester go at it hammer and tongs.

* * *

Artie and Lester are in trouble for cycling out into the countryside with a bottle of cider, drinking it under a bridge then riding nearby dairy cows around and around a paddock as if they were horses.

* * *

Geelong

New reports in papers. The Hindenburg line has been retaken. One hundred thousand American doughboys are now into the action.

Ten million Germans are starving. They are said to be croaking with hunger.

* * *

Royal Melbourne Show

From Argentina, a man known as Hard Head José Hernández arrives at the tent.

Not much of a boxer as much as a man who can take any punishment metered out. He wins his fights by outlasting his opponents.

Mr Sharman had heard of him and had written earlier requesting the presence of Señor Hernández in the tent for the entire Melbourne Show.

It proves a popular choice. Every able-bodied man at the show lines up to take the test.

First off, the locals will have a go hurting their fists on his hard blunt head.

Mr Sharman talks George or Stan up after Hernández outlasts yet another fight.

'Come back last house and see George Cook, half-man–half-mule, punch Hard Head Hernández halfway back to the

Pampas. There's no bigger punch in Australia! If he can't do it no-one can!'

Last house.

George starts easy in the first around, moving Hernández around. Hernández has his guard down and lets George in.

After the first bell in his corner, Mr Piggott tells Hernández to have a go at George.

'I go, I go, ok, ok,' Hernández replies, then returns to the ring where he fights like a wet lettuce leaf.

George throws a round-the-corner uppercut, with all his weight over his toes, slamming into Hernández's head.

He falls to the ground. Shakes his head and stands again.

Mr Sharman as referee is right there. Counting him back up to his feet.

'I go, I go, ok, ok.'

More punches from George and again nothing.

Final round. There is not a punch in George's arsenal that is big enough to do the job. Stan is the same; nothing works. Every time Hernández falls, he bounces back up again, looking Mr Sharman in the eye: 'I go, I go, ok, ok.'

* * *

Later we discuss the pain threshold. What's hurt the most …

A good square kick in the nuts.

Dislocated shoulder.

The poking and re-poking of sore ribs.

Falling off a horse.

Breaking a femur. Then some clumsy cur bumping into it.

Walking across a patch of bindi-eyes in bare feet.

Hearing the missus give birth.

Death.

Mr Sharman believes its part-mind, part-body. Hernández was about his body – he must have no nerves in certain parts, or a disconnection between the body and the brain. Joe Grimm was different again – he trained with Tommy Burns and Jack Johnson before the Rushcutters Bay fight. Neither of them could knock him out – he just kept on getting back up screaming, 'I am Joe Grimm and I fear no man!' Mind over matter. Hernández is a freak of nature, the body; Grimm, a freak of the mind, the brain.

* * *

Bert is back home, but I get a letter from Aunt Adelaide who somehow has got wind that Bert was in Broughton Hall. She writes:

> *Bert must have been exposed to some terrible things and because of some faulty family history he has had a 'turn'. Most ANZACs who proved themselves to be a rather shock-proof bunch by way of their heroic deeds, have had no problem, so it must be that Albert has been somewhat predisposed to some mental instability that led him not to tolerate the heat of the battle as well as others.*
>
> Aunt Adelaide hopes that the stay in the lunatic alyssum will allow him to *'regain the captaincy of his soul'*.

* * *

Castlemaine

Lester comes up against a very crafty type – one of those boxers who has so many tricks to him that he couldn't even lie straight in bed.

'Outfox the fox,' Mr Sharman tells Lester at the break.

Lester can't and Mr Sharman adds Mr Fox to his book.

* * *

Bendigo

In the hotels, groups of returned men gather to drown their sorrows.

The flotsam and jetsam of war.

Wooden legs squeak. They cough and stare their far away stares.

They refer to each other by hard-earned nickname … Hoppy, Wingy, Shifty, Stumpy, Gunner, Hooky.

* * *

Reports German civilians are killing and eating horses in the streets.

Reports that sections of the German army have mutinied or deserted and are fighting their own in the streets.

* * *

Rumours that a man cured himself of near-death influenza by eating pages from the Bible; in particular, the more relevant passages from First Corinthians.

* * *

Kyneton

One of the bluestone quarrymen fights particularly well. Mr Sharman writes down a name in his book; it has been a while since he has done that.

* * *

Gisborne

A billboard on a chemist's wall. A large picture of people coughing … The words:

Why catch their influenza? You need not! Just carry Formamint with you and suck these delicious tablets whenever you are in danger of being infected by other people.

'Suck at least four or five a day.' So says Dr Hopkirk in his standard work 'Influenza', 'for in Formamint we possess the best means of preventing the infective processes which, if neglected, may lead to serious complication'.

Seeing that such complication often leads to pneumonia, bronchitis and other dangerous diseases it is surely worthwhile to protect yourself by this safe certain and inexpensive means. Protect the children too, for their delicate little organisms are very exposed to germ attack especially during school epidemics.

Attack the germs before they attack you!

Formamint, the germ-killing throat tablet.

* * *

'What is this all about then, this influenza?' George asks.

I explain how it passes through the air, on the breath, on conversation, on coughs and colds, on sneezes and handshakes.

'Gripes! Sounds frightening.'

'It is, especially if it arrives here.'

* * *

Morwell

More news of a victory …

Thanks to an audacious operation executed with great verve during the night, Australian troops have taken the wood and village of Mont St Quentin to the north of Peronne, thereby assuring the possession of an important strategic position, which commands Peronne and the loop of the Somme ...

* * *

Billy's mother has written to us about what is to be recorded on poor Billy's headstone at Villers-Bretonneux. It is such an honour to help choose. She said that we all knew him well and he always spoke fondly of us. He was especially fond of Archie, she said. Mr Sharman reads out her suggestion.

Gone is our Will we loved so dear, gone is his voice we loved to hear.

We are all crying. Mr Sharman is crying too. 'I think it's perfect, absolutely perfect,' he says as he leaves the room.

* * *

Traralgon

It has been very wet overnight. The town is full of talk. A mile out past the butter factory there is a ditch full of thousands of eels. A dairy farmer had seen them at four in the morning, slithering en masse across one of his paddocks. They had reached a roadside ditch and were unable to crawl back out and are slowly dying there. By the time we arrived, detouring from our early morning walk, the whole town is there. One half-staring, one half helping themselves, wading into the slimy slippery mess.

* * *

The four hundred and twenty-fourth official casualty list is published. The latest success at Mont St Quentin brings its grief. As usual I scan through the list to check for anyone I know. I see one or two.

* * *

Sale

A recruiting sergeant has arranged a parade of little girls to walk up and down the main street in white dresses with stencilled black messages across their pretty skirts …

My Daddy is fighting for me, will you fight for me?

* * *

On the train a returned serviceman left without his leg jokes with me: 'Only one leg to be pulled now, eh?'

* * *

Bairnsdale

'The bigger they are the harder they fall.'

Someone in the crowd talks back.

'No, the bigger they are the harder we fall!'

'That might be true, but get up here and prove us wrong,' Mr Sharman says.

* * *

At restaurant tables, some of the wounded men sit with those who have lost their own loved ones.

Salt and pepper shakers, knives and forks become machine

gun points, lines of charging troops and trenches. The place where their son, or their friend, or brother, lies dead shown across a dinner table.

'It was all very sudden; never felt a thing, madam. Actually, it was all very peaceful, really,' the returned soldier lies.

* * *

Orbost

Last night Lester had a bare-knuckle fight, three against one – he was ganged up on in the main street. He's come out on the wrong side of the ledger and it looks like he's been chewing on a mouthful of wasps.

* * *

Melbourne

Kangaroo Court. Lester, Stan, Artie, George get ten pound fines each for 'the Port Fairy Incident' as Mr Sharman calls it. A further five pounds each for foodstuffs consumed and broken crockery.

And I have, in Mr Sharman's words, 'also blighted my copybook' by going along with all this. I feel terrible and lose twenty quid.

More fines and money lost for 'unscheduled street fights'.

Lester gets a five pound fine for his late night fight in Orbost. He complains that he was set upon. Mr Sharman tells him he shouldn't have been in such a setting to be set upon in the first place.

* * *

A few of us visit a menswear shop in Bourke Street. Each of us has a certain kind of dress sense …

Mr Piggott is a belt and braces man.

Nick likes to show off.

Rud wears his clothes thin before buying anything new.

Artie dresses well, but let's himself down in grooming; he is the most likely to have a shirt tail left hanging out.

Mr Sharman is both neat and sensible. He is dressed in the first suit he ever brought from Scharenberg's, Fitzmaurice Street, Wagga. The old suit Mick Shaw the bookie bought for him and another for Ted Moon the jockey after they came through for him.

I follow fashions middle path.

* * *

We hear that people apply a mixture of formalin, eucalyptus and creosote to the body to keep the flu virus at bay. What pungent odours!

'Might as well go throw yourself in a sheep dip!' Mr Piggott scoffs.

* * *

Night Watch wins the Melbourne Cup, but we don't go because of rumours of the flu.

* * *

New signs at Cole's Book Arcade …

Cole's predictions for the year 2000:

The world will be federated in politics, in religion, and in language. And men will wonder why they were fools so long. If all men throughout the world were better acquainted with one another there would be little or no war for then only the most wicked would need to be kept in order.

'Well, I hope Mr Cole is right,' says Artie in a weary voice, worn out and sounding much older than it should.

CHAPTER TWELVE

Peace

Camden

Again, each morning, there is the sound of my brother Bert retching, trying to clear the gas from his lungs.

* * *

Headlines …

German delegation arrives in France to conclude an armistice.

Streets are full with people mafficking.

Sedate businessman dance in the street with their employees. People skip arm in arm.

* * *

More news …

Premature result, armistice not yet signed.

* * *

Headlines …

Foch states his terms.

The Kaiser abdicates.

An effigy of him burns in the main street.

* * *

Monday evening.

Bells at schools and chapels are ringing.

The blasting of whistles.

Youths form a tin-can band, marching march around and around the town until well past midnight.

* * *

Tuesday morning.

Businesses put up closed signs.

Lusty cheers are given to the donors of lollies that are about to be scrambled for.

Hotels are Closed by Authority.

Confetti in limitless quantities.

An owner of a motorcar drapes it in flags, fills it with girls and does at least three dangerous high speed circumnavigations of the town.

We tie tricolours to our buttonholes and go for a picnic. Even Bert is cheery.

The band plays a selection of patriotic airs …

People singing their lungs out.

* * *

Peace!

I cannot believe it!

I am almost dizzy with happiness.

It is over. Finally ...

The war is over!

What a God-sent Christmas box for the world!

In Melbourne crowds derail a Carlton tram. Another tram, also overloaded, crashes through the Australian Electricity Company windows.

The four hundred and fortieth official casualty list is published. Names run down the page like rungs on a long ladder of misery.

Our war is over and so is theirs.

* * *

The *Sydney Morning Herald* ...

Every man, woman and child came into the city to 'celebrate', but they came in such numbers that they defeated their own purpose. At 9 o'clock, in Martin Place and Moore Street and in Pitt and George Streets adjoining, the crowds were so dense that no-one could move. They could only stand and cheer ...

The scenes of joy and excitement were necessarily not unattended by pathetic incidents. The reaction from the anxiety and tension which in some cases had been bravely borne almost ever since the outbreak of war by grey-headed parents in some cases proved too much, and they were overcome by their emotions ...

* * *

The war is over but the night visits from Bert continue ...

Shells, sausages and intestines, dead men killed twice.

Archie, are you listening?

Bayonets and eyes like prawns, a horse's sigh, rats and gas masks …

During the day he pours down the grog quicker than you could tip it down a drain.

* * *

The farm is falling apart. My father too old. The Blackmore brothers: one legless, one with a leg bent and the other quickly descending into lunacy.

* * *

There are a lot of returned men, just like my brother, standing alone on beaches, cliffs, in rowboats out in rough weather, alone, out in the open.

Or

Hiding in the dark underneath hedges, bridges, basements.

The war is over but now is their evil hour.

Afraid, confused, angry, weak, tired.

Staring off into the distance, looking away from the eyes of loved ones.

All tangled up too tight or starting to unravel.

Muttering.

Or

Screaming out aloud, screaming inside.

Pulling themselves together, then falling apart.

Putting on a brave face, then hanging out tears.

Trembling in fear, shaking in anger.

Off their tucker, hitting the grog.

There are strange hells within the minds war made.

* * *

My brother's hair has gone grey, and he is only twenty-eight.

* * *

Death notices …

Driver Henry Perkins. Tuberculosis of lungs and poison gas (war).

Percy Griffin. Suffered the effects of gas, haemorrhage brought on by consumption.

Fred Baker found dead. Strychnine poisoning self-administered.

Before Christmas, Bert, Frank and I are putting together the Christmas tree and its decorations. The red strips of crepe paper first.

Bert screaming, 'No, no, no!'

He curls up under the dining room table, sobbing.

It is the red crepe paper. It reminds poor old Bert of bits of blown-up men, their flesh hanging in dead trees or over the side timbers of rough trenches.

We both hold him. We hug him tight. We all hold on to each other as if the world has toppled off its axis and is tumbling through space, which, for us, in this world right at this moment, it is.

1919

CHAPTER THIRTEEN

Spanish influenza

Influenza is ripping through the country. It hops, it skips, it jumps, between the young and old mostly, family to family.

Lucy Baker, nine years old, influenza,

Herbert Basely, ninety-eight, influenza,

Mary Whitehorse, thirty years of age, influenza.

Her daughter Emily, six, also influenza.

Racecourses and showgrounds are being converted into hospitals.

* * *

New measures to control the Spanish flu:

Closure of public places, schools,

Cancellation of agricultural shows,

The compulsory wearing of masks on trams, trains and ferries,

It is an offence to remain in a public bar for longer than five minutes.

Road blocks between New South Wales and Victoria.

* * *

A letter to the paper complaining about young boys inside the Camden confectionery store, *'expectorating all about the place'.*

* * *

The compulsory wearing of gauze masks makes us all look like highwaymen.

The Camden Shire Council's Nuisance Inspector is severely troubled at the practice of people kissing incoming passengers at the railway station.

* * *

Quack remedies …

A towel soaked in hot vinegar placed over the face.

Snuff.

A mixture of ginger, soda, sugar in milk.

A good strong dose of whiskey.

* * *

It doesn't do any good. It is as if it only dies when we die ... There are stories of people finding the dead, blackened bodies. Corpses that look burned black due to cyanosis of the skin. Stories of black bodies sitting up in beds and on floors discovered by the town's helpful neighbours and young lads sent around to check.

* * *

The war is over but the battle of loss and sorrow has just begun. Groups of women, mothers, wives, begin to plant avenues of oak trees along straight roads before and after the approaches to towns and villages where their husbands, brothers and sons once walked.

Thousands of women now without their promised sweethearts look forward to a life of empty rooms, cold beds and lonely spinsterhood.

* * *

Bert visiting ...

'You know how long we sat under those bombs, Nipper?

'Seven weeks!'

Seven weeks, seven days, day and night, forty-nine days, forty-nine nights, one thousand, one hundred and seventy-six hours, seventy thousand five hundred and sixty minutes and us crouching under all that … dying or waiting to die and hoping we will die quick so it all stops, it all just stops.'

I have started a letter-writing storm with the Repatriation Department. Frank is having a lot of trouble with his stump, phantom pains; I am seeking to have his incapacity raised and see him get a decent pension. Bigger arguments about Bert: the department trying to say that his troubles are not WS (war service) related but more alcohol related. I write letter after letter to clarify the matter.

* * *

A returned soldier recently demobbed walked into a Sydney menswear store to receive his free civvies, handed over his chit and left his uniform behind. Left it right there crumpled on the middle of the shop floor, never ever wanting to wear it again.

* * *

There are courses for returned men.

Boot making.

Driving.

Auto-machinery courses.

There is also millinery for the widows.

CHAPTER FOURTEEN

Endings

Mr Sharman has asked to meet me at Narellan mid-morning. I drag myself up the main street.

I hardly recognise anyone now.

Frank Cashmere lost an arm, the blacksmiths where he bent steel is closed and the fire is cold.

Stanley Columbine is not at the Bank of New South Wales … Bullecourt … the manager tells me.

On the street and the dark underneath of cold verandahs I hear people explaining the absence of friends, brothers.

They attribute their loss to a strange place name we all now know too well:

Beersheba …

Passchendaele …

Fromelles …

Eddy Creese is gone … Messines ...

James Dixon still over there with the occupying forces.

Jack Scott is convalescing in England his father tells me.

William Sinclair was not so lucky … St Perrone …

Gordon Fife is in England, receiving skin grafts around the hole in the middle of his face. Amy Fairburn is stepping out with someone else.

I see Thomas Woodward back at the printers and he looks to be in one piece.

Billy O'Shea limps around up the back of the bakery.

Arthur Morrison at the telegraph office told me that Roy Shennan died of wounds after third Ypres and John Morrow went down at Villers-Bretonneux.

* * *

There is Mr Sharman sitting in the far corner of the hotel. The table is covered with his books, paperwork and empty beer glasses.

By his look I can tell it's going to be bad news.

Flu regulations have closed every agricultural show down until authorities are confident the pandemic is over. There is speculation that this could mean months or longer, even a year. The papers this morning had confirmed that all state borders are to remain closed.

'The rug's being pulled out from under us, Archie. No touring this year, maybe none next year … maybe even longer.'

I am needed to help him wind up the accounting side of things.

'Beaten by a bug, a tiny, tiny little bug.' He tries to measure it between his two held-up fingers. 'Who would have thought after the war and everything we have been through over the last four years and that's what stopping us.'

He has ordered more beer and there are two glasses. It looks and smells like he might have already had quite a few.

The avid teetotaller ... becoming softly drunk and it's not even noon.

Mr Sharman ... after five years of knowing him and he is still a conundrum ...

'Had a great tour planned. Back to the big houses, the New England run, Easter Show, the Queensland Show Train, the Riverina, trucks through Victoria ... lots of the old scrappers writing to me, asking me when we are coming. You should have seen who I had set up for the boards: Stan; good old Rud, of course, his shoulders mended and back in the ring again; and Tommy, well, he's back from France and raring to go; also some good mission kids and a young up-and-comer from our boys home right here in Camden. And then there's Nick and George and Mr Piggott as well. The old gang all back together.'

'Except for Billy,' I say.

'Except for Billy.' Mr Sharman sighs. 'Sorry.'

Mr Sharman looks away.

'Poor Billy, God rest him.'

His wet blue eyes blurring behind his taped-up reading glasses.

He stands.

'Excuse me, Archie, I have to use the men's.'

A firm and friendly hand on my shoulder.

'Lots to go through; do you want a sandwich? A pie? Anything?'

'No.'

'Back in a tick.'

The book of names is open on the table in front of me. The

notebook he was always writing or reading intently. All the troupe's names … all the fighters, the challengers, the ones to keep an eye on … from all over the place … all in alphabetical order.

Sharman's Book of Men.

I pick it up.

Ticks beside the names of those employed as part of the troupe. I see my name and address (under B for Blackmore). Asterisks beside the names of those who joined up and went to war. More than three quarters have these asterisks, hanging there like stars, with us waiting for all the names to come back.

Mr Sharman has written WW next to the names of those who have been war wounded.

Neatly ruled lines through the names of the boys who are not coming back.

Under D and crossed through is Les Darcy.

Under S … Billy ...

They are, even in death, still all Sharman's men.

'We both have our lists don't we, Archie?'

Mr Sharman is standing behind me.

'My memory isn't good as yours; but you remember all of them up here, don't you?' he says, softly tapping his head.

'Yes.'

'Every single one?

'Yes.'

'The name of every one of them?'

'Yes.'

'And the ones we all have lost, the whole country's lost … that's another list you keep, isn't it?

'Yes,' I say.

'From the papers, the casualty lists I have seen you read every day since this whole thing started. You remember every name right across the whole country, don't you? Every single one from the start of this whole thing right through to the finish?'

'Yes.'

... How could I forget any of them ...

'From the book ... ' I say, 'from your book, how many are gone? Out of the thousand or so?'

'Billy and one hundred and sixty-eight,' Mr Sharman says.

... This is the same number as the tally I have kept in my head all this time. Our grim ledgers balance ...

'All gone ... Mr Sharman ... so many of them ... taken from us ... never coming back,' I say.

I am trying not to cry, but it overwhelms me.

He is closer.

'Archie, just remember them as they were. Remember how well they all measured up.'

He has his arm around my shoulder.

'Reach back now and shake their hands. Remember every one of them, Archie. Gather them up and for their sakes never forget them, not a single one of them.'

Our falling tears spot across the open notebook.

Mr Sharman grabs my hand.

'Death divides us, Archie ... but memory ... memory stays. Remember them and they will stay right here with us.'

Epilogue

What happened to Sharman's men portrayed here? What happened to Grimes, Green and Kee? What about Hughes, Baker, McIntosh and Mannix? What mark did they leave? How did they measure up? Their lives now lived, how are they now remembered?

Firstly, I want to identify the fictionalised characters in this novel – there are several. However, as you will see in the following profiles, most were real people. I used fictional characters as narrative devices to depict real-life people and events.

Archie Blackmore is a fictional character, for storytelling purposes. I needed a 'nearby narrator' who was close enough to Jimmy Sharman to observe and describe his unique character and his reactions to events. Archie's disability (cerebral palsy) means he could remain with Sharman throughout the war. His powerful memory and mind enables accurate descriptions of people and events. Archie is based on a Massey University student hostel friend of mine, Craig D, who has cerebral palsy, is courageous and has a powerful mind and memory. There is also an Archie Blackmore in Queensland who is the son of good friends and he was born when I started writing this novel; thanks for allowing me to use your name!

As outlined in the statement on the portrayal of real-life people and First Nations people (see the appendices), all First Nations characters are not based specifically on any First Nations individual associated with Jimmy Sharman's Boxing Troupe during World War I.

Billy Spiers is a fictional character, in part based on the letters written by Australians serving overseas. Billy's character is an important narrative device to describe the pressure on larger, fit men to enlist. I also see Billy as the typical young Australian of the time and through his death I have, in a small way, expressed the enormous loss felt during the war and also my gratitude to those who served.

Archie Blackmore's family members were narrative devices to describe fighting at Gallipoli and on the Western Front and the trauma that came home.

Now, let's look at the real-life characters portrayed in the novel and how they lived the rest of their lives …

Billy Grimes won the Australian feather, light and welterweight titles between 1922 and 1927. He ended his career in the boxing tents. He retired from boxing and invested most of his savings in a travelling hardware business that visited farmers' wives on isolated stations across outback New South Wales. He went bust during the Depression. He worked in hotels, as a garage hand and at the Newcastle docks until he died from a heart attack aged forty-nine in 1952.

Jackie Green was a triple title holder, winning the flyweight title of 1916 at the age of fifteen. He also won the bantam and featherweight title in a seventy-four-fight career. He died in 1975 aged seventy-four.

Eric Barnes (aka Frank Burns) was an Australian middleweight champion. His son, George Barnes, was the 1950 welterweight champion.

In 1915 Tom Uren won the welterweight title. In 1917 he won the middleweight title fighting Fred Kay and went on to win the title another seven times. He suffered permanent double vision after fighting. In the 1920s, with his good looks and skipping prowess, Uren became a 'matinee idol', appearing at picture halls where large crowds of women were served free tea and biscuits while they closely watched Uren's afternoon training sessions. He managed a hotel in Orange before losing heavily in the Depression. He worked at Cockatoo dock until his death in 1954.

In 1915 Jack Johnson lost his title to Jess Willard at the Vedado Racetrack in Havana, Cuba; knocked out in the 26th round of the scheduled 45-round fight. Johnson constantly flouted conventions regarding the social and economic 'place' of Blacks in American society. He enjoyed expensive hobbies such as car racing and tailored clothing. Once, when he was pulled over for a $50 speeding ticket (a large sum at the time), he gave the officer a $100 bill; the officer protested that he couldn't make change for that much, and Johnson told him to keep the change, as he was going to make his return trip at the same speed. Johnson was married three times. All of his wives were white, a fact that caused considerable controversy at the time. Johnson continued fighting professionally until 1938. Jack Johnson died in a car accident in Franklin, North Carolina after racing angrily from a diner that refused to serve him. He was 68 and had no descendants.

Nugget Frater was a dairy farmer in the Townsville area who challenged boxers in Sharman's tent in the 1920s. The Osh Kosh letter in the novel was written in the late 1920s and is reproduced word for word from a local newspaper, except it was entitled 'Firpo of the North'.

Paddy Piggott was, according to newspaper comments by Jimmy Sharman, an Irishman who joined Jimmy Sharman's troupe in 1920. Jimmy Sharman remarked, with some concern, that Paddy used to gamble away too much on racehorses. In the novel he is fictionalised to provide a point of view about war that was needed to explore key themes about duty, war, courage and cowardice. He was not a Boer War veteran.

Legendary showman David Meekin started his sideshow act in the 1920s after trying to operate a boxing troupe in competition to Sharman. David Meekin developed a series of successful 'in and out shows' with many of the acts described in the novel. He 'exhibited' Ubangi Chilliwingi, a Pygmy woman from Cape Province. Their professional association over a generation established a Pygmy troupe that became famous. Meekin promised show crowds to 'Search the Universe for Strange People, Freaks and Novelties for the Entertainment of Show Patrons'. Meekin died on 19 March 1966 in hospital at North Sydney. Ubangi remained in Australia until her death, cared for by the extended 'showie family'.

Prime Minister Billy Hughes remained Prime Minister until 1922 and served as a government minister until 1949 when he left the Labor Party and joined the Liberal Party. A stalwart of Anzac Day marches, he died in 1952 aged ninety. Large numbers of ANZACs stood by as the funeral cortege passed by. A controversial figure all his life; to some a great patriot, to others a renegade. Overall, he remains one of Australia's more important politicians for his contribution to the early Labor movement and as a nation's wartime leader.

Archbishop Daniel Mannix was arguably one of Australia's most revered and reviled public figures. Mannix burned most of his personal documents and wrote short letters, so that, in his words, 'posterity could not analyse his soul'.

At a St Patrick's Day function in 1918 he did not doff his biretta as the national anthem played, leading to calls for his deportation. Mannix became a lightning rod for protestant bigotry. In 1920 he attempted to land in his native Ireland when the English forced him to land in Cornwall, England. Mannix quipped that it was 'the greatest victory the Royal Navy has had since Jutland and without the loss of a single British sailor'.

Although considered politically naïve and intellectually shallow, Mannix was quick witted and strongly led his constituency. He was regarded by many as 'one of the four wisest men in the world'. He oversaw improvements to churches and schools. He founded a number of educational societies.

Later he made comments about Hiroshima and communism that raised a few hackles. Mannix continued his subversive ways, often putting the postage stamp of the reigning monarch deliberately upside down on letters. He often prayed for five hours a day. He would walk from Raheen in Kew, through Collingwood to St Patrick's, wearing a frock coat and with a stick, handing out coins to the needy. After the death of Hughes' daughter, Mannix wrote a letter of condolence and Hughes visited Mannix. The two men maintained respectful communication until Hughes died.

On Melbourne Cup Day in 1963, after his annual sweepstake, Mannix collapsed. He died the next day aged ninety-nine.

Tommy Burns retired from boxing in 1920. He was involved with a number of business ventures until a religious calling led to his ordination as a minister in 1948. He died of a heart attack in 1955.

Hugh Donald (Huge Deal) McIntosh ran away from home at age seven and made his early fortune supplying pies to race tracks and prize fights. McIntosh made a huge profit from the Burns–Johnson fight and owned numerous theatres, newspapers and houses in Australia and England. He had a reputation for coarse language and was unscrupulousness. But his open, attractive personality aided his ambition to force his way into respectable society. His generosity and extravagance quickly became legendary. He contributed liberally to hospitals and other charities. By the mid-1920s McIntosh's luck had run out. He sold the *Sunday Times* in 1927 and was in heavy debt. Other schemes such as vaudeville production, selling angora rabbits, a cake shop, boxing promotion, guesthouses and a Fleet Street milk bar came to nothing. He died penniless in London on 2 February 1942 without descendants.

Reginald Leslie Baker (Snowy) (1884–1953) was a successful sportsman in many codes: swimming, rugby union, rowing and boxing. He developed a successful mail order coaching book and published *Snowy Baker's Magazine*. With HD McIntosh he operated Australian stadium boxing and also managed Les Darcy until he stowed away to the USA in 1916. Baker moved to the USA and starred in movies, then managed the Riviera Country Club at Santa Monica until his death in 1953.

George Cook (1898–1943) was nineteen when he toured with Sharman and as described in the Dubbo incident under military age. He was heavyweight champion of Australia and had one hundred and six fights around the world. Here is footage of him training: https://simple.wikipedia.org/wiki/George_Cook

Rud Kee (Cheong Lee) fought in Sharman's tent in the second half of World War I. He left the troupe during its temporary break-up in 1919 because of the flu epidemic. Back in Sydney, Taggie Young again challenged Rud to fights via local newspapers. They fought a furious fight at the Hippodrome, with Rud winning on points. The fight was so brutal it was reported that both fighters had faces like 'Pak-a-pu tickets'. The fight made the pair drawcards in the Sydney professional boxing scene. Rud fought Wave Keike, the Queensland featherweight champ, losing in a close decision.

Rud's last professional fight was a return bout with Taggie. Rud was suffering rheumatism in his shoulder, making one arm useless. He fought Taggie, who had returned from the Philippines ill with malaria. The fight was declared by the promoter as a no-contest. Rud, furious, vowed not to fight for the promoter again. Rud returned to Jimmy Sharman's troupe, fighting until the 1930s when his collarbone was broken at the Gladstone Show after he was dumped into the sawdust by a larger opponent. It was at this point he became Jimmy Sharman's permanent ticket seller and doorman. Known by many a tent visitor as an eagle-eyed and tenacious doorman, Rud famously once refused the Governor-General of Queensland access to the tent.

During the World War II, Rud and Jimmy Sharman ran a Sydney coal merchant business. After the war, Rud had a significant share in the business with Jimmy Sharman, the two being firm friends and business partners. When Jimmy Sharman (Senior) passed the business on to Jimmy Sharman (Junior) (or 'Young Jimmy') in the 1950s, Rud continued working for him. After touring business ended, Rud lived at Jimmy's property in Narellan and was provided with a lifetime annuity of 260 pounds per annum by Jimmy Sharman. He led a solitary life, never marrying and having no descendants.

He remained at the house until the mid-1970s when he moved to a nursing home. He was a favourite of nurses and residents. He passed away in 1980 aged eighty-four, taking much of the history of the troupe with him. Apparently an avid diarist, he recorded all aspects of the tour as it travelled … his diaries were never found.

Jimmy Sharman was born in Narellan in 1887 and was the fifth child of thirteen children. He had an interest in boxing at an early age. As described in the novel his first fight was at the Campbellfield races. He worked in the Riverina as a labourer and met a Mr Symonds, who provided early business mentoring to young Jimmy. Symonds was later a director of Peter's Ice Cream (J Sharman Jr NLA verbal history). He married and settled in the Riverina, primarily at Te Mora. He fought Jack Carter in Wagga Wagga on 1 January 1912, accidentally injuring him. Sharman visited Carter in hospital for months. Sharman then concentrated on fight promotion and developed the boxing tent operation.

Trove searches help explain Jimmy Sharman's development as a fight promoter and the development of the boxing tent format. Sharman is first recorded as refereeing a fight on 19 June 1912. He promoted a fight at the Star Theatre in Te Mora on 8 January

1913, then promoted a fight with the 'Page Midgets' on 18 February 1913. The first tent show was (according to Sharman personal papers, Te Mora local history and internet searches) was at Ardlethan in 1912.

Sharman's last fight was against Jack Smith for a Te Mora hospital fundraiser; he won after three rounds on 18 December 1919, raised 200 pounds personally and was made a life member of the hospital. During the war Sharman was a regular correspondent to the *Referee* (1886–1939), a boxing magazine based in Sydney, and was referred to as the 'Up Country' correspondent. He reported on good fighters he encountered at the tent as well as where his tents were successful and where he was touring next.

Sharman restarted full interstate touring in 1920. He received eye damage after an accident with cleaning fluid at the Pastoral Hotel in Wagga Wagga in 1922. He later used truck transport around this time, changing operations from accommodating the troupe in hotels to using a 'living-out' tent – boxers ate and slept in an annex tent next to the fight tent on site, travelling at night for shows in new towns the next day. He supported Roy Bell, another boxing tent promoter, after he suffered burns in a road accident and helped restart him. Many famous boxers started or finished in Sharman's tent. Film stars such as Errol Flynn and Victor McLaglen also trained or fought in Sharman's tent. He continued touring until handing over his business to 'Young Jimmy'. He would accompany his son on a number of trips, renewing friendships and quietly watching proceedings. He and Rud ran a coal delivery business during World War II. Jimmy died in 1965 aged seventy-eight and was buried in Camden with full Catholic Rites.

Before learning the business, Jimmy Sharman (Jimmy Sharman 2 or Young Jimmy) had a successful rugby league career with Wests. He continued touring until 1972, with the final show held at Shepparton after changes to laws about the number of fights a boxer could have in set time periods made it difficult to tour all shows each week.

Young Jimmy invested in dodgem cars and other sideshow rides and toured until the mid-1980s. Young Jimmy died in Sydney in 2007.

One of Young Jimmy's sons, 'Jimmy 3', became a successful stage director, producing many successful stage shows including *Jesus Christ Superstar* and the *Rocky Horror Picture Show*, and wrote *Blood and Tinsel* in 2008, which outlines Sharman family history.

An unknown Australian Soldier.
Killed in the war of 1914–1918.
Known unto God.
He is all of them and he is one of us.
Tomb of the Unknown Soldier, Canberra

Appendices

Portrayal of real-life people and/or First Nations people in this work

Storytellers often tell the stories of others. They are often compelled to tell these stories to correct an incorrect narrative or to retell the story so that it is not lost. I wrote this story for both reasons; it is also, I hope, so that it can teach us about the past and inform us about the future.

Throughout my life in New Zealand (Aotearoa) and Australia I have thought a great deal about how people and society change, particularly in terms of colonialism and First Nations people. My experience suggests that we need to keep sharing stories and talking, no matter how uncomfortable these discussions can be, as there is so much to reconcile. We must face the past and face the future together. A Māori whakatauki, or proverb, is 'He Waka Eke Noa', which is often translated as 'We are all in this waka [canoe] together.'

I have spent fifteen years of my life telling this story. It comes from the best intentions. It comes after an enormous amount of self-reflection and discussion with others and it also comes from a family – my family – and my life, which has involved a huge amount of work, thought and care as well as sacrifices.

I retell this story third hand, as a visitor to this country and with over one hundred years now passed. With all the characters now deceased, I have relied on historical reference data (archival, media of the time and research publications) to develop portraits of the characters and occurrences of the time; with that there may be some unintended omissions or inaccuracies. I cannot seek permission from persons portrayed in the work so I can only 'sketch up' their persona based on limited information. So, I have extended their character on what I do know, in a faithful manner. I can only ask that relatives, historians and readers understand the challenges in retelling a time where the writer was not present.

This story is primarily about Jimmy Sharman's activities during World War I. It depicts real-life persons and events. This story is based on extensive archival and historical research, it is a true story, fictionalised in parts in its telling. The endnotes detail what is fiction and what is fact, for the most part it is fact. Eighty to ninety per cent of the people and events that are depicted in the work are real, which is extraordinary, and drove me for over fifteen years, while I raised two children (with others), to work full or part time to write this work of over 94,000 words.

During World War I, Aboriginal and Torres Strait Islanders or First Nations people were boxers in Jimmy Sharman's tent. (I use at different times the term 'First Nations'.) Some depictions of First Nations boxers and Jimmy Sharman were made before further research was undertaken. There are still commonly held beliefs based on these depictions present today. Emeritus Professor of History at La Trobe University, Richard Broome AM, researched First Nations boxers and boxing troupes and offers a clear picture of the life of a First Nations boxer and Jimmy Sharman's Boxing Troupe. I have attempted to provide this more accurate portrayal here. As already outlined, it's important to tell the most accurate story about real-life people in this work. I also portray the First Nations boxers through an observer (Archie Blackmore); I am not telling the story from their perspective.

To portray First Nations people in this work I read and applied the concepts, principles and protocols of the Australia Council for the Arts' *Protocols for Using First Nations Cultural and Intellectual Property in the Arts.* I refer to this as ICIP. I also sought further legal and cultural/creative advice on the portrayal of real people and First Nations people.

In applying ICIP to this work I considered the 10 principles in the ICIP to fulfil my commitment to the protocols with respect to my work.

I pay my respects to all Aboriginal and Torres Strait Islander people, especially those associated with Jimmy Sharman's Boxing Troupe and who are broadly represented in this novel.

I acknowledge all Aboriginal and Torres Strait Islander people have authority to have custodianship of appropriate cultural knowledge and history in relation to their unceded lands. I acknowledge the importance of respect for all Indigenous people of Australia in owning and holding of stories and cultural knowledge from their own nations and clans.

In terms of these acknowledgements this work contains no cultural knowledge of any Indigenous people of Australia. Further, some Nations or clans claim or consider the names or images of their people as culturally important. When I researched the First Nations boxers involved with Jimmy Sharman's Boxing Troupe during World War I found no information about their names and identities. Only one is named and information on him is limited to boxing only; I could not confirm his nation or clan. Given these points and on advice, I have not named the First Nations boxer in this work. I have also not provided any personal identifying descriptions to this individual. Instead I have developed a number of character profiles of First Nations boxers based on Richard Broome's accurate research ('Theatres of Power, Tent Boxing circa 1910–1970' and Sideshow Alley, Broome and Jackomos). I have also sought legal and cultural creative advice to ensure my depiction of First Nations characters is a fair and accurate depiction.

While researching Jimmy Sharman's Boxing Troupe during World War I, I found some compelling stories about real-life people which are best told by others. As a writer I am now moving on to other stories in other lands and other times, but I hope to foster these stories with the people who are closer to them or could tell them with more authenticity.

One of the final principles of the Australia Council for the Arts' *Protocols for Using First Nations Cultural and Intellectual Property in the Arts* is benefit sharing. A donation has been made to the Indigenous Literary Foundation.

If you wish to discuss any aspects of this statement or the work overall, please contact me via the publisher.

I want to close now by going back to the start of this statement. Storytellers often tell the stories of others. They are often compelled to tell these stories to correct an incorrect narrative or to tell the story so that it is not lost. Given these risks I still had to decide whether I was the best person to tell this story. I did decide it was me. I have tried my absolute best; I hope I have done this story justice. I know it is a great story and I hope it is well told, and that it is shared and reflected upon.

Notes on depiction of social norms

As outlined at the fore pages of this novel the depiction of real-life persons and others as well as the events they react to closely reflects the social norms of the times portrayed. These may not be considered appropriate today. These are not the views of the author. Although the information may not reflect current understanding, it is provided in an historical context.

It is useful, especially for younger readers of this work, to discuss the five particular types of depiction in this work.

Firstly, the extreme racism First Nations people faced at this time. In this work it is described via dialogue and actions observed by the narrator as he observes others or reads media. Rud Kee and Taggie Young also faced extreme racism as Chinese men. People of colour or from different racial backgrounds – in particular, African-American Boxer Jack Johnson – faced extreme racism. Racist language such as name calling, institutional racism, racist actions and perspectives were and are vicious tools of oppression. This novel depicts how these people, particularly through the sport of boxing, challenged racism head on.

Secondly, there was significant prejudice towards Germans, Turks and the Irish because of events during World War I. There was significant prejudice directed towards Roman Catholics and the Church of England generated by the conscription debate. There was also significant prejudice towards people with disabilities as portrayed by what happens to Archie's character. This novel has a focus on these prejudices, as the characters in this novel would have been significantly impacted by these particular social norms.

Thirdly, there is some violence portrayed in this work. Boxing was regarded as a noble sport and a demonstration of manliness and courage. Fighting or violence in other settings or forms was a common way to assert dominance or resolve issues. Jimmy Sharman was renowned for operating a clean, fair and safe sporting event. This work reflects this fact as well as describing the wider violence prevalent at the time, but it does not condone it.

Fourthly, there was little interaction between the boxers and women and overall, in wider society, interactions between men and women were generally limited to family groups, church or work. Women were often home based and usually formed close relationships with men as part of a courtship process and then marriage. The work depicts the women involved in the conscription debate; however, the lack of female characters depicted generally reflects the life of a travelling boxing troupe as well as the role of women and the social norms of the time portrayed.

Lastly there are descriptions of war and in particular post-traumatic stress disorder (PTSD) (shellshock). There were misunderstood, cruel assumptions made about shellshock, some of which are made in this work. There are also graphic descriptions of war experiences in this work. These descriptions are used to examine the concepts of duty, courage and cowardliness as well as the effects of war.

In order to inform and examine the full context of Jimmy Sharman's activity during World War I, I based this work on carefully undertaken, extensive and accurate research. This was done to outline how Jimmy Sharman successfully navigated through this extraordinary time. It is always useful to reflect on the societal norms of the past, compare them to today and think about where we want to see them in our future.

Notes on sources

In order to provide an accurate and vivid account of real people and events that occurred well over 100 years ago, research for this novel has been extensive. I recognise the works and authors who guided me in writing this novel in the acknowledgements section of this book.

Source information is listed in the bibliography and the endnotes which follow. Source information was obtained by researching works by others, newspaper or other media articles, letters to the editor, archival material, and search engines, in particular, Trove via National Library Australia. I also acknowledge that researching of archival material managed by the New South Wales Library was important to this novel's historical accuracy.

Further, Trove via the NLA and the New South Wales Library archival material enabled my discovery that Sharman did not enlist and continued to operate the boxing troupe throughout the war, which is the most substantial theme depicted in this novel.

In the novel, source information such as a media article or from another source (not composed by the author) is displayed in italics. Some may be quotes from works listed as text in the references. Italics also indicates text from sources other than the writer such as Trove via the NLA or archival material. Characters letters are sometimes in italics to signal to the reader it is a letter.

The purpose of the notes is to allow readers to follow up on additional information not for accurate attribution as the material often occurred in multiple sources.

Again, I acknowledge the work of authors who I relied on to

develop this work and recognise that their work, combined with my writing, storytelling, collection and curation, has allowed an important Australian story to be told and is a great legacy of these authors.

If you wish to know more about the sources and their use, please contact the author via the publisher.

References

Adam-Smith, Patsy, *The ANZACs*, Nelson Publishers, 1978.

ANU, Australian Dictionary of Biography Online.

Baker, 'Snowy', *Snowy Bakers Magazine*, 1914, State Library of NSW.

BoxRec.com

Broome, Richard, 'Theatres of Power Tent Boxing 1910–1970', 1996.

Broome, Richard, 'Aboriginal boxers and social control in Australia', seminar paper, 1979.

Broome, Richard, Alick Jackomos, *Sideshow Alley*, Allen and Unwin, 1998.

Carlyon, Les, *The Great War*, Macmillan, 2006.

Carthew, N, *Voices from the Trenches: Letters to home*, New Holland Publishers, 2002.

Coleman, Emmet, Editor, *The Temperance Songbook*, Wolfe Publishing, 1972.

Corris, Peter, *Lords of the Ring*, Cassell Australia, 1979.

Drane, Robert, *Fighters by Trade: Highlights of Australia boxing*, ABC Books, 2008.

Facey, Albert, *A Fortunate Life*, Puffin, 1981.

Greaves, Geoff, *The Circus Comes to Town: Nostalgia of Australian big tops*, AH and AW Reed, 1980.

Hook, Alex, *World War I Day by Day*, Grange Books, 2004.

Larsson, Marina, *Shattered ANZACs: Living with the scars of war*, UNSW Press, 2009.

Lord, Fred, *Little Big Top*, Rigby Limited, 1965.

Lynch, E.P.F., edited by Davies, W, *Somme Mud: The war experiences of an infantryman in France 1916–1919*, Random House Australia, 2006.

McKernan, Michael, *The Australian People and the Great War*, Thomas Nelson Australia, 1980.

McQuilton, John, *Rural Australia and the Great War: From Tarrawingee to Tangambalanga*, Melbourne University Press, 2001.

Park, Ruth and Champion, Rafe, *Home before dark, the story of Les Darcy, a great Australian hero*. Viking Penguin Books, 1995.

Robson, L.L., *Australia and the Great War*, Macmillan of Australia, 1969.

Ruljancich, Sally, 'Cole's Book Arcade', *The Encyclopaedia of Melbourne*, Cambridge University Press, 2005.

Scott, Joanne and Laurie, Ross, *Showtime: A history of the Brisbane Exhibition*, UQP, 2008.

Sharman, Jimmy, Newspaper cuttings and personal collection, MLMSS 3672/Box 1x, MLMSS 5550X, 1912 to 1965, State Library of NSW and National Library of Australia.

Tatz, Colin, *Obstacle Race: Aborigines in sport*, UNSW Press, 1995.

Trove searches, via National Library of Australia.

UBD, *Road Atlas*, New South Wales, UBD publishing.

Ward, Geoffrey C., *Unforgiveable Blackness: The rise and fall of Jack Johnson*, Yellow Jacket Press, 2015.

Williams F John, *ANZACs, the Media and the Great War*, UNSW Press. 1999.

Notes

Chapter 1

1. The contract Archie signs is contained in Jimmy Sharman's personal collection at the Mitchell Library NSW and is an actual 4–5 page original document (undated) used by Sharman to sign up his boxers. Given the rate of pay was exceptionally good and the honour to work for Jimmy Sharman's Boxing Troupe was considerable, it is likely all boxers quickly signed the document.
2. A letter in a local paper from a Mr E Chipford of Goulburn is contained in Jimmy Sharman's collection at the Mitchell Library NSW.
3. The majority of the information on how Jimmy Sharman operated the boxing tent, how he followed the 'regional agricultural circuit' and how he spruiked is developed from multiple sources including *Lords of the Ring*, Peter Corris, Cassell Australia, 1979 and Broome, Richard, Alick Jackomos, *Sideshow Alley*, Allen and Unwin, 1998

Chapter 2

1. The description of 'war fervour' is developed from multiple sources including *Rural Australia and the Great War*, John McQuilton, MUP, 2001 and McKernan, Michael, *The Australian People and the Great War*, Thomas Nelson Australia, 1980
2. Sharman's early life as a Leeton billy boy is sourced from Jimmy Sharman's personal collection at the Mitchell Library NSW.
3. Boxing techniques is adapted from multiple sources including Jimmy Sharman's collection at the Mitchell Library NSW, *Snow Bakers* Magazine via the NLA collection, *Lords of the Ring*, Peter Corris, Cassell Australia,

1979, various boxing technique books and also from the author's own boxing tuition.

4. Young Griffo is sourced from Peter Corris, *Lords of the Ring*. Joe Grimm from Michael Winkler's groundbreaking work *Grimmish.*
5. Sharman versus Carter at Wagga Wagga is adapted from multiple sources including Peter Corris *Lords of the Ring*, Sharman's personal papers and local newspapers.
6. The Burns–Johnson fight at Rushcutters Bay is adapted from multiple sources including *Unforgiveable Blackness,* Ward, G.C., Yellow Jacket Press, 2015 and local newspaper reports.
7. The singing is from *Temperance Songbook*, Wolfe Publishing, 1972.
8. The masked wrestler letter is adapted from Broome, Richard, Alick Jackomos, *Sideshow Alley*, Allen and Unwin, 1998
9. Advertising of the time is adapted from multiple sources including McQuilton, John, *Rural Australia and the Great War: From Tarrawingee to Tangambalanga*, Melbourne University Press, 2001 and local newspapers.
10. Correspondence suggesting Germans are locked up to protect the harvest is a letter written to the editor of a local newspaper in the Hay District, NSW.
11. The account of the Sydney recruits via the *Sydney Morning Herald.*
12. Comments made regarding the traits of Aboriginal and African boxers is adapted from Broome, Richard, 'Aboriginal boxers and social control in Australia', seminar paper, 1979.
13. Melbourne attractions adapted from multiple sources including the *Encyclopaedia of Melbourne*, Cambridge University Press, 2005 and local newspapers.
14. Newspapers reported on when Sharman's tent was visiting local towns and agricultural shows. Sharman was a regular correspondent to the boxing magazine *The Referee*, reporting on fights he organised as 'prize fights' in local halls. Sharman lived in Te Mora rather than Narellan during the war and his tent touring and promotional fights focussed on the Riverina area. There is newspaper evidence of touring in New South Wales, Victoria and Tasmania during the war; Queensland touring occurred after the war. The exact numbers on fighters 'on tour' between venues is unconfirmed: at least four and up to ten to twelve. Some may have arrived at a show independently by arrangement with Sharman. In 1918, Sharman defended his boxers for not enlisting, stating that '70 different lads' were engaged in contests as part of Jimmy Sharman's Boxing Troupe during the war, which suggests a touring party size as portrayed in this work. Boxers profiled in this work's epilogue were members of the Boxing Troupe during the war. Trove via NLA provides further detail.

Chapter 3

1. The moving armies (snowball marches) occurred over the summer of 1914–1915. This is adapted from multiple sources including newspapers, McQuilton, John, *Rural Australia and the Great War: From Tarrawingee to Tangambalanga*, Melbourne University Press, 2001. McKernan, Michael, *The Australian People and the Great War*, Thomas Nelson Australia, 1980.
2. The route for Sharman's tour each was based on the dates of the NSW, Queensland and Victoria agricultural shows. I used modern-day schedules to set the schedule during Sharman's time; due to the farming seasons and practices the schedule has remained the same. I referred to the map in Broome, Richard, Alick Jackomos, *Sideshow Alley*, Allen and Unwin, 1998 that shows Sharman's route. I also referred to maps of NSW, Queensland and Victoria rail lines, timetables and stations to build up the routes details.
3. The letter from Frank is adapted from multiple sources including archival letters, Carthew, N, *Voices from the Trenches: Letters to home*, New Holland Publishers, 2002.
4. The plea for the 'bantams' to be able to enlist is sourced from McQuilton, John, *Rural Australia and the Great War: From Tarrawingee to Tangambalanga*, Melbourne University Press, 2001.
5. The fabulous Phelans are characters from a fictional short story I wrote called 'Six Foot Up'.
6. Sydney show history via various Sydney Royal Show Society histories and also the competition with Snowy Flynn's boxing troupe is sourced from Corris, Peter, *Lords of the Ring*, Cassell Australia. 1979.
7. The freak tent and other sideshow attractions, is adapted from multiple sources including Broome, Richard, Alick Jackomos, *Sideshow Alley*, Allen and Unwin, 1998. Greaves, Geoff, *The Circus Comes to Town: Nostalgia of Australian big tops*, AH and AW Reed, 1980. Lord, Fred, Little Big Top, Rigby Limited, 1965.
8. Les Darcy, is adapted from multiple sources including; newspaper reports and Park, Ruth and Champion, Rafe, *Home Before Dark: The story of Les Darcy, a great Australian hero*. Viking Penguin Books, 1995.
9. Tom Uren being a powder monkey, biting onto detonation devices, primary source: Sharman, Jimmy, Newspaper cuttings and personal collection, MLMSS 3672/Box 1x, MLMSS 5550X, 1912 to 1965, State Library of NSW.
10. Brisbane Exhibition history; Scott, Joanne and Laurie, Ross, Showtime: A history of the Brisbane Exhibition, UQP, 2008.
11. The slapping man is a reference to the novel of the same name by Andrew Lindsay.
12. The circus train, is adapted from multiple sources including; Greaves, Geoff, *The Circus Comes to Town: Nostalgia of Australian big tops*, AH and AW Reed, 1980. Lord, Fred, Little Big Top, Rigby Limited, 1965. Broome, Richard,

Alick Jackomos, *Sideshow Alley*, Allen and Unwin, 1998. I could not date when the train operated.

13. The selling of patriotic rams and the dental pavilion is sourced from Adam-Smith, Patsy, *The ANZACs*, Nelson Publishers, 1978.
14. The Frater letter from the Brisbane *Sun* was titled 'Firpo of the North' and was written in the 1930s. From Sharman, Jimmy, newspaper cuttings and personal collection, MLMSS 3672/Box 1x, MLMSS 5550X, 1912 to 1965, State Library of NSW.
15. Descriptions of Gallipoli campaign is adapted from multiple sources including newspapers, other works listed in references and CEW Bean.
16. Bert's farewell is adapted from multiple sources including newspapers and McQuilton, John, *Rural Australia and the Great War: From Tarrawingee to Tangambalanga*, Melbourne University Press, 2001.
17. Recruit Herbert Badgery is a reference to the key character and conman in Peter Carey's novel *Illywhacker*.

Chapter 4

1. Letter from Frank is adapted from multiple sources including archival letters and from Carthew, N, *Voices from the Trenches: Letters to home*, New Holland Publishers, 2002.
2. Anti-German actions, the association for recruitment, the need for brawn and vigour, war speeches, letters and Les Darcy needing to enlist is adapted from multiple sources including newspapers, McQuilton, John, *Rural Australia and the Great War: From Tarrawingee to Tangambalanga*, Melbourne University Press, 2001. McKernan, Michael, *The Australian People and the Great War*, Thomas Nelson Australia, 1980 and Park, Ruth and Champion, Rafe, *Home Before Dark: The story of Les Darcy, a great Australian hero*. Viking Penguin Books, 1995.
3. The war census is adapted from multiple sources including newspaper reports, McQuilton, John, *Rural Australia and the Great War: From Tarrawingee to Tangambalanga*, Melbourne University Press, 2001. McKernan, Michael, *The Australian People and the Great War*, Thomas Nelson Australia, 1980.

Chapter 5

1. Slackers letters etc. is adapted from multiple sources including newspaper reports, McQuilton, John, *Rural Australia and the Great War: From Tarrawingee to Tangambalanga*, Melbourne University Press, 2001.
2. The wowsers singing is from Coleman, Emmet, Editor, *The Temperance Songbook*, Wolfe Publishing, 1972.
3. At this time in history First Nations people were not allowed to travel interstate. It is likely Sharman either applied for travel permits on their behalf, was assigned the role of a protector or the fighters became wards of Sharman. Broome, Richard, 'Aboriginal boxers and social control in Australia', seminar paper, 1979.

4. Sharman received an unfit for service for World War II after an eye injury from a burst bottle of ammonia in 1922. There are no reasons given for not enlisting in World War I. Sharman was 27 and fit when war was declared; he may have avoided early pressure to enlist given his height, 5 foot 4 inches. He was also married with a child. He was Roman Catholic, of whom many were anti-war. He was also developing a business he was expert at, so these may have been other influencing factors; Jimmy Sharman confirmed nothing.
5. Good luck charms. My great grandfather was given a good luck charm with the symbols and words as described in the novel. I have this family heirloom.
6. Franz Ferdinand did tour Australia and this is adapted from an account from a Mrs Mack reported in the local newspaper.
7. Bert's letters refer to bird catching along the Nile, I saw this when I was in Egypt. His later mention of the dog wheel for churning butter is sourced and adapted from Carthew, N, *Voices from the Trenches: Letters to home*, New Holland Publishers, 2002.
8. The 'sensations of a bayonet charge' and the 'wake up poem' are from McQuilton, John, *Rural Australia and the Great War: From Tarrawingee to Tangambalanga*, Melbourne University Press, 2001.
9. Names for unenlisted men is from Adam-Smith, Patsy, *The ANZACs*, Nelson Publishers, 1978.
10. Fighting from Pozieres is from several newspaper accounts.

Chapter 6

1. Heavy losses from the Western Front is adapted from multiple sources including newspaper reports and from McKernan, Michael, *The Australian People and the Great War*, Thomas Nelson Australia, 1980.
   McQuilton, John, *Rural Australia and the Great War: From Tarrawingee to Tangambalanga*, Melbourne University Press, 2001. Robson, L.L., *Australia and the Great War*, Macmillan of Australia, 1969.
2. Details about Rud Kee (Cheong Lee) are sourced from Sharman, Jimmy, Newspaper cuttings and personal collection, MLMSS 3672/Box 1x, MLMSS 5550X, 1912 to 1965, State Library of NSW.
3. The Dr Haupt letter is sourced from McQuilton, John, *Rural Australia and the Great War: From Tarrawingee to Tangambalanga*, Melbourne University Press, 2001. McKernan, Michael, *The Australian People and the Great War*, Thomas Nelson Australia, 1980.
4. Conscription debate is adapted from multiple sources including newspapers, archival material, McQuilton, John, *Rural Australia and the Great War: From Tarrawingee to Tangambalanga*, Melbourne University Press, 2001 and McKernan, Michael, *The Australian People and the Great War*, Thomas Nelson Australia, 1980. The letter threatening men who are 'stepping out with our

best girls was from the *Ovens Murray Advertiser* via McQuilton, John, *Rural Australia and the Great War: From Tarrawingee to Tangambalanga*, Melbourne University Press, 2001.

5. The doctor's comment about Billy's weight was a conversation I had with a doctor when he realised I was an ex-rugby player.
6. Bert's letter is adapted from multiple sources including archival letters and Carthew, N, *Voices from the Trenches: Letters to home*, New Holland Publishers, 2002.
7. Meekin's shows began in the 1930s.
8. Comments made about Les Darcy stowing away are sourced from Park, Ruth and Champion, Rafe, *Home Before Dark: The story of Les Darcy, a great Australian hero*. Viking Penguin Books, 1995.

Chapter 7

1. Descriptions about First Nations boxers are based and adapted from multiple sources including Broome, Richard, 'Aboriginal boxers and social control in Australia', seminar paper, 1979. Broome, Richard, Alick Jackomos, *Sideshow Alley*, Allen and Unwin, 1998. Corris, Peter, *Lords of the Ring*, Cassell Australia. 1979. Drane, Robert, *Fighters by Trade: Highlights of Australia boxing*, ABC Books, 2008.

Chapter 8

1. Peter 'The Black Prince' Jackson sourced from Corris, Peter, *Lords of the Ring*, Cassell Australia. 1979.
2. Les Darcy's death, Rud sparring with Les and the statement made about Les dying of a broken heart, a man without a country, is adapted from multiple sources including newspaper reports and Park, Ruth and Champion, Rafe, *Home Before Dark: The story of Les Darcy, a great Australian hero*. Viking Penguin Books, 1995. Jimmy Sharman did not attend Les Darcy's funeral. For narrative purposes I portrayed them attending the funeral so the reader could appreciate the massive outpouring of grief for Les Darcy.
   On 4/7/17, Sharman donated 1 guinea towards the Les Darcy Memorial and wrote from Forbes, the following: *'Some people certainly give more, but none with more regret than me regarding poor Les sad end. I would very much have liked to have come down to the funeral but it was impossible for me to get away.'* Trove via NLA.
4. The Mallee mouse plaque is sourced from McKernan, Michael, *The Australian People and the Great War*, Thomas Nelson Australia, 1980.
5. The comment about hitting despondency to leg is sourced from McKernan, Michael, *The Australian People and the Great War*, Thomas Nelson Australia, 1980.
6. The letter from A Dawson NSW recruiting is fiction.

Chapter 9

1. The haranguing of men from balconies and other recruiting activities later in the war are sourced from McQuilton, John, *Rural Australia and the Great War: From Tarrawingee to Tangambalanga*, Melbourne University Press, 2001.

2. The mansion's full comment is sourced from Adam-Smith, Patsy, *The ANZACs*, Nelson Publishers, 1978.
3. The letter from Billy is adapted from multiple sources including archival letters and Carthew, N, *Voices from the Trenches: Letters to home*, New Holland Publishers, 2002.
4. Hughes being egged at Warwick was reported in the Brisbane *Courier* and outlined in Robson, L. L., *Australia and the Great War*, Macmillan of Australia, 1969.
5. The letter from A Dawson NSW Commander of recruitment was a fictional device only. Sharman did attend the Holdsworthy Barracks for six weeks in the summer of 1917–1918 teaching self- defence or close quarter combat; however, nothing is known about what compelled Sharman to do this. Source: Sharman, Jimmy, Newspaper cuttings and personal collection, MLMSS 3672/ Box 1x, MLMSS 5550X, 1912 to 1965, State Library of NSW.
6. The Mannix Speech on the referendum on 8/12/17 was reported via the *Advocate* and outlined in Robson, L.L., *Australia and the Great War*, Macmillan of Australia, 1969.

Chapter 10

1. This is the only written account found where Jimmy Sharman was questioned about his contribution to the war effort. This was found from Trove via the NLA. This reply was first published on 28 January 1918, occurring very late in the war. For most of the war, Sharman was celebrated for providing a clean, fair and entertaining show. Sharman's polite manner, his business sense and the 'charm offensive' he would unfold at gatherings before show night, whether it be a civic function or in the public bar, liaising with the town's hierarchy (the show chairman, the local mayor and significant landholders) and shoring up his reputation was a key factor to his success during the war. The potential of identifying or encouraging recruits via the boxing tent was probably another way Sharman defected pressure for him and his boxers to enlist. His First Nations boxers were regarded by society at the time as 'not suitable material for war', so he was probably able to maintain a boxing troupe of good numbers.

   Many of the white boxers were under military age. In other circumstances, I believe Sharman would delay his response to calls for his boxers to enlist or promise to consider their enlistment in the future. He would have used other reasons such as the enlistment of other siblings or the need to raise money for the family. He may have used the contract described as a method to stop his men enlisting or defend them for staying. Sharman's six-week period of training recruits in hand-to-hand combat was probably a well-timed commitment to avoid accusations that he was not contributing to the war effort.

Providing entertainment to bored locals and bringing some cheer to people depressed by the events of the war was probably another reason for his popularity.

Newspapers would actually celebrate Jimmy Sharman's success as a business throughout the war. *The Sportsman* 22/12/17: '*Jimmy is looking well and is getting big and quite like a capitalist.*' Mudgee 13/3/18: '*Perhaps the weighty treasury bag slung around his neck is the cause of the permanence of the smile. He's a straight goer and raked in the dollars.*'

Sharman would often donate a percentage of takings, allow side bets or provide a lump sum to local charities or the war effort. Donations were often made to the Red Cross or local hospital. The Te Mora District Hospital benefited from regular fundraising events by Sharman. Sharman was appointed as a life member in recognition of his frequent fundraising.

2. The newspaper article about Billy is adapted from multiple sources including archival letters, newspaper eulogies and from McQuilton, John, *Rural Australia and the Great War: From Tarrawingee to Tangambalanga*, Melbourne University Press, 2001.
3. Eureka Jones is a reference to the Delia Falconer novel *In the service of clouds*.
4. The conditions of fighting at Pozieres and Bullecourt are adapted from multiple sources including archival letters, Carthew, N, *Voices from the Trenches: Letters to home*, New Holland Publishers, 2002; Lynch, Davies (ed) *Somme Mud*, Random House Australia, 2006; as well as visits to the site by the author in 2008.

Chapter 11

1. The effects of PTSD on World War I soldiers is adapted from multiple sources and Larsson, Marina, *Shattered ANZACs: Living with the scars of war*, UNSW Press, 2009.
2. Curing hepatitis by eating beetroot was a successful technique for Cory Hutchings, who I was in surf lifesaving with back in New Zealand!
3. Helping a blinded digger is sourced from Adam-Smith, Patsy, *The ANZACs*, Nelson Publishers, 1978.
4. Digger Thompson is from McQuilton, John, *Rural Australia and the Great War: From Tarrawingee to Tangambalanga*, Melbourne University Press, 2001.
5. The racehorse dying after selling the business – this a famous McGrath family history story difficult to confirm!
6. The soldiers returning with war wounds, Broughton Hall, flotsam and jetsam of war and other suffering is adapted from multiple sources including archival material and from Adam-Smith, Patsy, *The ANZACs*, Nelson Publishers, 1978. Larsson, Marina, *Shattered ANZACs: Living with the scars of war*, UNSW Press, 2009.

7. Influenza advertising sourced from newspapers and McQuilton, John, *Rural Australia and the Great War: From Tarrawingee to Tangambalanga*, Melbourne University Press, 2001.
8. The words proposed for Billy's headstone are from an actual headstone from Villers-Bretonneux which I saw during a visit in 2008. For me, this was the tribute that demonstrated the huge loss and suffering of war but also the love of people lost to it. I will never forget reading this tribute; it has resonated with me ever since. This headstone compelled me to tell the personal stories of loss that war spread across the world through the character of Billy Spiers.
9. Cole's book store quotes at the end of the tour each November are from Ruljancich, Sally, Cole's Book Arcade, *The Encyclopaedia of Melbourne*, Cambridge University Press, 2005.

Chapter 12

1. The 11 November 1918 celebrations as directly reported from the *Sydney Morning Herald.* Sharman is recorded as showing in Ballarat on 13/11/18; however, I recreated the finish of the war at Archie's home with his family to reflect the heightened emotions of the war ending but the effects just beginning.

   Using a Trove search by date order via the NLA I was able to confirm the important key premise of this novel: that Sharman never enlisted and toured country towns during the war. I list location and date of all Sharman's shows recorded in local newspapers to demonstrate the frequency of small town touring; an extraordinary undertaking given the pressure to enlist and the loss of men from these towns to the war.

   Grenfell Show 9/9/14, Cowra, Wyalong 23/9/14, 9/10/14. Secretaries of 20 A&P Shows provide testimonials' of support for Jimmy Sharman's Tent Show, 9/12/14. Gunning, Camden 24/2/15, Cooma Show 8/4/15, Tamworth, Wingham, Dungog, Maitland (Boxers and wrestler), 14/4/15-28/4/15, Gunning 3/7/15, Forbes 14/7/15, Riverina 28/7/15, Narrandera, Coolamon Show, 18/8/15, Grenfell, Wagga Wagga, Cowra 1/9/15-21/9/15, 'Up Country' Cowra, Burrowa, Wyalong, Ardlethan, 13/10/15, Western Districts Victoria, Shepparton, Warrnambool, Colac, 10/11/15-8/12/15. Mossvale 26/2/16, Coolamon 1/3/16, Taralga 15/3/16, Monaro (Nimmitabel) 29/3/16, Bega 13/4/16, Cooma 19/4/16, Dungog, Kempsey, Wingham, 3/5/16, Northern Rivers (Grafton, Yamba, Casino, Lismore, Balina) 31/5/16. Parkes, Forbes 9/8/16, Grenfell 1/9/16, Cowra 15/9/16, Dubbo (Taggie Young leaves), 1/11/16, (Rud Kee joins) Adelong 24/11/16. Robertson (West of Dapto) 14/3/17, Bendigo Easter Fair 11/4/17, Gippsland, Mossvale, Leeton, Queanbeyan 25/4/17, Coonamble 9/5/17, *'Sports were loud in their praise for the clean sportsmanlike way in which Jimmy Sharman carried out his show and consider it was the best and cleanest combination of boxers that ever visited Coonamble.'* Forbes 22/5/17, Peak Hill 25/7/17, Parkes Show 28/8/17, Grenfell A&P Show 31/8/17 *Sideshows scarce but Jimmy Sharman had a tent.* Forbes 5/9/17, Young 11/9/17, Wyalong 22/9/17, Wimmera and Mallee 3/10/17, Horsham, Nhill, Warracknabeal 17/10/17. Goulburn 6/2/18, Nowra 22/2/18, Newcastle 6/3/18, Mudgee 11/2/18, Donations to the Les Darcy Testimonial Fund were made 27/3/18 after fights at Taree, Wyong, Newcastle, Mudgee, Wollongong, Queanbeyan, Camden, Goulburn. Bendigo 3/4/18, Maitland, Bathurst, Orange, (5 boxers recorded including George Cook), Wellington, Dubbo 17/4/18. The Dr Burkitt 'Dubbo incident' 3/6/18 reported in the Bathurst Times. Forbes hospital all takings donation 7/6/18, Nyngan 28/6/18, Te Mora hospital 80 pound donation 3/7/18, Trundle 16/8/18, Wagga Wagga 28/8/18, Peak Hill, Condobolin 11/9/18, Ballarat 13/11/18. Following the Spanish flu outbreak there are less shows, Sharman shows at Wollongong 28/3/19 and remains in NSW in 1919.

Chapter 13

1. Archie writing letters to the repatriation department, which was a common occurrence, adapted from Larsson, Marina, *Shattered ANZACs: Living with the scars of war*, UNSW Press, 2009.
2. Account of the flu, its effect and management is adapted from multiple sources including archival material newspapers and McQuilton, John, *Rural Australia and the Great War: From Tarrawingee to Tangambalanga*, Melbourne University Press, 2001.

Chapter 14

1. Sharman did close the troupe in response to the flu controls, particularly gatherings in public and travelling interstate; he re-opened in 1921. Sharman, Jimmy, Newspaper cuttings and personal collection, MLMSS 3672/Box 1x, MLMSS 5550X, 1912 to 1965, State Library of NSW. Also see Trove via the NLA.
2. Sharman was known to have notebooks which he paid close attention to. One was a profit/loss accounting ledger, one was income and outgoings by site, in which Sharman would add comments about what filled up the tent. And there was a book of fighters, their skills and temperaments; however, this has not been located. The primary source for this detail (where it is mentioned) is Sharman, Jimmy, Newspaper cuttings and personal collection, MLMSS 3672/Box 1x, MLMSS 5550X, 1912 to 1965, State Library of NSW.

Acknowledgements

I wish to acknowledge the Traditional Owners of the land where I wrote this novel, the Wurundjeri Woi Wurrung people, and recognise their continuing connection to the land and waterways. I pay my respects to their Elders past, present and emerging and extend this to all Aboriginal and Torres Strait Islander people.

I want to acknowledge the sacrifices made by service men and service women in war from the past to present day. LEST WE FORGET.

These include my relatives who fought in conflict.

- Private Michael McGrath 65th (2nd Yorkshire, North Riding) Regiment of Foot (The Hickety Pips), New Zealand Wars, 1860–61.
- Rifleman, Company Runner, Stanley Norgrove, New Zealand Rifle Brigade (The Dinks), the Somme, Messines and Passchendaele, World War 1, 1914–18.

- Sapper John Shennan, New Zealand Engineers, Gallipoli, World War 1, 1914–1918. My maternal great grandfather was at Gallipoli for nine days when a large shell from beachy bill dropped on the other side of a sandbag wall. Sapper Shennan was declared KIA near Christmas 1915. However, he was then found alive in the Hornchurch Hospital in the UK with medical notes stating the patient had 'bled from the ears and nose for three days and was prone to fits, as a result of shell concussion'. He returned to Wellington, New Zealand, where every Sunday my 12-year-old Grandfather Joe would row him out into Wellington Harbour to sit in the quiet for six hours so he could escape from the noise.

This story was introduced to me via Midnight Oil and their song 'Jimmy Sharman's Boxers' (*Red Sails in the Sunset* album). While at Massey University in New Zealand, my elderly neighbour, originally from Cairns, first told me about watching fights as a boy in Jimmy Sharman's Boxing Tent.

After moving to Australia in 1997 I started to visit many of the towns Jimmy Sharman toured and where Jimmy Sharman promoted his first fight at the Star Theatre in Temora, NSW; its residents and rural museum were very helpful. I also visited nearby Ardlethan, where it is suggested that Sharman showed his first boxing troupe in 1910 or 1911.

I visited the Mitchell Library in Sydney where a helpful librarian (they all are always very helpful! Thank you!) searched a strange number and returned with a parcel tied with string which turned out to have belonged to both Jimmy Sharman 1 and 2. It contained personal newspaper cuttings about the troupe, a copy of the fighters' contract document and a photo of boxers with a note on the back dated 1917.

Michael Hurley from the National Library of Australia taught me how to use Trove properly, which allowed me to confirm Sharman did tour extensively during the war. Via Trove I also found the remarkable Dr Burkitt speech at Dubbo about George Cook and the 1918 Te Mora letter in which Sharman defends his touring, pointing out that of the 70 boxers under his management 43 enlisted. Trove revealed that Sharman made a significant amount of money during the war and was celebrated for doing so. The combination of manners, a clean, entertaining show and generous fundraising endeared Sharman to all the people he met and to the country overall.

Jimmy Sharman and his son (Jimmy 2) entertained people from 1910 to 1975 with their boxing tent and there are many great stories still to be told; but for me, the discovery of the 1917 photo and knowing something about World War I was what has allowed me to tell a particularly remarkable part of Jimmy Sharman's life.

I want to say that Jimmy Sharman and his boxers were remarkable people living in remarkable times. It is an honour to tell their story here; again, I hope I do it justice.

I started to think about Jimmy Sharman in 1985. I started research in 2005. I started writing this novel in 2006. I heard once that writing a novel was like sailing single handed around the world. It was long and lonely, but there were people 'waiting on the shore' I want to thank.

My family: Michelle, Esther and Lawrence, sorry for my preoccupations and thank you for letting the characters come live in our house. Because of this novel I lost some precious time with you. I love you all.

Thanks to Bob for the help with 1915 accounting methods, currency and banking. Thanks to Barb, Naralle, Jan, Bruce, Jane for your interest, help and encouragement. Thank you to my mum, Sue, and Phil. Thanks to friends, especially Dan, David C, Brett D (the backyard crickets), Flick and Ella. Thanks to all my workmates at the 'Horse' and the 'Nash' in particular Dion, Ian, Chrissy, Jo, Colin, Kates B, J and W, Emms, Russ, Travis, Maz, Rob P, Lynn, David T, Patrick and many others for the encouragement and support. Thanks especially to Barb, for the photo.

Thanks to Tom and Pete, my coffee guys at Bin 3!

They say writing is a sedentary profession but I wouldn't have finished the novel without my 'medical team': a very special thank you to Louise N my chiropractor for always fixing my back after hours of poor computer posture then allowing me to do it all over again. Thanks to Merril B, Marcus H, Patrick M and Dr G for the running repairs and improvements to the carcass of an old worn-out rugby player-cum-author.

Thanks to my writing friends and acquaintances, Michelle W, Emily W, Katherine C, Bram P, Michael W and Tony B. Acknowledgement to Delia Falconer (*The Lost Thoughts of Soldiers*) and Lloyd Jones (*The Book of Fame*) for developing a new structural form of historical fiction novels with large character numbers for other writers, such as myself, to follow.

Thanks to those who provided cultural sensitivity advice. Special thanks to Ian M, who provided expert legal advice via Arts Law Australia.

Thanks to BSP for recognising this story. Thank you to the all word mechanics at BSP for getting this in print and on the shelves. Thanks to the copyeditor and sorry about my commas'! Thanks Especially to Di, Sharon and Denny.

Lastly, thank you to all the authors of World War I and boxing history who are found in the reference section of this work; in particular, John McQuilton, Michael McKernan, Peter Corris, Richard Broome and Alick Jackomos. You collectively helped me animate a new story about World War I. Thank you.

About the author

Stephen McGrath was born on Tainui land in the Waikato, Aotearoa (New Zealand) in 1968. He moved to Naarm/ Melbourne (Australia) in 1997 and has lived on Wurundjeri Woi Wurrung land, as a guest, ever since.

He won the *Age* short story competition in 2008 for his story 'A Parachute Landing in Siberia' and placed in the same competition in 2011 for his story 'The Yellow Chair'. He has won several other literary competitions. This is his first novel.

He studied town planning, sociology and anthropology at Massey University in New Zealand. He has worked as a planner in local government, was a volunteer firefighter in New Zealand, travelled widely and played a few games of rugby to a barely acceptable standard. He was a beekeeper until an anaphylactic reaction following 20+ stings made him concentrate on writing.

He lives in suburban Melbourne with his lovely wife Michelle and lovely children Esther and Lawrence as well as doggies Kookie and Field Marshall Otto Von Krump the 2nd.

He is keen to hear about your memories of Jimmy Sharman 1 and Jimmy Sharman 2. For more information about Stephen McGrath go to stephenmcgrath.com.au.

More from Big Sky Publishing

Suffering Redemption and Triumph

The first wave of postwar Australian immigrants

Peter Brune

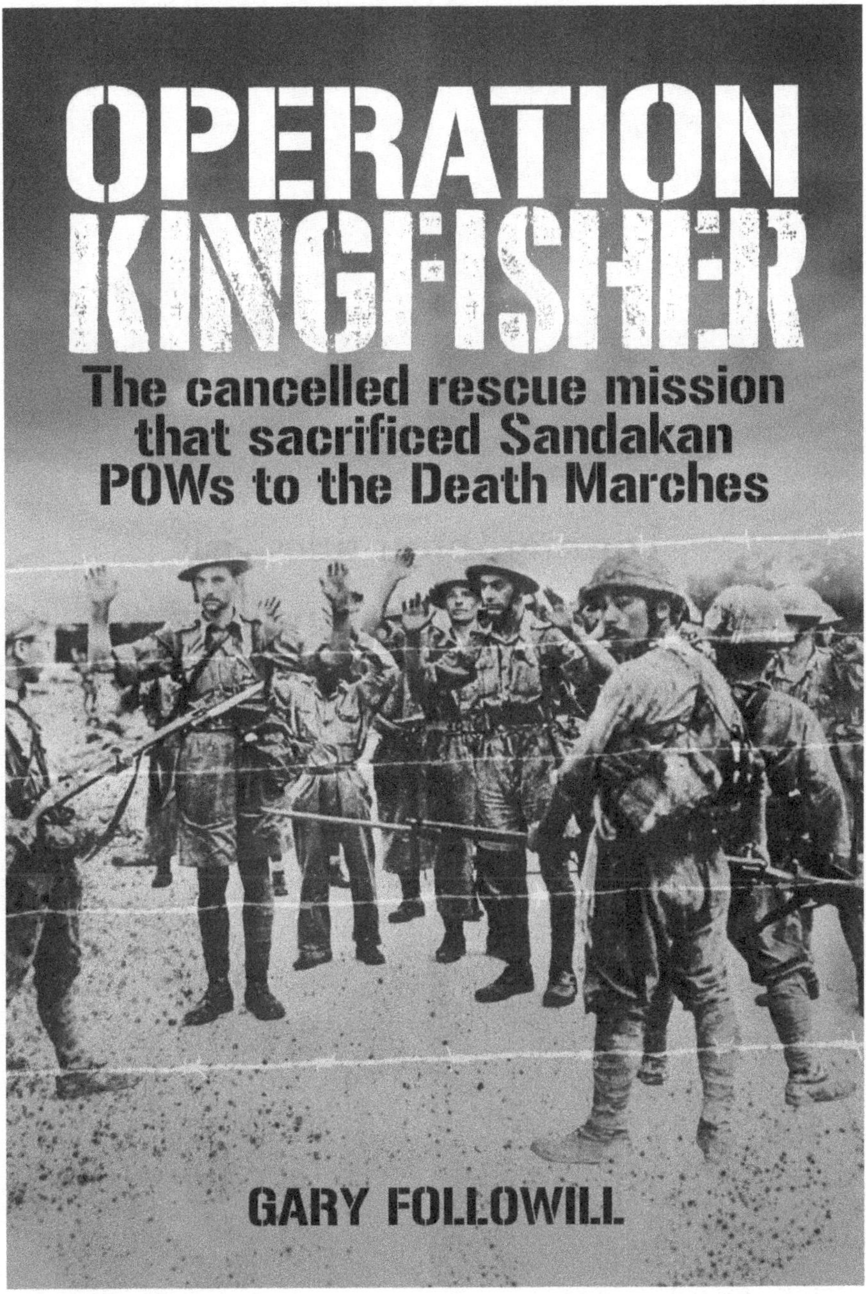